THE OAKWOOD PRESS

CW00536071

Tram~~~~~~ à Vapeur du Tarn

A 60 cm Railway in South West France

by
Sarah Wright
with illustrations and maps by Malcolm Wright

THE OAKWOOD PRESS

© Oakwood Press & Sarah Wright 2001

British Library Cataloguing in Publication Data
A Record for this book is available from the British Library
ISBN 0 85361 570 5

Typeset by Oakwood Graphics.
Repro by Ford Graphics, Ringwood, Hants.
Printed by Inkon Printers Ltd, Yateley, Hants.

Drivers, firemen and *chefs de train* are seen outside the shed at Graulhet. The date of this photograph is unknown, but probably early 1920s. Second from the right, middle row, is the Director who affected workmen's *sabots*. He can be seen, with *sabots*, in the photographs taken at the time of the strike in 1909. *ACOVA/Family of Auguste Cormary*

Title page: Graulhet, Caisse d'Épargne. View of the local bank, taken about 1909, showing the tortuous route and sharp inclines of the railway as it made its way through the centre of town. *J. Daffis/ACOVA*

Published by The Oakwood Press (Usk), P.O. Box 13, Usk, Mon., NP15 1YS.
E-mail: oakwood-press@dial.pipex.com
Website: www.oakwood-press.dial.pipex.com

Contents

The workshop workers at the engine shed at Graulhet between 1925 and 30. Second from left, standing, is M. Cloup, who came to the inaugural run of the CFTT. Fourth from left, also standing, is M. Cormary. His history is perhaps typical of the age. He started work in 1909, during the war, he saw service in the 'chemins de fer de campagne' a sort of nationalised service which kept transport ticking over. From 1919 to 1922, he was a driver, and then worked in maintenance until the closure of the line. He wears workman's *sabots*. Fourth from the right, standing, is M. Olivet, then a young engine driver, who worked on the St Sulpice branch until closure. His status is marked by the shoes that he is wearing.

ACOVA/Family of Auguste Cormary

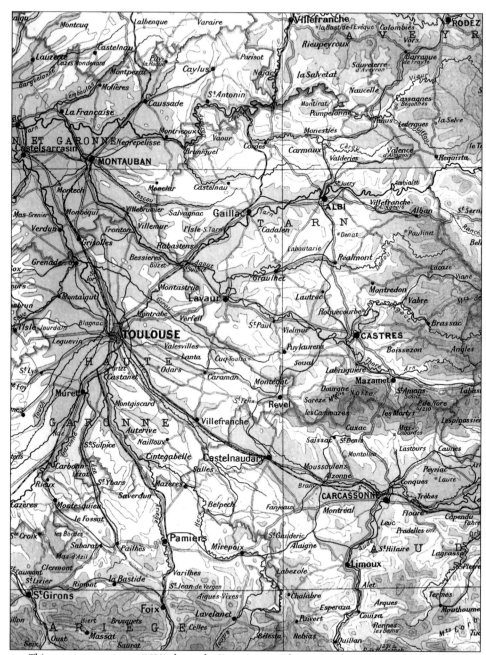

This contemporary map (1922) shows the Tarn area, and the relationship between the important cities, Toulouse, Albi and Castres, to the stations on the railways, Graulhet, Lavaur, St Sulpice and Réalmont. *Times Publishing*

Acknowledgements

Malcolm Wright provided illustrations, where not otherwise attributed, and generally co-authored this book.
The following are to be thanked for their help and encouragement in putting together this book:

ACOVA; Archives Départementales of Albi for illustrations and information; Roger Bailly for photographs; Institut Berliet for photographs; Jacqueline Bonnet for information; Louis Briand and the Carto-Club Tarnais for illustrations; Jacques Daffis for advice, encouragement and many photographs; Alison Ewan for illustrations; FACS for photographs; Graulhet Library for illustrations; Graulhet Tourist Office for information; Jim Hawkesworth for advice, encouragement and illustrations; Marthe Lacaze for photographs; *Éditions La Vie du Rail* for photographs; Henry Manavit for advice and information; *The Times* Publishers for a map; University of Aberdeen Geography Department: Michael Zappert and finally, my Dad.

Foreword

Increasing numbers of Britons visit French preserved railways, many now within a day's journey. They return with enthusiastic reports. A second and growing group have penetrated further into France, seeking out holiday homes. The preserved railways of western France and Provence are therefore also being discovered. These narrow gauge railways, now run for tourists, are the remains of a countrywide network once essential to the rural way of life.

Chance, luck and the presence of energetic personalities ensure the existence of the preserved French lines of today. They are the remnants of an extensive system, 22,364 kilometres in all (half the circumference of the globe), which brought almost all provincial France within reach of a railway. Through visits to the more popular destinations, we English-speakers glimpse the tips of this submerged 'iceberg' of rural communication.

For some years we have been selling French military narrow gauge models. Was there a civilian equivalent? Yes, there were several 60 centimetre gauge railways, one in the *département* of Tarn, 30 kilometres from Toulouse. The original network closed in 1937, but part of the route has been revived as a tourist railway. We paid our first visit in 1993.

Things started badly. Compared with the glorious scenery of Albi, the road to Castres had all the appeal of congealed porridge. We kept thinking of our picnic lunch and there was nowhere to pull off the interminable road. There was no sign even of the main line railway. When we reached the old Laboutarié station, our feelings began to change. Although both secondary and main line have been gone for years, the houses remain, recognisable from photographs taken a hundred years ago. Bulldozers were advancing from the south; an industrial estate was planned for the site. We experienced the thrill of capturing a scene that was soon to vanish.

Briatexte *BV* viewed from the river edge in 1993. The former WC is to the left and the corner of the municpal store which replaced the *halle* is to the right.   *Malcolm Wright*

We traced the route of the vanished Tramway westwards. As far as Graulhet, this was easy, but not very inspiring. All traces of the railway had vanished when the road was widened leaving a bland vista. To visitors, Graulhet wears a front of self-sufficient reserve and we never worked out where to park. We continued westward, as far as Briatexte, where, once again, the station remains, almost intact. We met an old lady who had travelled on the railway. Gradually, the quiet charm of the district began to work on us. At the old junction of La Ramière, we were once again able to photograph a scene which is soon to be modernised.

Westwards once again, at the historic village of Giroussens, gazing over the green valley where the little train once ran, we began at last to feel a real interest. Below us, was the section of the route which the Tarn Tourist Railway has revived. We descended to explore. The visitor is offered a banquet for the senses. The station is set in the village of St Lieux, and so trains set off through a village street. The route lies over a spectacular viaduct, overlooked in turn by the precipitous village of Giroussens. This is followed by woodland giving way to water meadows, until finally the terminus is reached just short of the main road. To our regret, trains run only on Sundays, and so we could only imagine the scents and sounds of a working railway, as well as the thrill of a ride.

On that spot, I was convinced that here lay a railway that would interest others outside France, as well as ourselves. The tourist railway is already well known in its own country, attracting 22,000 visitors in 2000 alone, impressive, as it only opens on Sundays or by appointment. The area is well known to French holiday makers, boasting many other attractions. Once I determined to find out more, Graulhet was revealed to be a welcoming town. .

I have therefore set out to produce a book which will appeal to several groups of readers. One group are the holiday makers who would like background information on an attractive area, and so the text has been allowed diversions into local history. The book has something for enthusiasts of railway history who will welcome an original study. Another readership are the modellers of railways, searching for inspiration. I hope that their needs are met by the maps, station layouts and drawings as well as my more general information.

Chapter One

Introduction

Paris 1889

Rocked by the small wheels below, Monsieur Bonnet, a respectable Frenchman visiting Paris, looked out of the railway carriage. The River Seine breathed out delicious breezes, and he could almost touch the trees as they passed. Beyond the river, the illustrious buildings of Paris marched to the skyline. Monsieur Bonnet had been to the capital before, but never had he been able to travel through it in such comfort.

His neighbour smiled, and then resumed her conversation with the child on the other side. Mother and daughter were clearly Parisians and knew this stretch of the river well but they too delighted in the ease and comfort of the journey. Everyone was caught up in the holiday mood. This was the summer of the 1889 Great Exhibition.

The line of trees swung away as the railway crossed the approach to the Alma bridge. Ahead, the steel tower built by Monsieur Eiffel dominated the view. No one French, man or woman, could see this triumph of art and engineering without a rush of warm emotion. At the same time, where the line curved, the Mallet compound locomotive at the head of the train could be glimpsed. When he had first seen it at Concorde station, it had seemed toy-like, full of charm but not capable of useful work. Now, as it approached the finest work of Gustave Eiffel, it could be appreciated as another masterpiece of French design.

The whole railway was living up to expectation. The system, designed and built by the Decauville Company, had won the tender to transport the crowds expected for the Great Exhibition at almost the last minute. The tender was awarded because Decauville promised to be cheap, and to keep disruption during construction to a minimum. The company had honoured these commitments with poetry that softened the heart.

All aboard! Though the passengers were on holiday, the little railway was not. The carriages glided on their way behind the engine. Instead of worrying about the route, the heat and pickpockets, passengers could concentrate on the sunshine and the breeze.

Monsieur Bonnet, canny provincial bourgeois, was in love. At the next stop, he hurried to the marriage broker's. The Société Des Établissements Decauville Aîné had placed its office next door to the Trocadero station, at the foot of the Eiffel Tower, conveniently for anyone wishing to enquire about its products. Naturally Paul Decauville himself was available to talk to a man with plans to build an entire railway.

A number of practical problems remained, but the town of Graulhet was about to acquire a rail link.

Two views of Graulhet station. The station building is as it would have been at the time of closure. The view of the track is toward the freight handling shed, of generous proportions.

Louis Briand/Carto-Club de Tarn

1935 Graulhet

The mixed service from Graulhet to Lavaur should have already left. There were few passengers, and the goods wagon was empty apart from a couple of parcels. Monsieur Cazals looked at his watch yet again and noticed with annoyance the soot settling on his sleeve. If he had made the journey by car he would have arrived spotless, and punctually. The hard seat cut into his back. Without an apology, the carriage with first class accommodation had been declared unavailable. He would look into it, to be sure, as he would look into the state of the platform, lack of maintenance in the carriage, unpunctuality, the surly apathy of the staff.

At last a reason for the delay was apparent. The slow, old and dirty 0-6-2 which had brought the train round shuffled off to be replaced by an equally slow and dirty 4-6-0. It coupled up to the first carriage with an ill-natured thud. The short train rocked. The child opposite dropped her ticket. When the train had apparently ceased moving, she bent forward to pick it up, but was again jolted off her seat.

'*Attention!*' grumbled a voice.

The child crept back to her seat and ill humoured silence resumed in the bare carriage. As the train left, M. Cazals determined to look into this business of the change of engines, unnecessary, surely, when both were so clearly under-used. A crazy lurch to the right brought his thoughts back to his seat. Now the train negotiated the descent to the river. They slowed almost to a halt, brakes whining, and then slewed to the left to take the bridge. The engine speeded up take a run at the other side, scattering pedestrians with a bad-tempered jangling of the bell. Now they were in Graulhet Old Town.

As he struggled to keep in his seat, his back to the view, his eye caught the eye of the small girl opposite. Was there just a glimpse of humour in that little face, as they both clung to the bench? A lurch to the right nearly pitched her to the floor. Again her neighbour muttered. Monsieur Cazals braced himself as the train negotiated another bend, this time labouring upwards. All the while, the bell rang at pedestrians and cars. They could stop, he wouldn't.

Anticipating the next halt, he put out a hand to the little girl. Her mother muttered suspiciously but the girl whispered '*Merci, monsieur*'. When the train stopped the two struggled out of the carriage on to the street, weighted with parcels, and M. Cazals had the grimy carriage to himself.

With his own eyes, he could see that the railway served little purpose. One woman and her daughter had gone one stop. He was alone now. Perhaps another passenger might be waiting further along the line. A bus service would be more convenient, certainly more comfortable for the passengers. And could the empty train justify the disruption it was causing to other road users as well as the money it was swallowing? The newspaper in his pocket had a report on the *autobahnen* that the fellow Hitler was building in Germany. As well as splendid new roads, the Germans had plans for a new car, clean, safe and convenient for every family. He thought of the girl, and of other children running away from the grimy wheels of his train. An old man now, he couldn't justify the railway any more, not to the young people, not to anyone.

At the next Council meeting, Monsieur Cazals listened in silence to the enemies of the railway and put up no defence. Local Government withdrew its support and the network was formally closed.

The railway, planned with high hopes, was unmourned at closure. What went wrong? How could such such a tiny railway survive for so long? Was the closure the end of the story? The following pages take a closer look at the Tramways à Vapeur du Tarn.

Background

Millions of years ago, the area now known as Tarn lay at the edge of a shallow sea. To the north was a volcanic massif, while a distance to the south lay the ancient Castilian plateau, now part of Spain. Forests at the edge of the volcanic massif were to form the basis of coalfields such as the ones round Carmaux. In the seabed, small shellfish lived, and died, lending a limestone character to the area. As the volcanic rock to the north degraded, clay and silt were deposited in the wash of rivers flowing into the ever more shallow sea.

A tremendous upheaval joined Spain to France. The Pyrenees were formed and Tarn became part of the new land bridge between central France and Spain. The watershed of this young country lies to the east; Tarn was and is geographically part of the basin of Aquitaine.

From then until now, three influences dominate the area, explaining much of its history. The Atlantic, as always, has made for a moist and mild climate, in contrast to the landscapes of Provence, geographically so close. It has also affected the attitude of local people. The food they eat, commerce and politics have been oriented westwards. 'The sea is in our soul' boasts the handbook put out by the Syndicat d'Initiative[1] of Graulhet. 'We have provided France with many admirals'. Perhaps the most celebrated local seaman was Laperouse, born at Albi. Graulhet boasts connections with two others.[2]

The second influence is the ancient Massif Central which comes within 50 kilometres of Graulhet. While the ocean is both boundary and gateway to the country, the Massif acts principally as a boundary, cutting the basin of Aquitaine off from the rest of France. Communication with the North has to go along the coast, while the East is reached by way of the Mediterranean. The rocks of the Massif have affected the geology of the region; its resources have also affected trade. Since ancient times, the rugged upland pastures have provided livestock of quality. The lusher pastures and more abundant water of the lowland provided supplementary grazing for the sheep goats and cattle, and in due course water for tanning the skins. The two rural economies were complementary, and that helped to foster an attitude of self-sufficiency. For centuries, the area has found new ways to dissociate itself from northern France, Paris especially. The old name Languedoc[3] has been welcomed back to an area which covers a large proportion of the regions of Aquitaine, Midi-Pyrénées and Languedoc-Roussillon.

To the South, lies the third great influence on Tarn, the Pyrenees, formed by the massive earth movements which joined France to Spain and now middle-aged fold mountains. Erosion has been working on them since the Tertiary era. They have added sandstone and clay to the ingredients of the basin of Aquitaine, giving a landscape known locally as *molasse* (literally, flabby). It is a fairly uniform, rolling landscape of loose sandstone and clay, the monotony broken by small beds of limestone. The sediment is carried down the rivers, to the flat sandy Atlantic shore, leaving ports marooned inland. Bordeaux, for example, struggles to retain the eminence it enjoyed as a trading centre for hundreds of years.

The Pyrenees, and the lower Sidobre hills both affect the weather. The prevailing wind is from the west, encouraging a dull and equable climate. Tarn is too distant from the mountain ranges to be affected by the intensity with which rain clouds form as the moist air is rapidly cooled. There tends to be a reasonable flow in the rivers, in summer as well as winter, thanks to precipitation on the distant peaks. Sudden storms can also cause dramatic floods. But when a depression passes over the lowlands, and the wind is sucked northwards from Spain, instead of the usual west, then the area suffers from the *autun*. This powerful wind blows in disconcerting gusts as far as Toulouse, causing damage and drying the soil. Thus a landscape that is usually temperate suffers from occasional buffeting by wind and rain. The well watered river valleys provided year-long growing conditions for grass and cereals, and of course trees, including oak, with some Mediterranean pine.

Prehistoric people, firstly the hunters then the herdsmen, seems to have preferred the uplands. The most celebrated remains in the area are at Le Bruc some 10 kilometres east of Graulhet. The Celts, still cautious of the river, also kept to higher ground. Remains have been found near Busque, north of Graulhet and Gabor near St Sulpice. The invading Romans made the area part of their province of Gallia, or Gaul.[4] As well as war and taxes, they brought new technology and communication. Settlement now crept into the river valleys. Lavaur on the Agout and St Sulpice on the Tarn were first occupied at that period. Christianity brought new local heroes, in the form of saints. People liked to remind themselves of this past; the names of St Hilaire, St Sernin and St Projet were landmarks on the Tramways à Vapeur du Tarn (TVT).[5]

In the later days of the Roman Empire, the title of *comes*[6] was created. Literally a companion to the Emperor, a *comes* became a leader in his own right, on to whom the responsibilities of a crumbling and threatened empire could be devolved. Tracing back to this idea, the *Comté* of Toulouse came into being in the Middle Ages and therefore can claim, in theory at least, to have existed before the kingdom of France. An army of Franks (Germans really) invaded Gaul, ending Roman domination. Under King Clovis 1st (481 to 511 AD) they overran the whole of present day France, but the kingdom that survived was in the Ile de France around Paris. Ile-de-France was the name given to the area bounded by the rivers Marne, Seine and Oise. Although not an island as the British would understand it, it was sufficiently surrounded by water to be considered an 'isle' in the French sense. It was, to be sure, a well-defined and easily defended heartland for the growing kingdom of the Franks. The Ile-de-France officially returned in 1981 as the name of the Paris region. The Franks gradually assimilated with the local people. St Gaston, St Sigismond and St Sulpice were acknowleged for their contribution in civilising the invaders; they too are commemorated in place names along the railway line.

Coat of arms of the town of Graulhet, *left*, the left side white, with a green ear of corn, the right side blue with a golden hammer. These symbolise the town's dual existence as a centre of industry and of agriculture. The hammer was added as a compliment to the town's leather workers in the reign of Henri IV, around 1600. The coat of arms of the city of Lavaur, *centre*, with the fleur de lys and the castle show a royal connection. The waters are the River Agout. The coat of arms of the *bastide* of St Sulpice, the crown and the fleur de lys again show a royal connection.

Within a century or so, the inhabitants of the various regions of present day France, though under different adminstrations, recognised important cultural and religious links and their languages, though distinct, were similar. When the Moors came over the Pyrenees in the 8th century, in search of new lands for Islam, it was Charles Martel from Paris who organised resistance. In 732, he defeated the Moors at the battle of Tours. Although he was never king himself, he was a forebear of the French monarchy.

For centuries, French kings struggled with principalities to their east to win territories such as Alsace. South of the Massif Central a fine civilisation existed in the *Comté* of Languedoc. Trade developed and the town of Graulhet had come into existence by 961, keeping to the limestone eminence beside the Dadou. The river provided water, and made the town more easily defensible while the hill provided a strong point, against sudden floods as well as human attack. It became a tradition for local people, in Graulhet and elsewhere, to have a house in town, and also a farm.

In the 12th century, a new sect[7] was brought to the area. Followers were called Cathars, or Albigensi (of Albi). Their beliefs were different from Catholicism; dedicated followers or *parfaits*[7] led austere lives renouncing all earthly pleasures. At the time, Catholic clergy had grown corrupt and the lives of many of them, including the Popes, were an embarassing contrast to this purity of these prominent Cathars. The rivalry grew so bitter that in 1208, Pope Innocent III ordered a crusade against them.

Unfortunately for the people of the region, the kings of Paris seized on this pretext to further their territorial ambitions. During the previous century, the neighbouring land of Aquitaine, had also been fairly independent. Eleanor of Aquitaine married Henry II of England (1154-89) and for a time it seemed that in the region's alliance with England, the kings of France could be resisted. The sons of Henry and Eleanor were ineffectual compared with their parents and bit by bit their French possessions were lost until only Gascony, a triangle of land between the Pyrenees, the Garonne and the ocean, remained. By 1200, French troops were regularly on the border with the Languedoc, looking covetously at the area. When the Pope provided a pretext, Simon de Montfort was sent south by King Philip II with an army.

In 1229, the *Comté* of Toulouse was formally annexed to France although the fortress of Montségur south of Lavelanet held out until 1244. The campaign was ferocious. The village of Touelles, for example, near the site of present day Briatexte, was destroyed and the city of Lavaur which put up a stiff resistance under Dame Giraude also suffered much loss. The *Comté* was divided into provinces, along the lines of the rest of France, Tarn being part of the province of Haut Languedoc. A new aristocracy was authorised, headed by governors who were directly answerable to Paris. Fortunately for everyone, the son of de Montfort, Simon junior, emigrated and put the family talents at the service of English politicians.

The area then enjoyed a remarkable renaissance. New towns were founded at the end of the war. Many of these were *bastides*,[8] St Sulpice, one of a chain of 'new towns' founded along the Tarn River, received its *Charte de Fondation* on 9th May, 1247. St Gauzens was established in 1270 and its neighbour Briatexte in 1287. Giroussens also dates from the end of the 13th century. Other *bastides* throughout Languedoc and neighbouring Aquitaine were established in the period. Instead of brooding over war crimes, the area capitalised on its resources and new markets which had been opened up in the rest of France.

In the Graulhet area since Celtic times, there had been trade between herdsmen of the upland pastures and valley dwellers who could fatten the livestock from the hills. With a reliable supply of lime-free river water, and oak bark from local forests, a trade in prepared skins grew up in all the local towns. Untreated animal skins would have smelt of putrid flesh and rotted fairly quickly and so it was necessary to clean and cure them. Tannin from sources such as oak bark reacts with the proteins in the animal skin to give the skin the durability characteristic of leather. The hides have to be steeped in progressively stronger baths of tannin solution, starting with a weak one of 0.5 per cent and ending with one that was 25 per cent in strength. It was a long process, requiring anything up to 18 months.In those days urine was often used for the cleaning agent, ammonia, which it contains. The town of Graulhet gave itself a competitive edge by devising in the 13th century an advanced tanning process. Bark from the roots of oak trees was used, and other advantages of the process were its comparative speed and effectiveness on large coarse ox skins. The hardwearing greenish leather, ideal for the soles of shoes, came to be in demand throughout France.

Variations on the basic colour came to be offered thanks to dyes such as cochineal, iron sulphate and, once it was available, logwood from the tropics. Unfortunately for the workers, there was demand for black, produced by steeping leather in logwood mixed with fermented female urine. Luxury work in materials such as kid and sheepskin also developed. Specialist trades proliferated.

In sum, the competitive 'secret' of the leatherworkers of the town was the care with which they undertook the unpleasant and laborious processes involved. These start with the grading and sorting of the raw skins, continue through scraping away any putrid flesh still adhering to the underside, cleaning, the steeping in tannin baths, and the conscientious rinsing in the Dadou river at each stage.

A new source of wealth was exploited in nearby towns and cities. This was pastel, a blue dye obtained from woad. In pockets of lime and clay with the mild climate, conditions for raising woad were ideal. By 1460, Toulouse and Lavaur were flourishing centres of trade and the best quality of dye came from Albi.

Extraction, carried out in small towns and villages where the woad was harvested, was a smelly process. Leaves from the plant were mashed and formed into balls. On contact with the air, they would go blue. They would be left to dry for two or three months and it was marketed in solid lumps. To produce a dye, the lump was broken up, heated in water and allowed to ferment. It was put into a vat with wood ash and other materials, chief of which seems to have been urine, that vital ingredient of medieval industry.

Woad was an important local source of wealth until indigo arrived from Bengal and Lavaur began to decline relative to Graulhet. With the discovery of aniline dyes in the mid-19th century, trade in woad appeared dead. Recently, with increasing concern for the environmental effects of chemically produced dye, the European Union have sponsored research into reviving woad production. Long Ashton Research Centre has developed a process whereby the leaves of woad are simply (we use the word advisedly!) put into hot water to release the indigo. Commercial woad may once again flourish.

Local clay provided the raw materials for pottery. There is evidence[9] of a local industry in Roman times. In medieval times, there were various centres of production. It was important to have reliable vessels to collect the industrial raw material for the leather and woad industries! The most famous pottery was to be at Giroussens. In 1618 the Confrérie des Potiers de Giroussens was founded.[10] By the 18th century, 100 potters were at work making 'china articles for everyday use'. Production slumped in the 18th century, arresting the growth of the little town, but studio pottery is once more being made.

The Languedoc had made a good recovery from the Cathar campaign but in 1337, Edward III of England initiated the Hundred Years War. In 1360, most of the area was ceded to England. By 1377, the English were ejected. They returned in 1415, but by 1453 had been expelled once more.[11] The wars of the previous century may have made the inhabitants particularly wary. There were *bastides* to retire to in case of attack.

By the mid-16th century, there were new troubles. The Reformation had swept Europe, gaining adherents who came to be known as Huguenots. As the Catholic Church was very much identified with the Paris Government, and backed the imposition of taxes, the Huguenots became identified as the party of lower taxation, sympathetic to boot with greasy foreigners such as the Dutch and English. Campaigns were waged on and off until Henri IV ascended the throne. During the trouble, the Bishop of Castres fled to Graulhet. Because the local church of Notre Dame du Val D'Amour was his temporary headquarters, it is still sometimes known as Graulhet Cathedral, even though the Bishop left four centuries ago and the church has since been rebuilt. The Château de Crins, really a large country house whose fortifications were largely cosmetic, was started in the year after King Henry succeeded to the throne. The residence of the principal family of Graulhet, it is associated with some famous names.[12] The Edict of Nantes passed in 1598 was supposed to guarantee tolerance.

7. GRAULHET — La Place du Château   *Edit. A. Vincent*

Castle terrace, Graulhet. The castle stood at the highest point of the old town. It was burned down during the Revolution and it is here that Bastille Day is commemorated every year with fireworks!   *Ville de Graulhet*

Peace was not guaranteed. In the period between the death of King Henry and Louis XIV[13] there were private wars. Briatexte was besieged in 1623. Although it saw off the attack, its fortifications were later demolished. Graulhet meanwhile, under the protection of François Jacques d'Aubijoux, who was appointed Governor of the whole province, and later prominent personalities, began to flourish. By the middle of the 18th century, Canada was an influential trading partner.[14]

The French administration, meanwhile was tottering. The luxurious court of Versailles established by Louis XIV in the 1660s, once the symbol and vector of stability, became a top heavy burden. National prestige was dented by constant wars and a succession of poor harvests showed just how fragile the economy had become. The French Revolution began in Paris in 1789 and officially ended when Napoléon established a Consulate in 1799. During the period, there was heavy fighting in the Toulouse area. To the east, the countryside was more calm but the château at the heart of Graulhet was demolished. Trade in luxury leather goods ceased as did the production of pottery, already in decline, at neighbouring Giroussens. The resourceful Graulhétois looked for new markets.

Napoléon who was first the Consul and then Emperor of post-Revolutionary France helped his adopted country to short-lived military glory but also to long-term social changes. A new basic unit was formed, called the *commune*.[15] This could be an area centred on a village, such as Montdragon, or a town the size of Graulhet. Each commune was to be administered by a *maire* and *conseil*. The legal representative of the State, the *maire* has gathered responsibilities, even in a country as centralised as France, over such things as building permits and organising local water supplies and drainage. In the days of the small local

5. Mines de Carmaux. — Ensemble des Usines

Mines of Carmaux. During the 19th century, heavy industry in Tarn developed around the coal basin of Carmaux. The illustrations show the central place that transport plays in mineral extraction. In the upper photograph are conventional winding gear, and chimneys for stationary steam engines. The lower photograph shows a delightful home-made piece of loading equipment.   *Louis Briand/Carto-Club de Tarn*

railway, such matters as the design and site of station buildings were the responsibilities of the *maire* and *conseil* and the commune could put forward requests for alterations in such matters as the schedule. Although the number of communes has declined there are still 36,300 in France.

The provinces of the old kingdom were replaced by a new system of *départements*,[16] usually named after the principal local river. Albi was the capital of the newly created *département* of Tarn, and was the meeting place of the Conseil Général. As Tarn was comparatively populous, a *sous-préfecture* was later set up in Castres.

Before the Revolution, French law had varied throughout the provinces. In 1800, Napoléon set up a Committee to continue the work of standardisation begun at the time of the Revolution. By 1804, the Code Napoléon was in being, giving France a unified system of law which has stood the test of time. A distinguishing feature was the eminence given to the notion of equality, a trademark of revolutionary France. It also incorporated features of existing laws, for example in the division of property among heirs. The French had always favoured giving all members of the family a share; in England the eldest son would take all his father's property. The Code Napoléon enshrined the right of other children and the wife to receive their due. Thus for both the Tramways à Vapeur du Tarn and the Tramway de Réalmont, the shareholding of the major investors passed to their widows without dispute.

Other institutions set up by Napoléon were the *Grandes Écoles*.[17] A programme of road building was put in place. France was to be linked as never before by a network of *routes nationales*. Literally meaning national roads, and benefiting travellers throughout the State, it was considered unfair and unwise to place the whole burden of maintenance on nearby rate payers. These were designed to follow the straightest practical route between centres of importance throughout France. Examples in Tarn include the N88 from Toulouse to St Étienne (almost in the Rhone valley) and the N112 from Albi to Béziers on the Mediterranean coast. They were considered too important to be left to local politicians; decisions regarding their use had to be referred to Paris. Other roads were the responsibility of the *département* although it was not until 1836 that a truly significant law was passed regarding their upkeep. Named as D roads, decisions regarding their use would be referred to the *Conseil Général*. Later in the century, engineers for the Ponts et Chaussées planned the railways, though at the time of that the department came into being, rail and steam hardly existed in France outside a few coalmines.[18]

After the defeat of Napoléon, France found herself far behind her neighbours in certain important respects. Britain and Prussia had a more modern manufacturing base and within 15 years a much better developed railway system. National as well as commercial pride was at stake, and state intervention was needed.

In Britain, and also the USA, a railway network grew up without needing state encouragement, privately planned and financed with a minimum of direction from Government. In France, a greater proportion of individual wealth was tied up in land, and wealthy people were on the whole more conservative than their counterparts across the Channel. In addition, the French already tended to look to the State to mastermind any transport initiative.

The Government in Paris would have to initiate a railway programme but at the same time not increase the tax burden too much. The restored monarchy of Louis

XVIII and his brother Charles depended very much on the goodwill of wealthy landowners but dared not increase taxes for ordinary people. High taxes had been a cause of the Revolution! But their timidness in not promoting economic reforms contributed to their downfall. Guizot, State Minister to their successor, Louis Philippe, steered the First Railway Law through the French Parliament in 1842, to overcome the difficulties as he saw them. This was known as La Loi Legrand after the Director of Les Ponts et Chaussées who had mapped out a desirable rail network for the country. The projected lines would be turned into concessions.[19]

At first, the Act seemed to be producing results. Companies such as the Paris Lyon Méditerranée, the Compagnie du Midi and the Paris Orléans (PO) were awarded these important concessions and their lines formed the basis of what became known as the *grands réseaux*.[20] Between 1844 and 1846, there was railway mania, and the railway network expanded rapidly. Then share prices collapsed and by 1848, a number of lines were bankrupt, and looking to the taxpayer for subsidy. Worse still, in spite of all the anger and expense, France still had only 1,921 kilometres of main line track compared to Britain's 6,349. Railways led, not to centres of profit and population, but where the whims of officialdom dictated, complicated by the desire of politicians to use public works as a way to distribute favours. The line connecting Paris to Lyon, the second city, was still incomplete, bogged down in bankruptcy proceedings.

Louis Philippe was succeded by the shortlived Second Republic after which the Second Empire of Louis Napoléon was established. He brought with him a new wave of financiers who founded banks specialising in commercial lending. The banker Isaac Pereire, for example, made the completion of the line to Lyon possible. By 1859, there were 6,000 kilometres of railway. France was also looking overseas. A foothold gained in Algeria became an empire by 1848 and colonies were established in equatorial Africa and Indo-China. In northern Tarn, coalfields were developed around Carmaux, with attendant heavy industries. Graulhet reflected the slow but steady growth. The *mégissiers* (craftsmen who purified hides), keeping abreast of developments in leather technology, were the most influential manufacturing sector of Graulhet, and their main trade link was along the D964 (N664) to Gaillac on the Paris Orléans.

In 1869, the Compagnie du Midi planned to link Albi to the north of Graulhet with Castres to the south. Naturally, a good case was put forward for routeing the proposed line through Graulhet. At the same, equally persuasive arguments were put forward in favour of Réalmont, just under 20 kilometres to the east. Bureaucratic rather than commercial reasoning prevailed at the Headquarters of the Midi, and the railway eventually ran between the two, 14 kilometres from Graulhet and five from Réalmont. The place to benefit from all the politics was a small village, Laboutarié, which got the station. The major network as envisaged by the planners of Paris was almost complete and there was little hope of another better placed railway.

Then the whole social and political climate changed. The Franco-Prussian war of 1870-1 ended the Second Empire. Admiral Jaurès, was one who distinguished himself in the resistance against the invaders. History swept away Emperor Louis Napoléon, his court and his liberal financiers. A defeated France had to surrender territory, and devise a new strategy of defence. Determined to halt future invasions, the new administration started to construct a line of military strongholds from the North Sea to the Mediterranean. These were built to the highest standards and the latest theories of military science. At the same time, the whole nation came to appreciate that the more fully integrated the country, the more it could be an efficient fighting machine like its rival Prussia. The Prussian Government had actively encouraged railway building and their country had one of the most developed systems in Europe. French national security as well as the existing demands of commerce were felt to require some sort of *réseaux sécondaires*[21] linking the many minor communities to the major railways.

During the time of Louis-Napoléon, attempts had already been made to address the problem. In 1865, the Loi Migneret had been passed. The State could open and subsidise a railway if it was considered sufficiently important, i.e. of *Intérêt Général* to the transport infrastructure of an entire region. The local authorities were empowered to do the same for routes of particular benefit to a district. The line would then be of *Intérêt Local*. As with the *Grands Réseaux*, once a concession was identified and the subsidy, if any, agreed, private individuals or companies could come forward to construct and operate the line. The first *chemin de fer d'intérêt local* was constructed in 1867 between Glos-Montfort and Pont-Audemer just south of the Seine estuary. The departement of Eure was encouraging to the development of a secondary network, but on the whole the mood was unenthusiastic.

By 1880, 2,189 kilometres of secondary railway had been constructed but there was still a vast French hinterland left to serve. Therefore in 1880, a second Light Railway Act was passed which, among other provisions, recognised the role that narrow gauge railways could play. Secondary networks would have to be cheaper to construct than a fully engineered main line; as building costs were reduced, so would more routes become viable. Reducing the gauge would mean than the trains could negotiate curves of comparatively small radius. This would be of great importance in hilly country or where wayleaves were restricted. A narrow gauge railway could more closely follow the contour of the ground thereby avoiding some of the embankments, cuttings and tunnels that added to basic costs. The greater flexibility of narrow gauge would allow the railway to approach the centres of population more readily and, by being able to use the streets of a town, clients could receive or deliver their goods with minimum use of intermediate transport.

Isolated narrow gauge lines already existed, mainly to serve a specific industry, quarry or agricultural concern. The Decauville Company was one which specialised in laying portable railways.[22] The public were used to seeing small scale railways at work. The revised Act seemed at last to be facing up to the challenges of 19th century transport.

A major problem in railway building was, as always, the acquisition of land for the trackbed. The Act made it possible to route the proposed line along the verges of existing roads. There were advantages in being able to use existing roadways, but customer convenience in selecting a route was sometimes ignored and the speed and comfort of any train following the line was severely restricted. If a proportion of over 70 per cent of the line ran at the side of public roads, the line was classified as a tramway. The width of the roadside that could be devoted to rail was limited (to 2.2 metres) and country road were often tortuous. The more narrow the gauge therefore, the better. The two official gauges were metre gauge which was almost too wide for a roadside tramway, and 75 centimetres.

Two views of the Decauville factory. The first shows the warehouses in which materials from Decauvilles's suppliers were stored. The second shows a workshop in which machining was taking place. Quite a high proportion of the machinists are women. In both pictures, railways are used almost as a production line. The pictures were taken in the early 20th century.

(Both) Confrérie Des Amateurs De Vapeur Vive

The Law also introduced the *Cahier des Charges*[23] which stipulated operating details of the light railway, according to gauge. From drizzly Brittany to the Mediterranean, the design of buildings, train running speeds and weight of track were all standardised. This may or may not have been a good idea at the time, but still in force 30 years later, it imposed old fashioned rules on an industry facing increased competition from the roads.

To solve the problem of finance, the original scheme of inviting private operators to actually build and run the line was left in place. Returns, however, were guaranteed by a system which rewarded inefficiency. Any gain in revenue from increased traffic would decrease the subsidy from State and *Département*. Central Government was careful to limit its responsibilities, exposing local ratepayers to the possibility of enormous losses. Attempts were made later to address these weaknesses, but it can be seen that once local administrations were sure that road transport offered a viable alternative, they had both the power and strong motivation to close secondary railways.

Many proposed routes were looked at afresh, and one line, the Chemin de Fer Économique Forestier des Landes adopted the gauge of 75 centimetres when it was constructed in 1906. Twelve kilometres long, it linked Lencouacq with Roquefort. In 1893, a tramway linking the suburb of Ste Foy with Lyon was built to this gauge but was upgraded to metre gauge in 1906. Nothing yet had come to serve the inhabitants of Graulhet though the possibility of a main line spur from Laboutarié to Graulhet was considered. In 1884, a tender was submitted by La Société Internationale des Travaux Publics.[24] This was for 1.7 million francs, an astronomical sum in those days. Two other concerns were induced to consider the project. The Chemins de Fer Économiques was unwilling to put a price on construction because it claimed that a spur only 12 kilometres long would not repay the expenses. La Société de Construction des Batignolles was prepared to consider the project as long as the *Département* undertook to give them preference when any other project was to be tendered. This was felt to be unreasonably onerous. And so, as with similar situations all over France, possibilities for building minor railways were explored and dismissed.

The second Light Railway Act had allowed for narrow gauge and in 1885, the possibility of a metre gauge line was duly explored. A feasibility study by the engineers Pot and Santoul concluded that the proposed line would run at a loss of 2,500 francs per kilometre. The communes concerned, the Department and the State all declined to make themselves responsible and the project was once more shelved. Metre gauge was felt to be a half-measure. Local people would be willing to subsidise a standard gauge line or nothing at all.

A power struggle in the Army now affected the story. In 1872, we left General Rivière planning a chain of fortifications down the eastern border of France. In 1880, gelignite was introduced by Alfred Nobel, making exploding artillery shells possible. Hitherto impregnable stone fortresses were now vulnerable to artillery. In the event of an attack, defenders and their equipment would actually be safer outside the forts which had for so long provided security. Mobility was once more a key problem, and the solution was to be found in rail.

The Génie (Military Engineers) planned to use metre gauge railways to move guns and heavy equipment while the Artillery, convinced by a single energetic officer, Prosper Péchot, preferred 60 centimetre gauge. In 1888, the Ministry of War decided in favour of 60 centimetre gauge, not only for military but also for civilian use. This was a triumph, not only for Péchot, but also for his friend Paul Decauville who was already marketing rail, locomotives and rolling stock to that gauge. The Decauville Company immediately gained military contracts, but also looked for civilian business. The company was awarded the contract to provide transport around the Exposition Universelle of 1889 in Paris.[25] The company did this to great acclaim, carrying six million passengers (including many admiring Prussians) and earned the Cross of the Legion of Honour from a grateful nation.

One visitor was Monsieur Bonnet[26] from Laboutarié. He was the *correspondant* for the Compagnie du Midi which was eager to gain business in Graulhet. As recounted above, the Midi had annoyed the citizens by failing to bring the main line into their town. Most freight still went up to Gaillac to be transported by the Paris Orleans line. As the leather industry alone generated nearly 4,000 tonnes of freight per annum, Graulhet was regarded as an important prize.

In Paris, Mr Bonnet was enchanted by the ride, but even more delighted by the economics of the railway. The concession for the Paris Exhibition was awarded to Decauville at, relatively speaking, the last minute. The railway was laid and, in the main, ready for operation by 6th May, in good time for the opening ceremony. From nine to midnight every day, trains left at eight minute intervals, a total of 113,000 kilometres run by the time that the exhibition closed in October. There was not one accident, not even an upset, perhaps because there were so many staff, 277 in all. Sweetest of all, the little railway made a 30 per cent profit. If it could so generously recoup an investment over a six month period, what could it do if it was permanent?

Full of enthusiasm, M. Bonnet made himself known at the handsome Decauville pavilion at the foot of the Eiffel Tower and spoke to Paul Decauville himself. He saw how innovation had made it possible for a small, lightly engineered railway to transport heavy goods. He had witnessed for himself the comfort possible in a carriage for 60 centimetre gauge. A display showed how Decauville track was contributing to celebrated projects such as the Panama Canal and the Channel Tunnel.[27]

Bonnet the younger was a trainee Engineer with the Ponts et Chaussées. The father and son put together a proposal for the *Conseil Général* of Tarn. A 60 centimetre line would run from Lavaur on the main line, to Laboutarié via Graulhet. It would then continue to Réalmont and Montredon. The line would serve the lead mines at Peyrebrune, if enough traffic could be guaranteed.[28]

A counter-proposal was being lodged almost simultaneously by M. Maire, the new Director at Peyrebrune (la Société des Mines du Dadou). It was metre gauge and considerably more ambitious in extent. It would follow the D63 from Montredon to Réalmont, the D631 on through Graulhet and Briatexte as far as the junction with the D87, then follow the D87 to Gaillac. The *Préfet* consulted the Paris Orleans Railway Company as its station at Gaillac would handle most of the traffic. The PO recommended turning it down.[29] The Bonnet proposal was therefore preferred; they had creditworthy backers, Paul Decauville of course, and a businessman from Toulouse, M. Mandement.

All the same, they were warned that government or departmental subsidies were unlikely to be approved. A revised version went therefore before the *Conseil Général* of the Department. The proposed line now simply ran from Graulhet to Laboutarié, the nearest main line station, financed almost entirely by leather merchants, M. Bonnet's friends and business associates. For the early years at least they felt it was their property. On 5th June, 1891, the Chambre Syndicale des Patrons Mégissiers de Graulhet[30] voted Bonnet their support and members bought shares in the enterprise. Building of the extension of the line would, it was proposed, be financed by profits from the existing operation.

The official steps towards opening the line were duly followed. The *Cahier des Charges* was approved on 4th March, 1893. This, as we have seen, regulated the railway according to Central Government rules. None of the rolling stock could be more than 1.8 metres wide, subject to an overall limit (all projections included) of 2.03 metres. Trains could be no more than 60 metres long and must consist of no more than six vehicles. The maximum speed was 20 kilometres per hour and there must be at least four trains in either direction per day.[31] Ticket and freight charges were also fixed. Any revision was subject to approval by the *Conseil Général*. On 26th April, 1893, the project, still the personal responsibility of the Bonnets and M. Mandement, was officially granted the concession by the *Département*.

On 25th July, the line was declared of *utilité publique*,[23] and the *Conseil* reiterated that the Department had not promised to provide guarantees or subsidies. This seemed a fairly reasonable disclaimer at the time; it looked as though the line would pay for itself and the local traders were willing to put up the initial capital. Once the Department had reassured itself, the line was declared of *intérêt local*.

On 28th March, 1894, the Articles of the new company, now styled the Compagnie des Chemins de fer et Tramways à Vapeur du Tarn[32] were formally deposited with the lawyer Maître Léon Frezoul at Albi. The popular abbreviation for the name was the TVT, short for Tramways à Vapeur du Tarn. The company logo, consisting of a shield displaying the initials STT (Société des Tramways de Tarn) was also officially registered, as it would appear on the smokebox door of each locomotive.

The capital of the company was 300,000 francs, divided into 1,500 shares worth 200 francs each. The Directors, Bonnet and Mandement owned 200 shares, and a further 20 were in the name of Georges Berges of Toulouse, the local representative of the Decauville Company. A further 500 shares were later to be issued when the Lavaur section was built, bringing the total share capital to 400,000 francs. On 15th April, 1895, the TVT replaced Bonnet and Mandement as the nominee for the official concession.

On 30th June, the line connecting Graulhet to the main line at Laboutarié was opened. Politics and personalities, as much as commercial consideration had shaped the Company Articles to make the STT a child of its time. While M. Bonnet was bringing the line into being, 60 centimetre gauge had been fashionable. The networks around Pithiviers and Calvados had been started in 1891, the one around Royan in the previous year. But by 1894, the commercial genius of 60 centimetres, Paul Decauville, had been forced to resign.[33] The Tarn

Graulhet in 1900. The most important crossroads of the city was where the east-west D631 met the D84 to Albi. The upper picture shows the Avenue St Paul, now Avenue de la Résistance, going south. The lower photograph shows the view north.   *Ville de Graulhet*

network, followed by the Tramway de Réalmont were the last public lines to commit themselves to that gauge. All over France of the period, secondary lines continued to open, but this was the last of 60 centimetres.

There were similar histories throughout France. The necessary legislation had been in place for some years; at first local people were reluctant to commit themselves to the expense. As lines were built, and success stories could be told, initial reluctance was overcome. Transport increased the prosperity of a remote district and therefore in itself generated demand. With increasing prosperity and increasing revenues, more investment was justified.

In the case of the TVT trade in the Graulhet area did increase. Leather traffic which had been under 4,000 tonnes before the railway opened, was the major part of the 10,629 tonnes of raw materials and finished goods carried by the railway in 1911. Much of this increase was due to the merino trade. Sheep rearing in Australia had made available top quality sheepskins, as long as there was transport. Once Graulhet was connected to the rail network, new freight appeared, red quebracho, *Schinopsis lorentzii*, from South America. This hardwood was a rich source of tannin. Until then, the leatherworkers had relied on local oak, which was not available in sufficient quantities to supply the explosion in demand. From almost nothing, the weight of quebracho imported, usually in powder form, increased to nearly 4,000 tonnes at the peak of demand. Up until World War I, railways were demonstrably increasing trade, and rail networks were extended throughout France.

It is hard to imagine now the impact of World War I on ordinary people in Graulhet. National feeling was strong against the Prussian foe. The humiliations of 1871 were kept fresh in the popular memory, even though France could boast many achievements since. The bullying behaviour of the Austrians in the Balkans at once outraged the French sense of fair play and awoke old fears. These feelings were irritated beyond bearing when the Prussians treated small, neutral Belgium, in a similar way.

The war began with huge public gestures, some of them futile. Thousands, eventually millions, of Frenchmen were called up for the Army. In Graulhet passenger services ceased. Goods traffic on the other hand boomed, thanks to orders for boots and other leather equipment placed by the military. As the war proceeded, the farms and factories of the area were drained of men of fighting age while steadily orders arrived arrived for more and more material. By late 1915, the goods yard at Graulhet was choked with goods, awaiting collection by the depleted workforces of the factories. During February 1916, M. Valiech, M. Bonnet's successor as Director, was forced to close the railway to further goods traffic. It was reopened when the 40 waiting wagons were unloaded. Imported hides were a problem, but the principal encumbrance were the barrels of quebracho powder, no less than 1,500 of them.

Services gradually improved for passengers. At first there were two round services per day three times a week, that was on Mondays, Thursdays and Saturdays. As the war dragged on, a Sunday service was added. The tranquil estate of Nabeillou, on the line to the west of Graulhet was turned into a military hospital. For years after, staff and visitors must have remembered their trips on the 'little train' to attend the wounded and dying.

The war as it dragged on seemed to justify the reliance on railways. In Graulhet and elsewhere, they were the arteries through which coursed the blood of France. On the battlefield, it seemed a similar story. By the end of 1918, the French forces possessed 3,800 kilometres of narrow gauge track (not all in service) simply for connecting the military front with its railhead. But the war also nurtured potential rivals to rail transport. With each side striving for advantage, the internal combustion engine was greatly improved, road vehicles and aeroplanes. Afterwards, an industry that had produced tanks and military lorries now turned to selling cars and lorries to civilians.

In post-war France, the signs were often ignored. Instead of planning to meet increased competition from road transport, the TVT expanded. The Depression which swept the Western World in the late 1920s affected France as a drawn out pressure[34] rather than a sharp agony. In the harsh conditions of the 1920s and 1930s, enterprises already dependent on subsidies, suffered decline. The TVT was closed in 1935, and dismantling began in 1936. Those railways which survived until World War II, had a brief period of business. Frequently military targets, never repaired, stigmatised by memories of war-time austerity, and very old-fashioned, the secondary network went into final decline in the 1950s.

France meanwhile began reconstruction. At Graulhet, the old station was swept away; the *stade* Noël Pélissou,[35] overlooked by social housing, was built on the station grounds. All along this line, as with others, the old buildings and station yards took on new functions, the railway dead and almost forgotten.

The Dadou valley in the late 20th century, west of Laboutarié station, looking down the valley.   *Malcolm Wright*

Chapter Two

A History of the Company

As described in the previous chapter, the Articles of the Compagnie des Chemins de Fer et Tramways à Vapeur du Tarn were finalised on 28th March, 1894 and the company was recognised as the official holder of the transport concession on 15th April, 1895. The official abbreviation, as appearing on company property, of the fulsome title was STT. MM. Bonnet and Mandement, the previous concessionaires, were principal shareholders in the new company, and M. Marius-Dominique Bonnet the new Director.

The 12.7 kilometres of the proposed line offered few engineering difficulties, apart from passing the main line at Laboutarié, or problems in securing a right of way. M. Bonnet acted as chief engineering contractor, assisted by M. François Daney. A conflict of interests might have been expected in the dual rôle accorded the new Director. In fact, the economist won over the engineer in those early days and major rebuilding had to take place later.

The line followed existing roads for almost all its route and stopped just outside the old town of Graulhet. It had originally been planned to build the station in the town market place but there was opposition and the purchase of existing buildings would have been costly. The rest of the route had been provided at almost no expense and so a station in the centre of the town seemed a needless extravagance. A tract of open field was purchased from a M. Albigot just to the east of the Dadou river, then the town boundary. Passengers had to disembark, then walk to the Pont Neuf[36] to reach their destination. The Dadou river, well known for being relatively limefree, was to provide the steam locomotives with water.

Early on, the portable track recommended by Decauville was abandoned in favour of a more conventional 15 kilogramme per metre rail laid on oak sleepers. The Departmental Engineer had been in touch with his colleague in Loiret. It was the responsibility of an officer of Local Government to ensure that secondary railways conformed to the agreed standards. The 60 cm gauge Tramway de Pithiviers à Toury was already running. It had been found that 12 kilogramme rail bonded to metal sleepers was unsatisfactory for the demands of a commercial freight railway.

In 1895, there were a total of 20 employees on company books. One was M. Bonnet, now aged 78, who worked from a small wooden office built on to the station at Laboutarié. There were 11 staff for stations and engine sheds, three gangers and five engine drivers. Three 0-6-2 tank locomotives, four carriages, 18 wagons and two brake vans were supplied. The success of the Graulhet line was noted. On 1st September, 1901, a tramway connecting Réalmont to Laboutarié was opened. For the full story see the chapter on the Tramway de Réalmont. The two towns, and indeed the sponsors of the two tramways, considered themselves to be rivals. The thrift which animated the Graulhet line was even more in evidence on the Réalmont one - there were no steam engines, just horses. Rivalry between the two tramways was to persist until 1932 when an exasperated *Département* obliged the bankrupt Tramway de Réalmont to hand over services to the nearly bankrupt TVT.

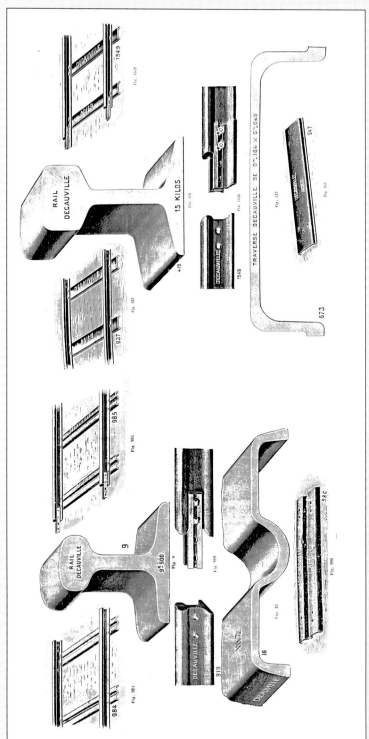

Rail from Decauville catalogue. The 9.5 kilogramme weight portable rail was standard for military use. 12 kilogramme rail was originally recommended for the Royan and Tarn lines but 15 kilogramme rail was eventually adopted, laid on conventional creosoted wooden sleepers rather than metal prefabrications. The weight given is per metre of each rail. A prefabricated section would of course weigh more than double the given weight per metre.

Jim Hawkesworth

The work at Réalmont and the success of the TVT persuaded the authorities to allow the second part of the project, the extension to Lavaur. Unlike 1891, there was no resolution affirming the independence of the line. A contract was drawn up in 1900 and received the all-important Declaration of *utilité publique* on 5th September. The Departmental ratepayers thus became guarantors of the railway, and were instantly called on for a contribution. As was noted in Chapter One, the line was supposed to repay them from profits. M. François Daney, who had assisted M. Bonnet during the first phase, was the Director of Construction. Daydé and Pillé, rue de Chateaudun, Paris, were the successful contractors for the largest single engineering work, the bridge over the Dadou at Briatexte.

The planned route, like the original, made extensive use of the roads. But unlike before, the maximum gradient was fixed at 2.5 per cent, and the minimum curve at 40 metres radius, with certain exceptions. Improvements were also to be made to the existing line to bring it up to these new standards. Most notably, the sharp turn at the road junction at Laboutarié was realigned so that the original 30 metre radius was increased to 50. At 20.8 kilometres, the extension was longer than the original, presented more engineering challenges, and required a route through Graulhet. The railway was able to make use of the existing Pont Neuf to cross the Dadou river into the town, but seven major engineering works were required. These included an embankment followed by a cutting at the eastern side of Briatexte, a railway bridge across the Dadou to the west of that village, the widening of six existing bridges and the shifting of 10,000 metric tonnes of spoil to construct the embankment and cutting at the Col d'Ambres above Lavaur. Relatively little work was done in Graulhet although the route was steep and tortuous. The official maximum gradient of 2.5 per cent was exceeded for nearly half a kilometre, with a gradient of more than 5 per cent for 130 metres. Given the cost of the engineering works on the rest of the line, it would have been wise to invest more on the route through the town.

The *parc de materiel* (or rolling stock) was officially fixed at five locomotives, carriages offering a total of 350 passenger places, and freight wagons with a capacity of 350 tonnes. (This total included existing stock.) Two new locomotives were purchased, this time from Weidknecht (*see Chapter Six*). The Weidknecht 4-6-0T had a slightly more powerful output and promised to cope with the challenging conditions.

As this was a line of *utilité publique,* the *Département* agreed to contribute 618,750 francs towards the construction. In return, it was to receive half of any receipts when these exceeded 4,240 francs per kilometre. The Departmental interest was further secured by a charge on three out of the company's five locomotives, and similar charges on the rolling stock. Additions to the *parc de materiel* were the responsibilty of the company which issued 500 shares with a total value of 100,000 francs.

On 30th April, the bridge at Briatexte was tested with a train consisting of two locomotives and six wagons each weighing 14 tonnes. Trials were satisfactory, and the line was opened for passengers on 26th May, 1903, in time to carry the Minister for the Navy, Camille Pelletan, to Graulhet. As part of a celebration of the exploits of Admiral Jaurès, Minister Pelletan unveiled a statue. The Lavaur line was opened for goods on 26th October and became the route for Australian

Briatexte viaduct, from south of the viaduct. The ruined mill can be seen under the bridge. The house which appears to be perched on the bridge is not!   *J. Daffis/ACOVA*

Weidknecht 4-6-0 on Briatexte viaduct.   *J. Daffis/ACOVA*

Statue of Admiral Jaurès. The statue is near the site of the station. Here it is in the position where Camille Pelletan and the jubilant crowd of local people would have seen it, on the lower part of the Place du Foirail (Jourdain). The houses on the right are actually built into the castle terrace. The steps lead to the upper level.
Ville de Graulhet

Graulhet station during the strike of 1909. Two views of the station side of the *Bâtiment des Voyageurs*, showing a strong military presence. The Weidknecht is almost hidden by its numerous miltary escort. The strike was the occasion for many postcards since both sides of the conflict, which was highly politicised, published them to raise funds.

Louis Briand/Carto-Club Tarnais

merino skins coming from the Atlantic ports. Coal and other raw materials, mostly from the industrial complex north of Albi, continued to be brought in via Laboutarié. Although this original branch was always to be the most profitable section of the railway, extending the network helped to increase traffic in general. The whole line also benefited from a chance for a complete refit.

The increase in administrative work was given as a reason to move the headquarters of the TVT to Toulouse while the operating office was moved from Laboutarié to Graulhet. In October 1903, M. Théodose Valiech, the new Director, approved the updated timetable from the Toulouse office, and it was from Toulouse that came letters of appointment. Graulhet dealt with matters such as payslips. The once formidable M. Bonnet died in Toulouse aged 88. His son, who had also been involved in the railway was now aged 52 and took the chance to retire to a nearby village.

From 1903 onwards, Graulhet began to feel new pressures, some of them the products of local success stories. Improvements in transport had helped to make Graulhet a world class centre of production but it was suffering growing pains as a result. The steadily increasing labour force had by now completely lost their traditional links with local agriculture and lived in squalid isolation over an increasingly polluted river. The river was so filthy that the company was forced to use hard water from a local well. There was bad feeling everywhere, rising expectations, coupled with an actual decline in conditions.

In 1907, there was a leatherworkers' strike, followed by more bitter one which began in December 1909. Leather workers demanded an increase in wages and a reduction in working hours. Two detachments of militia occupied the station while the strikers and sympathisers picketed the street of the town. Throughout the winter months the strike dragged on. Soup kitchens were established for the needy. Vincent Auriol, a future French President, peeled potatoes at one of these, while Jean Jaurès[37] provided good offices at a higher level. The strike collapsed on 2nd May, 1910.

Although issues raised by the strike could not totally be ignored, this was generally a prosperous time for the railway. Trade and receipts increased in equal measure. The staff on the railway now numbered 30. There were two extra station masters because of the newly opened stretch of line, and the team of gangers was increased to six. There was a chance to make jobs more specialised. Five 'auxiliaries' under the old dispensation became three drivers, three firemen and a night driver, the same applying in the engine shed. Costs in general increased. The mood throughout the country was optimistic, 'invest and expand' the watchwords. As early as 1906, the PO approached M. Valiech, because it was driving a line down the Tarn valley to Toulouse. If he extended the line westward a mere 14 kilometres to the planned station at St Sulpice, they would have an outlet to Toulouse.

At first the *Conseil Général* refused its backing. By 1908 it had relented sufficiently to permit a feasibility study and by early 1913 had declared of *utilité publique* not only a line to St Sulpice but also an extension to Salvagnac. The share capital of the reorganised railway was to be as follows. The existing line was to be revalued at 825,000 francs. 725,000 francs was to be raised for the extension to St Sulpice and a further 885,000 francs for the 17 kilometres to Salvagnac. In return, Central Government would subsidise the existing line by 16,500 francs per year, the St Sulpice extension by 15,000 francs and the Salvagnac branch by 17,000 francs. In other words, there was to be a guaranteed return on the existing line of 2 per cent, 2 per cent return on an extension to St Sulpice and 1.9 per cent on the Salvagnac one. In those years when 4 per cent interest could be expected on securities, the guaranteed return[38] was not very tempting. Added to that, an independent review demonstrated that the estimates of costs fell considerably short of what would be needed. (The eventual cost was to be more than 2½ million francs.)

It is rather surprising that an agreement concerning freight transfer was actually signed by both TVT and PO on 17th April, 1914. Weidknecht supplied another 4-6-0T locomotive, and 10 more wagons were purchased, in anticipation of this extension. Then all eyes in France turned to the Balkans where a certain Austrian was assassinated by a Serb, and Austria was soon calling on its ally, Prussia. The Prussian threat and a chance to avenge their defeat in 1871 exacted the total commitment of all French citizens. All plans were put on hold, including the extension to St Sulpice, and a proposal to link Paris with Narbonne through Graulhet.

The outbreak of World War I disrupted normal life and put all plans into abeyance. In the year before the outbreak of hostilities, the TVT offered three daily services in each direction, and two on the Lavaur line, as well as many 'specials', e.g. for market days, and a substantial goods traffic. There were just under 140,000 fare paying passengers and over 29,000 tonnes of goods were carried. Everything was to change. Rolling stock was requisitioned, four wagons going to the 60 cm gauge Ordnance Works at Bergerac, and the war effort absorbed almost all available fuel. As the war dragged on, semblances of normal service returned. Leather was much in demand. At the same time because of conscription, all factories in France were hampered by shortages of manpower. By February 1916, the station yard at Laboutarié was at a standstill, as has been previously described. Forty wagons were released from front line duty and a sort of equilibrium returned. There were passenger services on Mondays, Thursdays, Saturdays, and, towards the end of the war, Sundays.

New tyres for locomotive wheels were ordered from Le Creusot in March 1918, but were not supplied until after the end of the war. By 1919, the railway depended on just two locomotives, through the lack of spares. The entire system was run down and in need of investment. The purchase of six Pershing type war surplus tipper wagons was a small help in restoring stock. Yet in these conditions, the TVT returned to its pre-war plan of expansion.[39]

In 1922, State and Departmental aid offered were much more generous than had been offered before. As part of the Armistice terms, Germany was obliged to pay reparations to France, which were to be used for reconstruction. Infrastructure, especially railways, benefited from the rebuilding programme, although Graulhet was well away from the combat area.

The conditions under which the St Sulpice line was to be built altered the whole operation of the TVT. With the existing network, it would form a *Voie Ferré d'Intérêt Local*. The line to Lavaur would be relegated to branch line status. Now that the TVT was declared of *Intérêt Local* it could attract more grants, considerably more. Of the 2,657,632 francs required before the line could open, the shareholders would provide the 750,000 francs already spent and Central Government 81,767 francs. Small contributions were also made by the Communes of St Lieux and Giroussens towards the cost of the station buildings. The *Département* had to make up the remainder, which turned out to be substantial. Not only did this commit local ratepayers to being major contributors, but also exposed them to making good any unforeseen deficit for the duration of the concession which was revised to run until 1963. In return, more of the assets of the TVT were made over to the *Département*, already titular owner of half the rolling stock. Central Government continued to control fares and salaries.

The company's running stock was now to consist of seven locomotives, six *fourgons* (guard's vans), carriages with accommodation for 530 passengers and freight capacity totalling 370 tonnes. Of these five locomotives, five *fourgons*, accommodation for 280 passengers and 260 tonnes of goods would revert to the Department at the end of the concession. The Department would also receive 70 per cent of all operating profits in excess of 4,240 francs per kilometre. This seems only fair to what was in effect the major shareholder. In practice, as public servants know relatively little about railway management, it was easy enough not to run at a profit.

Construction was approved by the Ministre de Travaux Publics and backed by the Ministre de l'Intérieur and the Ministre des Finances in 1921. Some works had already begun, this was recognised at the time of authorisation. Fraisse Frères of Albi[40] successfully tendered to build the largest single engineering works on the line, the viaduct over the Agout near Giroussens. They were then entrusted with the work of building the entire extension of the line. Readers may be interested to know that although the tender for the bridge submitted by Fraisse Frères was the lowest of the three submitted, the company managed to increase its receipts by 20 per cent and claim a share of traffic revenue.

In May 1924, the Berliet Company of Lyon provided a petrol driven 30 hp railcar for 106,500 francs. It was hoped to operate the railcar with one man, but the Government Inspector declined permission. Another purchase was of a Decauville 2-6-0T locomotive delivered in January 1925. The Decauville Company had developed this model during the war, quite an improvement on the old 0-6-2. In working order, it was a tonne and a half heavier than its forebear.

The line opened on 2nd April, 1925 for passengers and for goods the following June. Omens for the future health of minor railways in France were not good. The rail for the new line was bought for a reasonable price as it came second-hand from the Tramways of Ardèche[41] which were all but closed. That very month, the most serious accident in the history of the line occurred and staff were officially cautioned (*see Chapter Five*). It was soon clear that the line was not attracting passengers; for three months, there were three services daily in each direction, but in July this was cut to two.

After the comparatively free spending of the period of reconstruction, France was sliding into a period of austerity. The cost of living was rising, as was unemployment. At the same time, road transport was advancing rapidly in convenience and economy. Important among the 'sunrise industries' which had been encouraged in the early post-war period were car and lorry makers such as Renault, Citroen and Peugeot, and their production, now well established, was attracting both goods and passengers away from the railway. Caught by the economic downturn and increased competition, the authorities shelved the planned extension to Salvagnac.

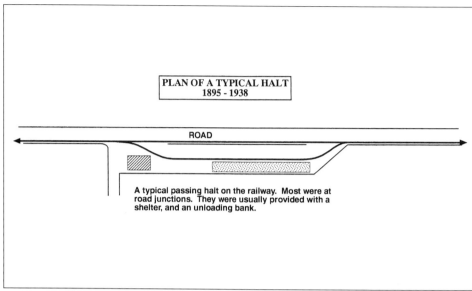

PLAN OF A TYPICAL HALT
1895 - 1938

ROAD

A typical passing halt on the railway. Most were at road junctions. They were usually provided with a shelter, and an unloading bank.

Plan of typical Halt 1895-1938.

The Salles viaduct. The single most expensive engineering work on the TVT. *Malcolm Wright*

Soon the existing railway was fighting for its life. Since the turn of the century, one of the main cargoes was sheepskins. The bottom fell out of the market the very year that the St Sulpice line opened, and tonnage dropped by a quarter. For three years, the TVT managed to keep up receipts, but from 1928 onwards the decline both of tonnage and of profitability (even with all the subsidies received) was irreversible. In 1929, almost all the coal traffic, once amounting to almost 6,000 tonnes a year, had gone; there were only eight 10 tonne wagons needed for the entire system. Another staple, quebracho, faded abruptly. In 1931 the railway carried nearly 4,000 tonnes of the tanning agent. The following year, it carried only 84.

To improve the service, the TVT raised prices again and squeezed more productivity out of the system. The number of staff had drifted upwards, as often happens, and had been increased by the opening of the St Sulpice line. In 1928, well after the decline was evident, the railway employed 65 people, admittedly down from a maximum of 67. Now the trend had to be reversed. For example, seven station staff lost their jobs or were retired on 1st May, 1931. In 1930, a clause was inserted into Company Articles making it a road as well as rail transport provider. A bus service, originally a temporary expedient because of flood damage, became permanent. Once these were working the railway route, it was clear that road traffic was at once cheaper and more convenient.

In 1931, most trains were replaced by buses. Monsieur J. Cazals who had replaced M. Valiech after 1924 as Director presided over an agreement with Monsieur Legrand of the STED of neighbouring Haute Garonne.[42] The STED (Société Anonyme des Transports Économiques Départementaux) would organise bus services, leaving the railway to provide transport for goods, two daily railcar services between Graulhet and Lavaur, and a steam engine service to Lavaur on Saturdays. The railcar only lasted until August of that year, but a mixed service from Graulhet to Laboutarié was re-established. In spite of the intervention of the *Préfet*, the steam service to Lavaur was discontinued in 1934, and buses substituted. At first, the bus services were overcrowded and on 24th October, 1934, so many were waiting *en route* for Lavaur that the regular bus, with two supplementary cars, had to shuttle back and forth no less than eight times before the passengers, all 128 of them, had been taken to their destination.

In 1932, the TVT had proposed a rescue plan. The most profitable section of line, the original link with Laboutarié, would be kept and the Department would be responsible for running costs. Not impressed, the Department made a counter-proposal. It would buy out the company. The TVT claimed that the concession was worth 120,000 francs per year, payable until 1963. Not surprisingly, agreement was impossible to reach.

The bus services provided by the STED proved costly and the TVT sought to join forces with Peyre Enterprises of Laboutarié. They already provided direct bus services to Lavaur and Toulouse. It was logical, no doubt, to hand over transport to a successful company, but it demonstrated that the railway was in terminal decline.

The loss of goods traffic followed the same pattern. The TVT looked to road transport to help cut its costs, thereby helping to prove that the railway was no longer necessary. The company employed a lorry, a classic case of 'if you can't beat 'em, join 'em'. In addition, staff who could attract a cargo on to the railway

This early 20th century view of the D631 looking west shows the railway hugging the verge.
J. Daffis/ACOVA

The railway and other road users. This photograph shows how closely the road was followed by the tramway. At first treated with good humour, the presence of the rails was regarded with growing irritation over the years.   *Louis Briand/Carto-Club Tarnais*

A 6 tonne wagon at Graulhet. The photo was taken before 1928 when the wooden *halle* with small office was to have been demolished. The cargo is probably chipped quebracho wood. *J. Daffis/ACOVA*

were to be rewarded with a meal at their choice of restaurant in Laboutarié. But even this classic appeal to the French stomach could not stave off decline. In 1931, the railway carried just over 19,000 tonnes of goods, well down from the prewar figure of 29,000 tonnes. It is true that all aspects of French economic life were now suffering from the worldwide Depression. Exports, especially of luxury goods were hit hard, and this was reflected in the continual decline of exports. The traditional markets declined but the railway failed to pick up new traffic.

Under 6,000 tonnes of goods were carried in 1935 and the railway now only employed 14 people. All the others had received their letters from the Company Administrator. 'Because of the persistent downturn in traffic and our crumbling financial base, the Company regretfully must cease to employ you as of . . .' For some, it would be early retirement, underwritten by the *Conseil Général*. For others, the search for work had to begin. The underlying finances were, as the Administration claimed, bad. Passenger numbers had also steadily declined, even when bus services run by the TVT were included. The St Sulpice line was taken up in 1936. World-wide recession could not be entirely blamed; in 1935, when the St Sulpice extension was still open, rail transport accounted for a mere three per cent of transport in the area.

The County Engineer asked for the closure of the network. It was, in his opinion, no longer needed. The local people did not want to travel to Laboutarié or St Sulpice, the termini of the railway. Their journeys began and ended at Toulouse, Albi and Castres. Motor buses could convey them the entire way without the inconvenience of a change from one train to another. The same could be argued about freight. Real destinations and points of entry were the mines, ports and markets of France and lorries could transport the goods more conveniently. Attempts to invest and upgrade the railway had not justified the expense, and in his opinion there was nothing that could be done to make a 60 cm gauge line cost-effective. But the Engineer's most forceful argument was that the line from Graulhet to Laboutarié, constructed as it was on the road verge, was a nuisance to other traffic. Once it was gone, the road could enjoy improvements such as road widening and resurfacing.

Even as the line to Lavaur was being taken up, a compromise was considered; if the railway abandoned the Laboutarié stretch which was throttling road traffic, it could continue to operate on the western side of Graulhet. But as the Laboutarié line was the only remaining part of the network still in operation, Monsieur Cazals could see no point in trying to run the system without it. Thus failed the final rescue plan. Closure was discussed once more at the *Conseil Général* in May 1936 and a resolution to this effect was passed, the closure to take effect from 20th May, 1937. Activity had, in any case, ceased leaving nothing to be administered but company debt. The remaining section of line was closed in 1938 and officially struck off the list of *chemins de fer d'utilité publique* on 11th May, 1939. As far as the County Hall was concerned, the Tramways à Vapeur du Tarn no longer existed.

According to the agreement made with the *Département* when the St Sulpice line was built, most of the surviving locomotives and rolling stock now belonged to the ratepayers. A sale was held in January 1938, to realise the best prices possible.[43] The *Équipe* (local Engineering Department) bought some of the tools, equipment and buildings, others where appropriate reverted to the communal authorities which had provided them. Graulhet station, which had been built by the original shareholders on land which was bought with company money, was rented to the Graullhet authorities.

The track on the Lavaur and St Sulpice sections had already been taken up. In 1938, the date of the final closure, it was the turn of the Laboutarié section. Some material lingered until the fall of France. Then the need for scrap metal was acute and everything was sold and recycled. Some rail was buried in road metal under the streets of Graulhet. There it remained, safe from the invading Germans throughout the Occupation.

Although the railway had ceased to be active, the company was a little harder to dismiss. Shareholders continued to insist that the concession was still a valuable asset, worth over three million francs, the rolling stock (long since vanished) and railway buildings, a further million or so. The *Département* offered half a million. On 20th April, 1949, the municipal authorities of Graulhet took possession of the Graulhet station buildings in lieu of unsettled debts. It was used, firstly as a *Collège d'Enseignement Général*,[44] and later became a club house for the local rugby team. As the TVT had lost its last asset, the company was formally dissolved at a general meeting on 27th May, 1949. Mme. Cazals, widow of the late Director, chaired the meeting.

We are left to wonder if things could have been different. If the railway could have survived the war, it might have reached the era of conservation intact, as did some others. Perhaps if Cazals had been more realistic about rescue plans, or if the general political climate in the years preceding World War II had been different, the railway could have survived. His predecessor, M. Valiech, made a number of mistakes, some expensive, especially the line to St Sulpice. The ratepayers bore the brunt of the engineering costs, it is true, but the workforce nearly doubled while receipts fell. The railcar was another white elephant, expensive untried technology, which was always breaking down. It was brand-

New uses for Graulhet station, 1955. At the bottom left can be seen the old *Bâtiment des Voyageurs* and the engine shed at the covergence of Allée des Mûriers and Avenue de la Gare (Avenue Amiral Jaurès) The station yard has been replaced with playing fields and many of the trees which used to line the Avenue have gone. Beyond, on land which has evidently been fields until recently, are springing up factory units and blocks of residential buildings. *Editions LaPie*

new; second-hand stock, tried and tested, was available at the time as the French War Department ran down its massive park of 60 cm material. Railways such as the Tramways de Pithiviers à Toury which made more use of military cast-offs survived longer - part is running still!

Hindsight makes sages of us all. At the time, there were arguments in favour of more rather than less investment. Purchases made in the past had paid off. Indeed, during the Great War, the railway depended on the new 4-6-0T and rolling stock supplied in 1913. The Lavaur line had been a commercial success, despite the misgivings of the *Département*. The cheeseparing of M. Bonnet had in itself contributed to the decline. The Laboutarié link, needed to be re-engineered in the days of heavy traffic and made enemies of the growing motoring lobby, proving that economies can be expensive.

In effect, our little railway, like most other light railways was damned if it retrenched and damned if it invested, to some extent suffering the worst of both, the economies practised at the outset as much to blame as later modest extravagances. The rest of the network, though built to higher standards, was still unable to adapt to modern demands. Trains were still slow and labour-intensive transhipment was required. By the 1930s, road transport, directly connecting supplier with customer, could move faster and require less labour than the roadside tramways. The network never succeeded in finding the new commercial niche so desperately required.

Yet, although closed and completely dismantled, the narrow gauge Tramway was not completely extinct, as described in a later chapter.

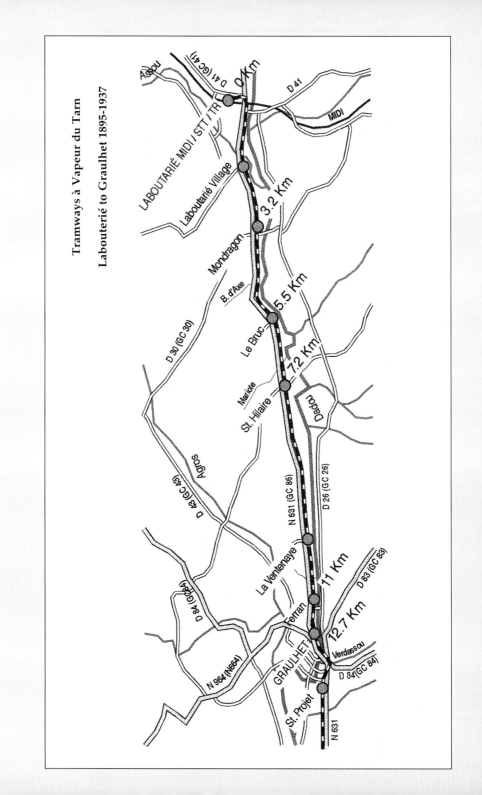

Tramways à Vapeur du Tarn

Labouterié to Graulhet 1895-1937

Chapter Three

Laboutarié to Graulhet

For reasons outlined in the Introduction, the gauge chosen for the network was 60 centimetres. The original section linked Laboutarié Midi station to Graulhet. Sometimes known as 'the mother line' it was the first to be opened, 30th June, 1895, using rail weighing 15 kilograms per metre. The line officially closed 30th June, 1937.

The line from Laboutarié to Graulhet was built using capital raised by local merchants to connect the industrial centre of Graulhet with the Midi main line from Albi south to Castres. 300,000 francs were raised to cover the cost of the line and the equipment, a comparatively modest sum compared to the total cost of the network, 4,268,000 fr. The line followed the valley of the Dadou river, on the north side, on comparatively level ground, keeping to the beds of existing roads, the GC41 and GC86 (now the D41 and D631). Little structural engineering was performed, apart from widening existing culverts. This kept costs down, but means that, because of subsequent road widening schemes, few traces of the railway are visible today.

The eastern terminus of the TVT was Laboutarié station. The station building still exists, in 1999, in a state of decay. The old main line has gone and the rest of the station complex is now a depot of an agricultural cooperative and light industrial units. Rural industry apart, this is a very quiet corner, situated to the east of the original village which has, itself, not grown appreciably. The narrow gauge station was sandwiched between the main line and the D41. There was an embankment on the west side of the railway and it was considered too expensive to landfill the site and move the existing main line goods facilities to the western, more convenient, side of the station. The railway continued to use the existing station approach.

The Midi station track layout was to a standard design of a main running line with loop. The goods facilities were serviced by a line on the east side of the station terminating in storage sidings serviced by wagon turntables. The Midi building at Laboutarié provided generous facilities. It was a three-windowed, double-storey building with an office annexe at the south end. As of 1993, the building still existed. An interesting quirk is that the roadside station nameplate is La Boutarié, a spelling occasionally used by some inhabitants, whereas the railside name is the more normal Laboutarié.

As before mentioned, the former Midi line is now closed and the derelict track terminates just to the north of the station. Around the station, many contemporary buildings survive. It is possible to make out the foundations of the transhipment hall, the refreshment bar and the water tower in the photos taken in 1995. Perhaps because the Midi had provided a fairly substantial *Bâtiment des Voyageurs (BV)*,[45] the TVT only had a small *BV* 7.5 by 3.8 metres, with a wooden office tacked on to the side. This was the office of M. Bonnet, that once formidable figure in the affairs of the company. He hired and fired. He quarrelled with his rivals, M. Benoît and the restauranteurs of Laboutarié. He

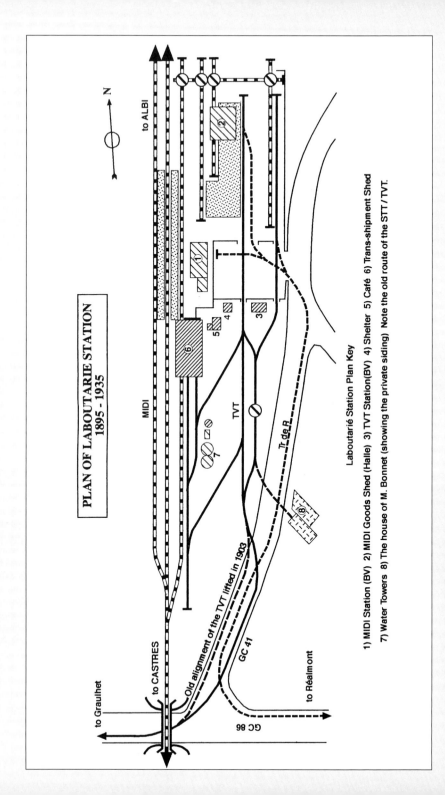

PLAN OF LABOUTARIE STATION
1895 - 1935

N

to Graulhet

to CASTRES

to ALBI

to Réalmont

MIDI

TVT

Tr de R

GC 41

GC 86

Old alignment of the TVT lifted in 1903

Laboutarié Station Plan Key

1) MIDI Station (BV) 2) MIDI Goods Shed (Halle) 3) TVT Station(BV) 4) Shelter 5) Café 6) Trans-shipment Shed
7) Water Towers 8) The house of M. Bonnet (showing the private siding) Note the old route of the STT / TVT.

Laboutarié station yard, early 20th century viewed from across the main line tracks.
J. Daffis/ACOVA

Laboutarié station yard, late 20th century. This is viewed in the same direction but from the TVT side.
Malcolm Wright

Eastern side of *BV*. The *BV* is viewed across the TVT station yard. A headshunt would once have crossed in front of the building, ending to the right. The track from Réalmont would have crossed the yard passing a little to the right of where the photographer was standing, with buffers to the right of the station door. *Malcolm Wright*

Western side of *BV*. The photographer was standing on the site of the Midi main line track. *Malcolm Wright*

sent out proud invitations in the summer of 1895. 'The President and Members of the Council of the TVT have the honour to invite you to the official inauguration of the line' The party lasted all of 30th June, beginning and ending with a trip on the train. The building was demolished when the D41 was widened. The travellers' refreshment bar, already mentioned, was a larger building. When M. Bonnet opened it, there were protests of the very strongest from the restauranteurs in Laboutarié village. In 1903, when the Director's office moved from Laboutarié, the bar closed.

Within the station grounds, the TVT provided itself quite generous track facilities. The main line came in from the west. The head shunt went north as far as the main line goods hall. Before this was the turning loop with turntable. Spurs to the west connected with sidings on the main line and the *halle de transbordement*.[46] This shed was originally 21 metres long, spanning a section of main line siding. At the other side of a 3 metre platform was the narrow gauge line. To this side, labourers and freight were sheltered by an extension of the roof. The original building was destroyed by high winds in 1915 to be replaced by a larger, open building, 24 by 6.8 metres which covered main and narrow gauge line. During the reconstruction, the station trackplans were altered and a parallel siding laid which could also be protected, by an awning. During bad weather, blinds could be pulled down the open sides of the shed to protect freight. (Nothing is said about the workers!) To help transfer of goods, the narrow gauge line was elevated so that on both sides the wagon floors were at the same height. A crane was introduced, to help with moving particularly heavy loads.

To the south of the *halle de transbordement* stood the imposing twin water towers which served the main line trains. They were nicknamed the belltowers. Beside them was the more modest tower for the TVT. All three were supplied by a local pumping station.

Along the course of the railway, except where it cut the corner ran the telephone cable. A private spur linked M. Bonnet's house which still exists, easily recognised since it is built at a sharp angle to the D41.

The Tramway de Réalmont also came into the station along the D41, and shared the Midi goods shed. Although both lines were to the same gauge, there is little evidence of co-operation and only the tiniest stretch of shared line. To some extent this absence of co-operation was justified. Both lines, one from the east, the other from the west, had to negotiate a sharp bend, and needed to extend the curve of the track to the opposite side of the road. Originally only 30 metres radius in order to keep to the western side of the road, the radius in its widened form was 50 metres when improvements were effected in 1899. The tramway crossed under the main line and so the gradient was steep, about 3 per cent, 4 per cent in two places. The tight curve combined with the fight against gravity must have generated considerable wheel flange friction and stretched the tractive effort of the locomotives to the full.

The Tramway de Réalmont, as mentioned before, shared only two areas of track with the TVT. One was at the door of the Midi goods shed, the other a roadside siding. Where the rival tramways crossed, there was friction because M. Benoît, the champion of Réalmont, insisted that the weight of steam-drawn

A view of a 6 tonne Decauville wagon type 'B' in Laboutarié station yard. We can assume that the sacks contain freight of a bulky rather than dense nature - probably corn. The contraversial *buvette* can be seen to the right, behind the wagon. The condition of the original is poor but we have included the illustration in view of its importance.   *J. Daffis/ACOVA*

Another wagon type 'B'. Behind it can be seen the loading crane and the distinctive buildings at Graulhet station. There is also a nice view of a Decauville point lever in the foreground.

                     J. Daffis/ACOVA

The station is to the left of the picture. Trains would have come out of the station, crossed the road and travelled along the right-hand side of the road towards the spot where the photographer was standing.   *Malcolm Wright*

trains would cause rail distortion. He insisted on special ramps to protect his rail and hand held turnouts for the modest requirements of his system. Historians have pointed out discrepancies between M. Benoît's demands and the photographic evidence; it is possible that a lot of recorded resolutions were never translated into fact. To win verbal victory was enough!

The rival tramways parted at the D631, going east and west respectively. Once under the main line bridge, the TVT followed the road on the south side along a straight and level kilometre or so to the village of Laboutarié which was, and is, entered along a gentle curve. The Assou, tributary of the Dadou, was crossed using the existing road bridge, span 12 metres. Nothing remains of the two locations of the village halt which was moved from Mas de Bourne, a local farmhouse, to the Mairie in 1903. The original consisted of a passing loop to the south of the line and a simple shelter, 1.8 by 4 metres, open on the railway side, providing a bench for waiting travellers. Laboutarié is the largest village on this part of the route to have had trains running down the high street. In those days when a number of houses still had thatched roofs, cinders from the engine frequently started fires. Graulhet boasted a volunteer Fire Brigade, and they would be summoned by trumpet and bugle to swell the local group fighting the blaze.

In those days, the village was also noted for its two restaurants. They competed with M. Bonnet's buffet bar until it was closed in 1903. Friendly relations were restored when the Directors took to using the restaurants as employee incentives. If a special train was ordered for rapid delivery of goods the entire crew were treated to a meal, the certain way to a Frenchman's heart.

Passing under the main line a locomotive completes the sharp turn to take it under the Midi bridge just west of Laboutarié station. It would then cross the road and come along the right-hand side towards the photographer.   *Louis Briand/Carto-Club Tarnais*

Train in Laboutarié village, a Decauville 0-6-2 hauling two carriages and a brake van towards Laboutarié station. It is passing close to the houses on the south side of the village street which were in danger, especially in summer, from cinders.   *Louis Briand/Carto-Club Tarnais*

The line followed the road round a gentle curve. In just under a kilometre was the halt for Montdragon, a slightly more important village sited on the south bank of the Dadou. Although the passenger shelter was just the standard design, the goods siding was a relatively generous 90 metres long with a stone platform five metres wide to the south. Travellers had to walk over the Dadou river to the village, once a stronghold of the Salvetat estate. Remains of its past include a romanesque chapel.

The road and line continue straight for roughly two kilometres, reaching the former halt at the hamlet of Pont Vieux, so called because there has long been another bridge over the Dadou. The course of the line continues straight and level until after it crosses the Labit brook. Between here and the hamlet Le Bruc, there are a number of fairly tight curves to be negotiated and a gradient of 2.5 per cent. This climb, and the bends, three of 200 metres radius, one of 400 and a fairly gentle one, radius 1,200 metres, made this a slow stretch of the journey.

The halt at Le Bruc, a small hamlet now, was situated opposite the junction with a small road leading up into the hills. Le Bruc derived its name from the Occitan word for heather, the French word being *bruyère*. It is an area of heathland centred on a hamlet which was once an independent commune. Provisions were basic, put in under pressure from the local Commune after the line opened. It had the standard shelter, but no passing loop. Between Le Bruc and St Hilaire, line and river were close together. A curve radius 550 metres was followed by one of 950 metres. The river valley then opens out once more and the line crosses a small stream called Bouquet d'Axe before reaching St Hilaire, the next halt.

It always was a small settlement, no church in spite of the pious name, marked by the bridge which took the D26 (GC26) over the river . The village kept the feast of St Hilaire, which was a good excuse for a party, and the railway ran 'specials' to enable the Graulhétois to join the fun. Vigorous dancing and warm food would have been almost essential because the feast falls on 14th January. At the junction with the road down to the river, was the standard shelter and siding, this time a mere 58 metres long. Less freight was expected here than at Montdragon. In the early days of the railway, when the Dadou upstream of Graulhet provided the only source of clean water, washerwomen used to take the train from Graulhet to St Hilaire taking the D26 to the riverside. A flat wagon would accompany these 'washerwomen's specials' to carry all the baskets of laundry.

The local commune wanted another halt where the railway crossed the Mariote brook, but the TVT refused. As far as it was concerned, passengers could easily walk from St Hilaire.

Continuing westwards, there is a hamet set back from the road. In the days of Napoléon, long before the train, the D631 was straightened, taking it away from the river and bypassing the original settlements. The old road meanders past the church of Notre Dame de Besplaux, a diminutive 17th century church.[47] It is served by the halt of La Ventenaye, at the crossroads with the D43. This halt was the result of a successful application by the local commune after the opening of the railway, never consisting of more than a shelter.

Station Avenue, Graulhet, 1910. Taken during the leatherworkers' strike, the *BV* is being guarded. Behind, and to the left, the pumping house is visible. *Louis Briand/Carto-Club Tarnais*

This was also taken at the time of the strike, with the strikers and sympathisers outside the *BV* at Graulhet. To the right, the travellers' conveniences can just be seen.

Louis Briand/Carto-Club Tarnais

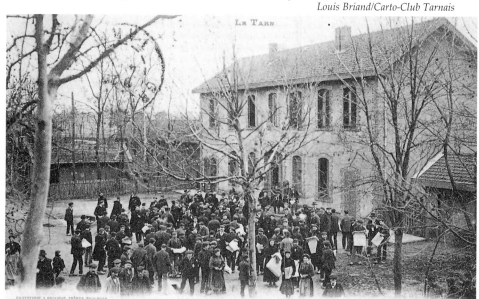

One kilometre nearer Graulhet was the halt for Ferran where the Chemin de Ferran crosses the Dadou and meets the D631. The siding was a substantial one, 90 metres long, like the one at Montdragon with a shelter built to the standard pattern. In the heyday of the railway, this was a bustling village with its share of leatherworkers, set in a bend of the Dadou. Today it has been swallowed up by the town. To the north is a light airport, with a miniature runway for model enthusiasts. An industrial estate is named La Molière on the site of a farm.

Past Ferran, the modern road passes along a series of roundabouts, from which notices proclaim that Graulhet is the town of flowers. Green fields existed here until the early 1950s when the area was designated as a zone of development, with new housing and factories. At the junction with the road to the suburb of St Pierre, the modern bypass sweeps motorists north.

The ghost of the train would have gone straight over the roundabout and down the Avenue de l'Europe. In 1590 the petit palais des Crins was built here, home to the Abijoux family; the remains are in private hands. François Jacques d'Aubijoux was a noted patron of the arts and an author of the town's prosperity. At the junction with the Allée des Pins, the railway executed a sharp turn to the left, of no more than 50 metres radius, to run into the station in what is now the municipal sports ground.

On the day that the line officially opened, Sunday 30th June, 1895, there was a party of celebration. Sunday was chosen to ensure that as many people as possible could be present. Formal invitations from the *Conseil d'Administration*[48] asked official guests to be at Laboutarié station by 12 minutes past 9 in the morning returning at an unspecified time in the evening. The party was swelled by the townsfolk of Graulhet.

When this was the terminus, the station layout consisted of a main running line that ended in a headshunt combined with a turntable and locomotive shed. Halfway along the running line, a crossover gave access to the platform. At the far end (south) of the platform the line continued into another headshunt, connected by another crossover to the main running line, so providing a run-round loop.

Passenger traffic facilities were adequate from the beginning. The *Bâtiment des Voyageurs*, a stucco building with brick detailing of the corners, window and door openings was originally 21.1 metres by 8.1. On the platform side at least, the building was unusual. No windows were visible on the upper storey although there was a station master's flat above the public rooms; all the windows must have been on the road side. On the ground floor were to be found the waiting room, ticket hall, office and newsagent.

The station was rebuilt when the line was extended to Lavaur. It is interesting to note that the very decorative gas lamp on the south corner was retained. The new part of the building commenced about a metre above this lamp. Not only was an upper storey added and the building reroofed but it was extended in length. The detailing though, continued to conform to the original pattern. Separate from the building was a one storey WC. Beside the station building was a wooden carriage-shed that gave covered storage to two coaches. Attached to this was a duty room, 5 metres by 4 metres with cellar.

The extensive goods facilities were accessed by a set of three crossovers providing a very flexible layout with one significant disadvantage. Access to the goods yard was only possible by reversing the train from the platform, there being no separate goods arrival line. This defect was remedied when the layout was

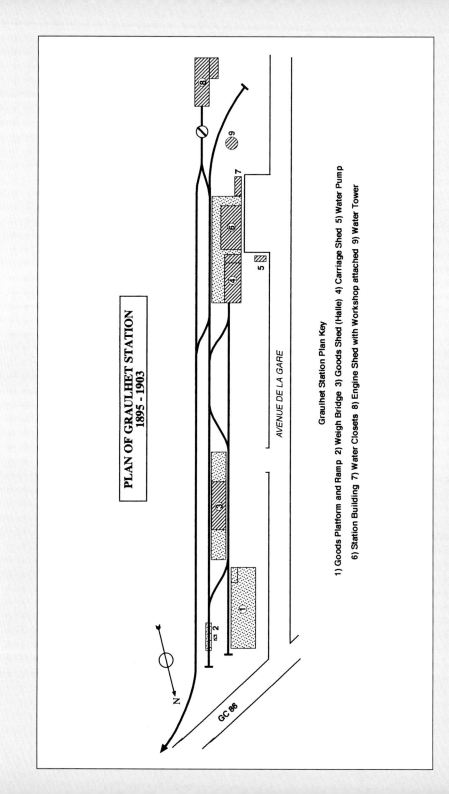

PLAN OF GRAULHET STATION
1895 - 1903

AVENUE DE LA GARE

GC 86

N

Graulhet Station Plan Key

1) Goods Platform and Ramp 2) Weigh Bridge 3) Goods Shed (Halle) 4) Carriage Shed 5) Water Pump

6) Station Building 7) Water Closets 8) Engine Shed with Workshop attached 9) Water Tower

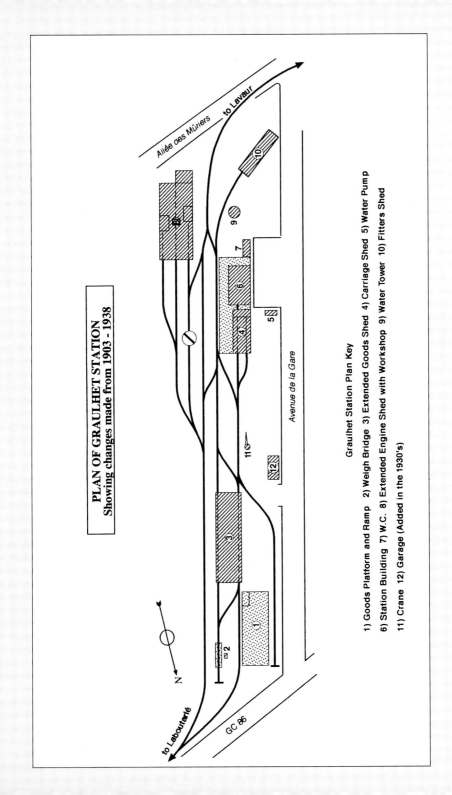

PLAN OF GRAULHET STATION
Showing changes made from 1903 - 1938

Graulhet Station Plan Key

1) Goods Platform and Ramp 2) Weigh Bridge 3) Extended Goods Shed 4) Carriage Shed 5) Water Pump

6) Station Building 7) W.C. 8) Extended Engine Shed with Workshop 9) Water Tower 10) Fitters Shed

11) Crane 12) Garage (Added in the 1930's)

Allée des Mûriers   to Lavaur

Avenue de la Gare

to Laboutarié

GC 86

N

Taken during the leatherworkers' strike of 1910, troops pose in front of the water tower at the south end of Graulhet station. *Louis Briand/Carto-Club Tarnais*

Weidknecht poses with military escort. There is a good view of the details of the station architecture of the period, including the lamp and the station clock. The person in formal dress but with *sabots* is M. le Directeur. *Louis Briand/Carto-Club Tarnais*

changed in 1903. The original facilities consisted of a weighbridge set on a siding and then the *halle à marchandises*, 25 metres long but relatively narrow, set in a loop and flanked by two open platforms 10 and 15 metres long. These were built parallel to the Avenue Amiral Jaurès (formerly the Boulevard de la Gare). A raised loading dock was adjacent to the street and was provided with a siding. We infer from the layout that the station would have been provided with a pilot engine to keep the station run-round loop free whilst goods were loaded and unloaded in the yards. The line had three engines, two would have been steamed each day, leaving one in reserve, or undergoing maintenance or boiler washout.

The headshunt served the water tower. For years the railway took its water from the river. As the leather industry expanded, and as chemicals joined the standard organic waste of a built-up area, the river became rapidly less suitable as a supply of boiler water. Water could alternatively be supplied from a well. There was a little pumping house on the far side of the *BV*. The well water had a high lime content, therefore was just as unsatisfactory in its own way. It is interesting that a contemporary recipe for water treatment uses two of the ingredients required by the leather industry, logwood and quebracho.[49]

From its inception, the railway sought to be linked to the Municipal water supply, already barely sufficient for local needs. For years, efforts to establish a better supply foundered, because of the perceived cost. At length in 1927, the money was spent and the Miquelou reservoir made clean water available in realistic quantity. In 1929, the station was at long last connected to the town supply. French locomotive design was sophisticated and the only boiler replenishment was by injectors. Any particulate matter can block them. Failure of the water supply would require the fire to be dropped immediately. Before 1929, one wonders how often a locomotive roster was lost because there was a **** in a pipe?

The 1903 station building is still recognisable, but a recreation park now occupies the rest of the site. This is a run-down area of town; when the leather industry still flourished, Algerian labourers were welcomed in. Only a couple of factories now survive and most of them are unemployed. Tucked behind the old station and more clearly visible from the Allée des Mûriers, the rebuilt engine shed of 1903 survives as a store. The leather-works visible in some contemporary photos also survives, in 1999, a shop.

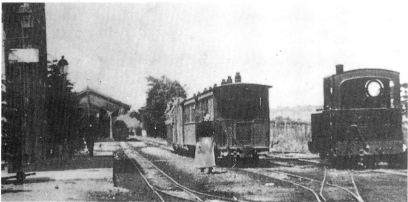

Graulhet station as it was after 1905 looking in the direction of Laboutarié. To the left, the *BV* can just be seen, with the *halle des marchandises* beyond.   *J. Daffis/ACOVA*

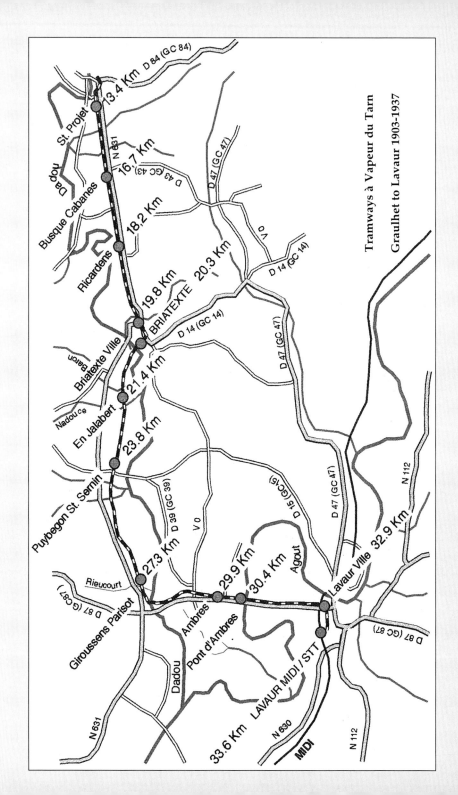

Tramways à Vapeur du Tarn

Graulhet to Lavaur 1903-1937

Chapter Four

Graulhet to Lavaur

The second phase of construction, this came into being thanks to the success of the first. Political pressure and subsidy from local government also played a part. The line is characterised by inconsistency. Overall it received greater investment relative to likely financial return than was evident in the Laboutarié line, but, within Graulhet town especially, economy ruled.

From Graulhet station to Lavaur Midi main line station. Opened to passenger traffic 26th May, 1903. Opened to freight 26th October, 1903. Dismantling begun 1936. Closure 1937. Weight of rail: Decauville 15 kilograms per metre laid on oak sleepers.

As with the original line, there were celebrations when it was opened. This time, a Government Minister presided. The party started on 27th September, 1903 and continued all the next day. The railway conveyed the Ministre de la Marine Camille Pelletan to the town to unveil a statue of Amiral Jaurès and inaugurate the railway.[50] For two days, a train full of dignitaries toured the town, followed by one of musicians, in turn followed by a 'scratch' train filled with local people. With plenty of the right spirit, music resounding in the narrow streets and the sharp gradients, the atmosphere must have been unforgettable!

The previous chapter describes how the *BV* was affected by the extension of the line, and the tale of the water supply. The Lavaur extension had other consequences. The track layout was improved by a turnout at the station throat, giving direct access to the goods yard. A crossover adjacent to the station buildings was reversed giving an immediate entry to the goods yard at this end of the layout. The middle crossover was amended with the provision of a double slip, giving access to a new siding that not only served the loading bank but would have been a convenient goods headshunt. Additional to this new loop further loops were provided to give a platform release road independent of the locomotive servicing arrangements. The main line that originally terminated in the engine shed was extended and realigned becoming the running line towards Lavaur.

A new engine shed and works were accessed by the additional loops already mentioned. The wooden loco shed with workshop and the carriage shed were both dismantled and taken to the new terminus at Lavaur. The turntable was moved to the south of the new *BV* and incorporated into one of the new loops. The big new engine shed, 32 by 10.2 metres, was entered by three sets of rails, allowing five locomotives inside. The other end of this building was taken up by the workshop and a stationary steam engine to provide power for the workshop equipment. The old headshunt was retained, enclosed by a workshop for painting and joinery. The carriage shed was provided with an additional siding, certainly by 1916, allowing most of the coaching stock to be kept under cover.

The goods shed was extended over the open platforms which flanked it. The substantial island platform remained, served by a second siding to cope with increased traffic. A stationary crane was installed to the north of the carriage shed.

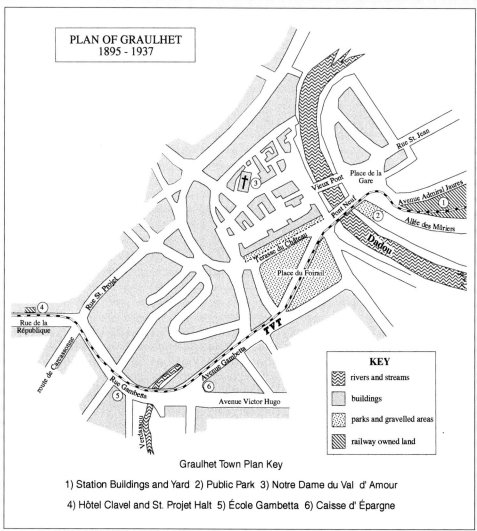

PLAN OF GRAULHET
1895 - 1937

Rue St. Jean

Place de la
Gare

Vieux Pont

Avenue Admiral Jaures

Pont Neuf

Allée des Mûriers

Terrasse du Château

Dadou

Place du Foirail

Rue St. Projet

TYT

Rue de la
République

route de Carcassonne

Rue Gambetta

Avenue Gambetta

Avenue Victor Hugo

Verlassou

KEY

▨ rivers and streams

▢ buildings

░ parks and gravelled areas

▨ railway owned land

Graulhet Town Plan Key

1) Station Buildings and Yard 2) Public Park 3) Notre Dame du Val d' Amour

4) Hôtel Clavel and St. Projet Halt 5) École Gambetta 6) Caisse d' Épargne

Map of Graulhet town showing the route taken by the railway.   © *Malcolm Wright 1995*

The station was scheduled to enjoy improvements yet again in 1928 when it was judged that the wooden goods shed had reached the end of its service life. In addition, a bigger turntable was needed for the railcar. Approval had to be sought from the *Conseil Général*. For the time being, the politicians still smiled on the railway, and permission was granted. The old shed was to be replaced by a 60 metre structure in reinforced concrete, with awnings over the lines. The island platform was to be moved alongside the shed to simplify goods handling. The weighbridge would be transferred to a new siding. This was possible because a strip of land had been acquired for the new carriage shed plus joiner's workshop. The planned layout required over half a kilometre of new track.

But in fact very little work was carried out because, in 1929, the fortunes of the railway crashed. The company had to be content with repairing and extending the goods shed and with an improved water supply piped directly from the new reservoir. Of all the new track envisaged, only one line was laid, and that was for the contractors' benefit. In 1932, there was a new building, ironically, a garage measuring 6.8 by 3.38 metres for a lorry. The stationary engine was removed from the works shed, and its place was taken by washing facilities.

The line to Lavaur left the station on a bend of 60 metres radius. It came out into the Allée des Muriers also once known as the Chemin de Crins (alley of mulberry trees). The track then swung briefly into the Avenue Amiral Jaurès where the roads converge into the Place Languedoc. In 1989, the statue of the Admiral was moved here from its original site. The line followed Place de la Languedoc into Square Foch, formerly Place de la Gare, overlooking the river. In the days of the railway, this was the site of the War Memorial.[51] The public showers were built here in the early 1930s when the town acquired its water supply. The building now houses the Syndicat d'Initiative. Until 1970, when it was destroyed by a fire, a large building dominated the approaches to the bridge. It has now been replaced by the smaller Hôtel des Postes.[52] With greenery and river views, this is an agreeable spot.

Around are reminders that the river was once literally the economic powerhouse for the town, driving several watermills. Here also was a drying house; right up to the eve of World War I the river was used for rinsing tanned leather, as well as a local water source. There were always problems. Either waterpower was all too abundant, especially during the days of the spring spate, or there was enforced idleness in dry weather. Some problems were solved when the reservoir was built, although this initially meant that the river was even more neglected and for a while attained the dubious distinction of being the most polluted in France. Things could only get better. From 1950 onwards, new industry was sited away from the river, and, as mentioned, leather working has sharply declined. One of the aims of the Syndicat d'Initiative, founded 1961, was to assure water quality. The Dadou (in 1993) is a pleasant smelling river, even on a July afternoon; the local fish endorse our opinion and angling is once more possible.

The railway followed a curve of 40 metres radius round to the left and then crossed the road to bring it in line with the Pont Neuf. This was widened, and a flight of steps down to the river demolished to make way for the trains. The Pont Vieux also crosses the Dadou at this point. The area had always been a popular

Graulhet, over the bridge, early 20th century. The track can be seen swinging across the Pont Neuf, before snaking up the hill into old Graulhet. To the right is the Café de la Gare, with the market place behind. The tower of the Caisse d'Épargne marks the top of the hill.

J. Daffis/ACOVA

Graulhet, Caisse d'Épargne.   *J. Daffis/ACOVA*

centre for celebration at Carnival time and the new bridge rapidly became itself a social hub on market day, the railway bringing fairgoers and equally importantly, taking them home. On the left bank, buildings and café-restaurants especially the Tivoli hosted their share of parties, literary and otherwise.

The Old Town dating back to the 10th century lies to the west of the river. As previously described, a castle once dominated the mound above the bridge, the terrace still remains, overlooking the lower market square. On 14th July, the Revolution is commemorated with fireworks on the site. Behind can be seen the twin towers of Notre Dame du Val d'Amour, still sometimes known as 'Graulhet Cathedral'.[53] The market square, also known as the Place du Jourdain, is on two levels. The castle terrace constitutes the upper one, and used to be the scene of lively poultry markets. Larger beasts such as cattle were bought and sold on the lower level. The railway cut diagonally across the lower square, the Place du Foirail, to the left of a band stand and the statue of Admiral Jaurès. On market days, the steam train would have puffed through a picturesque crowd. All these have gone, to be replaced ironically by a bus station and a vast car park. The square also was the site of the old Théron, an Occitan word meaning spring water. This was, until the 1920s, the town's supply of drinking water, piped in from a distance. To make life easier for the old ladies who used to stagger away with heavy buckets, there were stone benches on either side. A piped water supply within the town must have been a blessing!

At the far end of the square, the railway turned into Avenue Gambetta. The route required a stiff climb and a sharp turn to the right as it joined rue Gambetta. At this crossroads loomed the impressive Caisse d'Épargne, the town's main Bank, still there today. Opposite used to stand a public weighbridge, with café-restaurants occupying the other corners, but the modern site, though clean and well maintained has a slightly forlorn air as though nothing much happens here nowadays. There was another sharp curve, of 40 metres radius, and a gradient exceeding 2.5 per cent as the route crossed the bridge over the Verdaussou brook.[54] This once ran through a gorge, with precipitous medieval buildings to each side. The original bridge was widened to take the railway and in modern times, the road has been straightened and improved yet again so that the area, though clean, is dull. Downstream of the bridge, the old insanitary gorge has been covered over. Sandwiched between a cul-de-sac and a lane survives the distinctive building of the École Gambetta, built on the site of the chapel of St Projet.[55]

The railway crossed the road from south side to north and negotiated the junction with the D84 on a bend to the left of no more than 40 metres radius. Originally called the St Projet crossroad, a statue of the saint looked down from a wall. The D84 northward bound, which used to be the Rue St Projet, now commemorates Jean Jaurès. The route of the railway ran along the north side of the Avenue de la Republique, now Avenue Charles de Gaulle. The halt of St Projet, just before the junction with the modern Boulevard de la Liberté, was in front of the Hôtel Clavel, a popular subject for period postcards. This was the commercial centre of the town. The Hôtel Clavel would accept and forward parcels and items for express delivery and so for many years, the arrival of the little train would generate much interest.

Two views of the Hôtel Clavel. Convenient for the commercial quarter, this was the site of the
halt within Graulhet town. It was obviously a popular subject for period postcards. They were
taken between 1903 and World War I. In the lower photograph, the Hôtel and the area in general
are enjoying prosperity, skirts are slightly shorter, and there is the faintly ominous presence of
a military uniform.   *Louis Briand/Carto-Club Tarnais*

When planning the route, the TVT applied for a siding where it could park a pilot locomotive. Crossing Graulhet involved not only negotiating five bends of less than 60 metres radius, but also a veritable switchback over the first 474 metres. For a total of 130 metres, the gradient exceeded 5 per cent. The little 10 tonne Decauville locomotives could, in theory, manage to pull 40 tonnes up a 4 per cent slope at a speed of 6 kilometres per hour, but in practice, they could only be relied upon to pull a train totalling 28 tonnes under these conditions. When a train exceeded two carriages plus wagon a second engine was required. They must have been a fine sight , the double headed trains on the tortuous streets, but safest watched from a distance. The Weidknecht 4-6-0T locomotives employed on the route had better adhesion and the occasions upon which they needed assistance fewer. The days of bustle and theatre are long since over and the empty street given over to its dreams.

St Projet was near the edge of town at the turn of the century. Now the Avenue Charles de Gaulle makes its way through the western suburbs to become once more the D631. The railway kept to its north side all the way to Briatexte. In the days before Napoléon, the road meandered south, quitting its present course at the site of the Collège d'Enseignement Sécondaire Louis Pasteur and its playing fields. This a modern comprehensive built on an open site with playing fields. As in Britain, selective schools fell from favour and comrehensives were built in France, following the pattern already established in the USA. Louis Pasteur, a leading scientist, was a Frenchman and has many schools named after him.

3.75 kilometres from the station, was the halt for Busque-Cabanes, consisting of a simple shelter. This and other passenger halts on the Lavaur section were provided for in a more lavish style more generous than that of the original. The main building, a standard 4 by 2 metres, had concrete foundations. The front consisted of a central opening in a wood framed wall with brick nogging. Here and at some other halts, the shelter had a brick lean-to resting on a wooden base. Like the other halts on this section, there was no siding and the site has been swallowed up by the Rhine/Danube roundabout.

Busques, settled since before Roman times, once a centre for wool preparation, and boasting a 16th century château, is about three kilometres to the north of the halt to which it lent its name. Cabanes is approximately the same distance south. It is fair to guess that the inhabitants did not find the railway particularly convenient and they would have turned early to road transport.

Along here, fruit has always flourished, thanks to the gentle valley slope. Several attractive *pigeonnières* survive; they were carefully designed collecting points for that valuable resource, pigeon dung. The obliging birds would deposit their precious cargo on the first floor. A wagon would be driven into the loading bay at ground level and the floor would be tipped, filling it with guano - no hands, lovely muck!

The gothic church of Notre Dame des Vignes also witnesses to the local culture. Originally N.D. des Pignes, it took its name from the local pines. When vines were planted on the sloping valley sides, it seemed logical to make the small name-change. For centuries, it had been a place of some importance, a magnet for ocal pilgrims, particularly in the week leading up to the Feast of the Virgin, 8th September. Infants were brought here to be blessed by the queen of mothers. The tradition was going strong in the days of the railway which was

Church Square, Briatexte, about 1910.   *J. Daffis/ACOVA*

The route through Briatexte.   *Louis Briand/Carto-Club Tarnais*

the focus for mother and baby outings. It is almost certain that the Camille Pelletan included the church in his tour of the town in late September 1903, because Admiral Jaurès, whose statue was at the centre of the celebration, is buried in the churchyard. Here too on 18th April, 1685 was baptised Admiral Pierre Jacques de Taffanel de la Jonquière, once governor of Canada.

The area keeps up its links with the past; from here towards Lavaur can be seen orchards. Local growing conditions have helped, obviously, but the new impetus came from people of French origin (the *pieds noirs*) displaced from Algeria. They planted new orchards, tree fruits mainly, which an imposing new feature of the landscape.

To the west is the Nabeillou estate, transformed into a military hospital during World War I. The hospital's presence was one of the factors which persuaded the authorities to re-open the line during the Emergency. It is now a leisure centre run by a lay Catholic organisation. The junction with the road to Cabanes is a little to the west of the roundabout, running south past the new science park and the Nabeillou reservoir.

A kilometre further on, and still on the north side of the D631, the train reached Ricardens halt, a request stop. Since leaving Graulhet Old Town, the road had offered the railway a relatively straight and even shoulder to follow. Now the road approached Briatexte set in the bottom of the river valley by a series of bends and gradients.

Founded in 1287, Briatexte was designed originally for defence not for ease of access.[56] Planning an approach for the railway caused the thrifty Directors of the TVT, like many previous would-be entrants to the town, much anxiety. The cheapest option was to site the station where the D631 enters the town and to follow the road round bends with a radius tighter than the recommended minimum of 50 metres and up gradients greater than 2.5 per cent. It was decided to deviate from the road so that more tolerable bends and gradients could be engineered.

The chosen route required, by the frugal standards of the TVT, much construction work. The railway followed the D631 almost into Briatexte. At the town boundary, it turned right and followed a lane called the chemin de la Gascoune. An embankment and a cutting were created to keep the gradient within 2.5 per cent. It briefly rejoined the D631 just outside the Mairie. This was the halt for Briatexte *ville*. Road and railway carried on to the junction with the D14, formerly known as Avenue de la Gare, now as Avenue St Paul. The railway now executed a tight turn to the left of no more than 40 metres radius. It passed the Place du Foirail, then executed another sharp turn this time to the right, to reach the station on a plot on open land by the Dadou. No less than 20 small bridges and culverts had to be re-engineered to allow the passage of the trains. Market day for Briatexte was a Monday, and in the early days at least, there was an extra daily service on the Lavaur-Graulhet section. The big annual fêtes were on the Mondays preceding Easter and All Saints' Day (*see Chapter Seven*). They were the occasions for special trains to convey visitors to the fun.

The station layout was simple, consisting of a double loop with a fairly short siding to the east. Another siding was added after 1915, to the south of the *Halle des Marchandises*. In relation to the population of less than 2,000, the buildings of Briatexte station were generous. The company wanted them even more

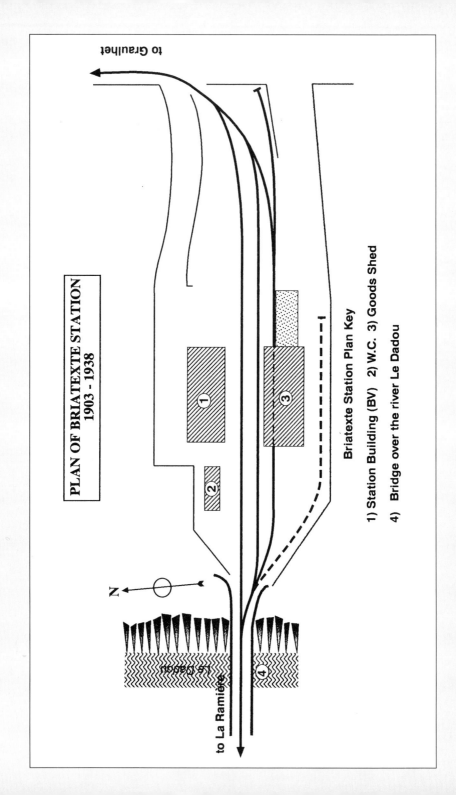

PLAN OF BRIATEXTE STATION
1903 - 1938

to Graulhet

to La Ramière

Le Dadou

N

Briatexte Station Plan Key

1) Station Building (BV)   2) W.C.   3) Goods Shed

4) Bridge over the river Le Dadou

Briatexte station before 1915. Viewed from the town, looking towards the viaduct. The *halle* is the original one, and the ground on the near side of the *BV* has not yet been cleared. Note the interesting little shelter in the foreground. *J. Daffis/ACOVA*

Later view from the same angle. The new *halle* has been built, in response to a petition, to replace the old one which was destroyed by high winds in 1915. It is more substantial than the original. To please local opinion further, the wilderness beside the *BV* has been dug up and is being planted, and a brand-new fence has been erected. *J. Daffis/ACOVA*

BRIATEXTE (Tarn). — La Gare

The company logo survives at the front door of Briatexte station, worked in pebble mosaic.
Malcolm Wright

substantial, with a two-storey *Bâtiment des Voyageurs*, but this was refused by Departmental planners, no doubt anxious to restrain spending on a venture for which they had part of the financial responsibility. The one-storey building measured 22.2 metres by 10, comprising waiting room, office, shop, and a four room flat. At a discreet distance stood the shed which housed the WC and store.

Across the double loop stood the *halle à marchandises*. In 1915, the original shed was destroyed by the same storm which ruined the one at Laboutarié. The new one, a substantial wood framed shelter, which provided a canopy for a siding and partially enclosed platform, was built after a petition was mounted. It occupied a site of 16 by 10 metres. A well surrounded by a kerb supplied water with the help of a chain pump.

After 1938, the commune took over the shed, which was still in good condition, as a store and most of the grounds, apart from the area round the *BV* which became a private house; in 1993, its resident remembered travelling on *le petit train*. When she died, the area was turned into a Community Hall with associated Council stores. The wooden-framed building now has brick piers and the old WC building has been extended to provide extra storage.

Immediately to the west of the station is the site of the old bridge. The Dadou river flows at the bottom of a gorge nearly 100 feet below the level of the station. When the railway was built, the engineering firm Daydé and Pillé, with workshops at Creil just north of Paris, won the building contract. 104 metres long, this was the most ambitious piece of engineering to date on the line. The steel bridge was supported on three masonry pillars; above the river itself, the bridge attained a height of 24 metres. Resting on these pillars was a trestle bridge composed of steel girders. The uprights were 3 metres high and 2.4 metres apart. The bridge accommodated a cantilevered wooden walkway on each side of the track and was a total of 4 metres wide inside the guard rails. Before the bridge went into service, a train consisting of two locomotives and six wagons of ballast crossed it with no mishap. The metal trestles were dismantled for scrap after the war, being too large and remote to tackle during the time of Occupation. Before the job was completed, a workman was killed. In 1999, the foundations and the piers still remain.

On the western bank of the Dadou, travellers could look back to the village of St Gauzens, a short walk from the station. The course of the railway now left the existing road and struck out across open country. Here and there, its course can still be inferred from the pattern of tree growth and field margins. It crossed the Baron stream by a purpose-built bridge before reaching the request stop of En Jalabert, 1.14 kilometres from the viaduct. This was closed a mere seven months after the opening of the line to be replaced by one at La Bataille, 50 metres further on. Neither halt would have had a shelter. The line now joined a country lane taking advantage of an existing bridge, which had to be widened, to cross the Nadouce stream. It passed the hamlet of la Barrière, then crossed the stream of the same name by a small metal bridge.

Where the line crossed the D39, and where a local school had been built, was the halt for Puybegon-St Sernin. This has always been a bustling corner of the commune where the D631, the railway, and the Dadou draw together. By the riverside is the church of St Peter. Constructed in the 15th and 16th century, the

Briatexte station from the viaduct. This shows the station from the other side. The new *halle* is being built. A works train can be seen on a siding to its right, a siding which was subsequently removed.   *J. Daffis/ACOVA*

Plan of Briatexte viaduct. The overall length of the metal viaduct was 104.4 metres. The distance from rail height to the river bed was 24 metres.   © *Malcolm Wright*

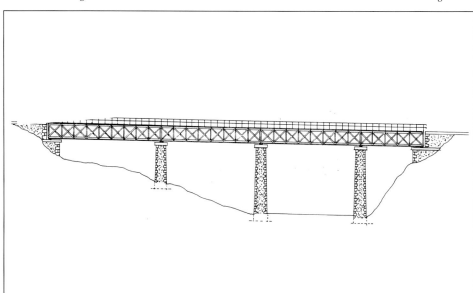

Briatexte viaduct, between the wars. The view is from the far side of the river on the northern side of the viaduct. There is a good view of the *BV* and *halle,* new version. Below them can be seen the remains of an old mill, destroyed by fire. *Louis Briand/Carto-Club Tarnais*

Site of Briatexte viaduct viewed from the eastern side 1993. *Malcolm Wright*

building incorporates a medieval doorway. To its side, a mill and millpond suggest both tranquility and bygone industry. Just to the north, the more modern church of St Sernin and the rest of the hamlet skirt the main road.

The village of Puybegon, in former times a fortress, is perched above the valley at least three kilometres away from the railway. The inhabitants had a stiff climb down to the railway. This too would have been a minor halt with no suggestion of a siding for freight, though there would have been a shelter of the same pattern as the one for Busque-Cabanes. Goods traffic from the plateau would have been funnelled into Briatexte along the D14 and D15.

The railway crossed the D39 to the west of the village, and still a little to the south of the D631, across farmland. Even in 1999, the atmosphere was rural. We are outside the sphere of influence of any of the local towns. The Mediterranean pines celebrated in old place names still flourish in local fields.

A kilometre further on, the railway rejoins the southern side of the road. This was, and still is, open countryside. Road and rail run nearly parallel for two kilometres or so to the next halt. This stretch was far from straight, boasting no less than four bends of 50 metres radius.

A small halt originally called Giroussens-Parisot was established to the east of the junction of the D631 with the D87 (GC87). This was sited just to the east of the Rieucourt brook which runs south to the Dadou. Of the two settlements which lent the halt its name, Giroussens is about four kilometres to the west along the D637 and Parisot six to the north.[57] The halt consisted of a standard shelter between the line and the road with a passing loop to the south. Some freight was anticipated from the north along the D87, and also from the west and so there was provision for wagons.

The line and passing loop reunited before the road bridge over the brook and then turned south. The manoevre involved a bend to the left of 50 metres radius, and a gradient of 2.5 per cent as briefly the line followed the course of the stream. Then the railway curved away to the right round a radius of 100 metres and by a curve to the left, radius 50 metres, it joined the D87 en route for Lavaur. Tight bends were necessary if the thrifty tramway was to make use of the road bridge over the Dadou which was just over 70 metres long and constructed in three spans.

On the south bank is the hamlet of La Ramière (a local word for pigeon). There is no evidence that this was ever an official halt and later it was to lend its name to the station. Half a kilometre from the bridge, road and rail part company once more as they separately negotiated the steep climb out of the valley of the Dadou and into that of the Agout. The line twisted away from the road, first by a shallow bend to the left and then to the right. This stretch was known as the Col d'Ambres. A col is literally a neck, and by extension a narrow or a pass. (The Col d'Ambres runs below the village of Ambres which is perched on the watershed between the Agout and the Dadou.) It consisted of 600 metres of fairly straight track, first of embankment, then of a steadily deeper cutting, the gradient sometimes as steep as 2.6 per cent and rarely dropping below 2.1 per cent. At the summit, the D39 crossed the railway cutting on a metal trestle bridge.

Near the summit, was situated the halt for Ambres, a short but stiff climb away. Today, the small village terminates as it always did in a splendid view of the valley, useful for the knights of yore, splendid for the visitor. Little goods traffic was expected; although a siding was planned, it was never constructed; it was a constricted site. It would have had a shelter of the standard pattern. The route was now downhill for 300 metres with once again gradients ranging from 2.1 per cent to 2.5 per cent, with the cutting becoming more shallow until it vanished. At this point, the tramway rejoined the D87. It kept to the left of the road all the way to Lavaur.

About 100 metres along the D87, and just under half a kilometre from the summit, was the request stop for the village of Port d'Ambres. Just to the south, a three-arched road bridge provided the railway with a crossing of the Agout river. Over the next kilometre, there were a series of gentle curves (only one being tighter than 100 metres radius) and slight gradients to be negotiated.

Road and tramway crossed over the Midi line by a metal bridge. The town of Lavaur has grown out beyond the railway (now a itself a branch line terminating at Montauban), originally, the main line would have run through open country. The tramway followed the D87 into the town as far as what is now known as Place Pont St Roche. The distinctive buildings beloved of the old postcards survive today. Just before the crossroads, was the Lavaur *ville* request stop; and it then executed a sharp turn to the right into Avenue Auguste Malroux (the St Sulpice road) taking the left-hand side of the road.

Between the railway and the river, is the cathedral of St Alain, built in the 12th century, with a celebrated Jaquemart of bell tower automata. The cathedral gardens look over the Agout, crossed by the 18th century Pont St Roch and a railway viaduct built by Séjourné in the 19th century. In the town are other tourist attractions, evidence of the wealth and trade of bygone days. The Compagnie du Midi routed the main line from Montauban to Castres through Lavaur. Important main roads intersect here. Yet by the middle of the 20th century it had 8,000 inhabitants, whereas Graulhet with far fewer natural advantages had over 13,500. In 1999, it is agreeable enough, but quiet. Growth is concentrated to the west.

The tramway turned out of Avenue Auguste Malroux into Avenue de la Gare which it followed on the right towards the main line station. Many of the buildings which can be seen in old photos, including the Hotel de la Gare, survive in 1999. The Midi building faces the Avenue, dominating the Place de la Gare. By means of a triangular track arrangement (*triangle Américain*) in the small station square, trains from Graulhet could enter and leave the station grounds, take passengers from the *Bâtiment des Voyageurs,* and gain access to the TVT freight yard. The triangle also made turning a locomotive or railcar a simple manoeuvre. The water tank was fitted in the western apex of the triangle. It was made of cement, had a diameter of 1.8 metres and stood on a stone base.

Passenger trains coming into Lavaur station therefore kept to the eastern side of the turning triangle. Following a curve of 43 metres radius, they stopped at a spur on the south side of the main line passenger platform. The *BV* of the TVT was to the side of the main station building on this passenger platform. It consisted of a small office and waiting room for travellers. Measuring 7.3 by 5 metres, it was a little more ample than the standard wayside shelter, but was constructed in the same way with brick and timber. A small building on the other side of the main line *BV* housed the travellers' conveniences.

Lavaur town. A Decauville carriage is turning out of the picture, part of a train on its way to La Ramière. It has just stopped for Lavaur *ville* (another name for this square was Place du Pont) and is turning into the D87.   *Louis Briand/Carto-Club Tarnais*

Another train, more clearly visible, is turning out of the Avenue Auguste Malroux, towards Graulhet.   *Louis Briand/Carto-Club Tarnais*

Station Avenue, Lavaur. The train has come up from Station Square. The *BV* of the Midi can be seen in the background. *Louis Briand/Carto-Club Tarnais*

View of Weidknecht 4-6-0T coming from the direction of Lavaur station. *J. Daffis/ACOVA*

LE TARN ILLUSTRÉ
890 LAVAUR — Avenue de la Gare   Phototypie Tarnaise, Poux, Directeur, Albi

Taken about 1910, this view shows the Station Hotel, Lavaur, with the *BV* for the Midi in the
background.   *Louis Briand/Carto-Club Tarnais*

A view taken from the same angle in 1999, shows the Station Hotel and *BV* still standing, but
most of the evidence of the existence of the petit train has been swept away.   *M.D. Wright*

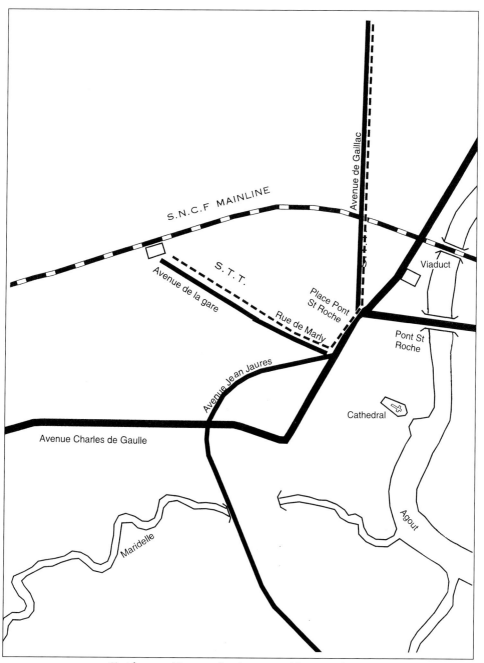

Sketch map of Lavaur, showing route of former railway.

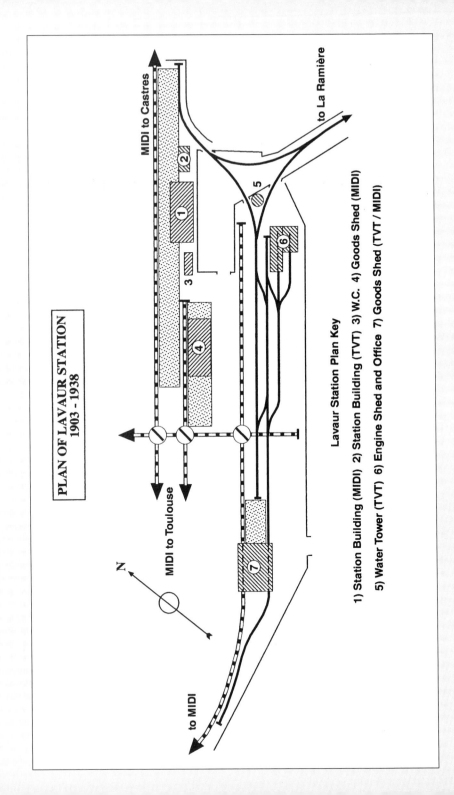

PLAN OF LAVAUR STATION
1903 - 1938

N

MIDI to Toulouse

MIDI to Castres

to La Ramière

to MIDI

Lavaur Station Plan Key

1) Station Building (MIDI) 2) Station Building (TVT) 3) W.C. 4) Goods Shed (MIDI)

5) Water Tower (TVT) 6) Engine Shed and Office 7) Goods Shed (TVT / MIDI)

The *BV* of the Midi at Lavaur. To the right is part of the TVT *BV*. In the foreground can be seen the apex of the turning triangle and the waiting Weidkneckt.   *Louis Briand/Carto-Club Tarnais*

A view showing all the *BV* of the TVT. The plans submitted to County Hall suggest that it was a detached building, but in fact the two were joined.   *ACOVA*

TVT Timetable Winter 1903/1904
*Issued by the President of the Board, Valiech, at Toulouse 27th October, 1903
Inspected and approved by the Préfet of Tarn at Albi, 27th November, 1903*

Connections from Albi	8.58	10.54		8.38
At Laboutarié from Castres	8.53		4.26	9.11

Train No.	*1*	*3*	*5*	*7*
	am	*am*	*pm*	*pm*
Laboutarié Station	9.07	11.30	4.47	9.20
Laboutarié Village (Halt)	9.14	11.37	4.54	9.27
Montdragon (Halt)	9.19	11.42	4.59	9.32
Le Bruc (Halt)	9.27	11.50	5.07	9.40
St Hilaire (Halt)	9.33	11.56	5.13	9.46
Fernan (Halt)	9.45	12.08	5.25	9.58
Graulhet Station	9.50	12.13	5.30	10.03

Train No.	*10*	*20*	*12*	*14*
	am	*am*	*pm*	*pm*
		SO		
Graulhet Station	6.25	10.28	12.30	5.35
Graulhet St Projet (Halt)	6.31	10.34	12.36	5.41
Busque Cabanès (Halt)	6.39	10.42	12.44	5.49
Briatexte St Gauzens *arr.*	6.52	10.55	12.36	6.01
Briatexte St Gauzens *dep.*	6.54	10.58	12.59	6.03
Puybegon St Sernin (Halt)	7.06	11.10	1.11	6.13
Giroussens Parisot (Halt)	7.16	11.20	1.21	6.23
Ambres (Halt)	7.26	11.30	1.31	6.35
Lavaur Town (request stop)	7.38	11.42	1.43	6.47
Lavaur Station	7.41	11.45	1.46	6.50

Connections for St Sulpice	8.05		2.10	7.07
At Lavaur for Castres	9.56		2.08	8.08

As in the original, the word 'halt' has been omitted in the following part of the timetable.

Connections from St Sulpice	9.52	2.30		8.03
At Lavaur from Castres	8.59	2.15		9.03

Train No.	*9*	*11*	*21*	*13*
	am	*pm*	*pm*	*pm*
			SO	
Lavaur Station	10.10	2.16	4.00	8.20
Lavaur Town	10.14	2.20	4.04	8.24
Ambres	10.24	2.30	4.14	8.34
Giroussens Parisot	10.34	2.40	4.24	8.44
Puybegon St Sernin	10.44	2.50	4.34	8.54
Briatexte St Gauzens *arr.*	10.57	3.01	4.45	9.05
dep.	10.59	3.02	4.47	9.07
Busque Cabanès	11.15	3.17	5.03	9.23
Graulhet St Projet	11.24	3.26	5.12	9.32
Graulhet Station	11.28	3.30	5.16	9.36

Train No.	*2*	*4*	*6*	*8*
	am	*am*	*pm*	*pm*
Graulhet Station	7.40	10.00	3.32	7.50
Ferran	7.45	10.00	3.38	7.56
St Hilaire	7.58	10.18	3.50	8.08
Le Bruc	8.04	10.24	3.56	8.14
Montdragon	8.12	10.32	4.04	8.22
Laboutarié Village	8.17	10.37	4.09	8.27
Laboutarié Station	8.25	10.45	4.17	8.35

Connections for Albi	9.06		4.28	9.15
At Laboutarié for Castres	9.01	10.58		9.12

Notes: There are request stops at pont Vieux, La Ventenayé, Ricardens, Briatexte (town), En Jalabert and north side of the river at pont d'Ambres. SO - Saturdays only.

View of Lavaur station in 1999.   *M.D. Wright*

The goods yard was to the west of the turning triangle, reached along a curve radius 35 metres. Three lines linked by crossovers gave access to the engine shed at one end and the *halle de transbordement* (transhipment shed) and platform at the other. The *halle* was of generous proportions, measuring 20.7 by 11.7 metres, and there was a further 10 metres of open platform. A headshunt ran under an awning past the *halle* to terminate about 50 metres beyond. Another spur reached the nearside of the platform. Two main line sidings ran to the north of the *halle de transbordement* and to the north of the main *halle des marchandises*. To add flexibility to the arrangement, the Midi dropped a 'vertical' siding through the sidings and the parallel main line with a wagon turntable at each intersection. Where it crossed the two narrow gauge sidings it was protected by stop blocks at each.

The TVT *remise* consisted of the wooden building which was at Graulhet before 1903. It was dismantled and moved to the new terminus with the internal wall removed so that it could serve as engine shed and workshop combined. Following TVT tradition, these installations were built on land belonging to the Midi. When the line closed, it was reclaimed by the original owners. The track was taken up and the SNCF[58] took over the *Bâtiment des Voyageurs* which was turned into an office for the track maintenance squad. The *halle* survives as a store for animal food, but otherwise the old yard is a flat space of tarmac.

The transhipment shed at Lavaur in 1999, put to new uses.   *M.D. Wright*

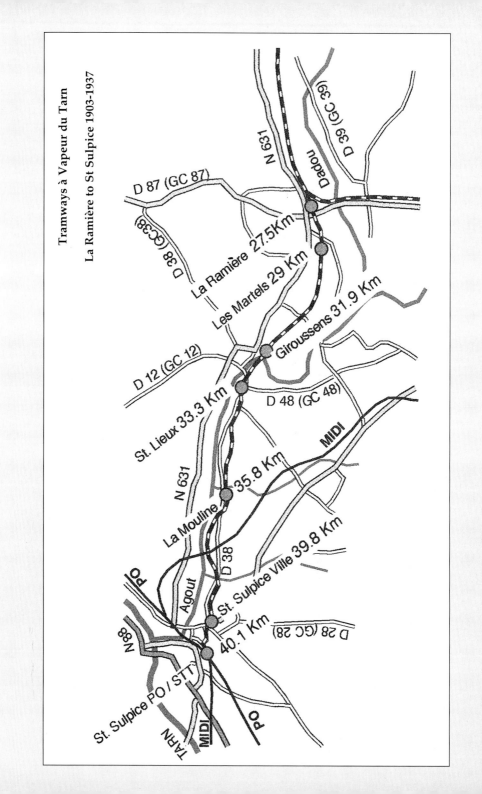

Tramways à Vapeur du Tarn

La Ramière to St Sulpice 1903-1937

D 87 (GC 87)

D 38 (GC 38)

D 39 (GC 39)

N 631

Dadou

La Ramière 27.5Km

Les Martels 29 Km

Giroussens 31.9 Km

D 12 (GC 12)

D 48 (GC 48)

St. Lieux 33.3 Km

MIDI

N 631

La Mouline 35.8 Km

St. Sulpice Ville 39.8 Km

D 38

Agout

D 28 (GC 28)

40.1 Km

N 88

PO

St. Sulpice PO / STT

TARN

MIDI

PO

Chapter Five

La Ramière to St Sulpice

In May 1903, the TVT had a network of over 33 kilometres of railway linking Graulhet and area to the main line at Laboutarié and Lavaur. Freight and passenger numbers were growing as were, to some extent, profits. Almost immediately plans were considered to construct a third main line outlet. In 1906 the Director approached the Paris Orléans with a scheme for extending the existing line to the station at St Sulpice and then on to Salvagnac to the North-West. The Compagnie Paris-Orleans was the *grand réseau* which built and ran the railway from Toulouse to Albi along the Tarn valley. St Sulpice was one of the stations *en route*. The town is also known as St Sulpice-sur-Tarn or St Sulpice-la-Pointe to distinguish it from others of the same name. The original St Sulpice was the seventh century Bishop of Bourges in Burgundy who helped to Gallicise the Germanic Franks. For a number of reasons, schemes were abandoned or deferred, only to be periodically resurrected.

If engineering studies are included and the cost of the third Weidknecht 4-6-0 tank locomotive delivered before the war, as much as one-tenth of the project was completed by 1922, using company and local funds. In that year, as mentioned in Chapter Two, Paris decided that construction should go ahead, initially as far as St Sulpice. Central Government fixed its subsidy, the shareholders escaped without further charge and the *Département* was to pay the balance. This was, as it turned out, at least 60 per cent of the total! On 2nd April, 1925, the line was completed, and opened to passengers on the 11th of the month and goods on 1st June. Official closure was 30th June, 1937.

The line was, as previously mentioned, engineered to a much higher standard than the rest of the system. The rail weighed in at a relatively substantial 20 kg per metre, purchased second-hand from a railway that was closing; it seems that no significance was read into this. Though the most significant expenditure was on bridges, culverts and the Salles viaduct, the whole line enjoyed the same uncompromising standards. A local quarry had to be opened to provide ballast because, compared with previous sections of the railway, so much permanent way was to be laid from scratch. To build this 13 kilometre stretch was to cost more than double the existing 33 or so kilometres of railway, and it added to the area served by the network one commune, Giroussens, with 1,500 inhabitants, and one, St Lieux with about half that.

The line joined the existing line at *Point Kilométrique* 27.332, that is, at the station of Giroussens-Parisot. As Giroussens was to have a more convenient halt on the new line, the station was renamed La Ramière after the hamlet on the south bank of the river. A plot of 800 square metres on the west side of the Rieucourt brook was purchased to provide a station yard. The original installation consisted, as described in the previous chapter, of a shelter and passing loop to the east of the stream. The passing loop was lengthened and taken over the bridge, which had to be widened. The passenger shelter on the east side of the stream was dismantled and moved to Giroussens.

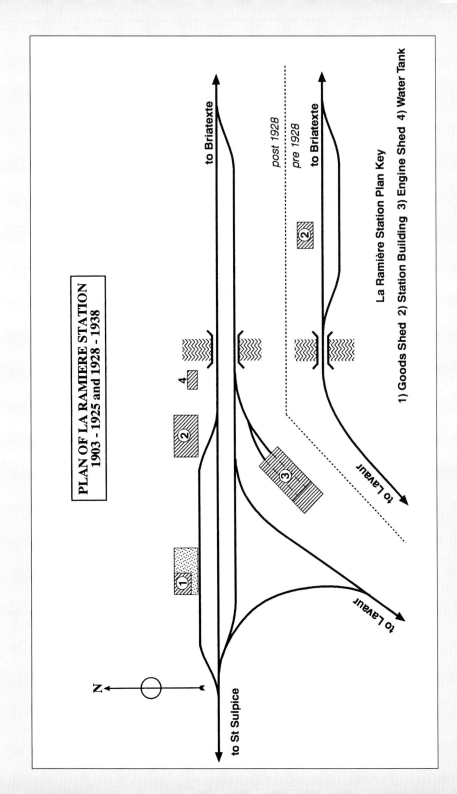

PLAN OF LA RAMIERE STATION
1903 - 1925 and 1928 - 1938

to Briatexte

post 1928

pre 1928

to Briatexte

to Lavaur

to Lavaur

to St Sulpice

N

La Ramière Station Plan Key

1) Goods Shed 2) Station Building 3) Engine Shed 4) Water Tank

La Ramière *BV* in 1993. This modern view of the old *BV* was taken from the road.
Malcolm Wright

La Ramière *remise*. The engine shed is now also a private house, with a mature garden! The photograph was taken from the road; the angle at which the shed was built can be seen, as can the old engine shed door.   *Malcolm Wright*

La Ramière *halle*. It is clearly of small proportions. *Malcolm Wright*

Another view of the *halle* 1993. This was taken from the east and shows the diminutive platform. Some distance beyond is the crossroad with the D87. *Malcolm Wright*

In keeping with its new status as a 'T' junction, the essential trackplan of the station was triangular, each side measuring approximately 20 metres. The passing loop extended across the northern face of the triangle. The Lavaur and St Sulpice lines formed the eastern and western faces and a spur leading to an engine shed was built on the trace of the original line south. The comparatively substantial station building and goods shed were built parallel to the D631 to the north of the triangle. This trackplan made La Ramière one of two stations where it was possible to turn the railcar. The other station was Lavaur and so it spent its working life plying between the two.

The *BV*, measuring 10.2 by 8 metres, consisted of a waiting room, ticket office and a four room flat for the station master, who was in fact a woman. The conveniences were accommodated in an extension to the building, most probably on the western side.

In the original design, the *remise* (engine shed) was served by a single track spur but in due course the track was doubled so that it could also house the railcar. The *remise* measured 14 by 7.8 metres providing an inspection pit and rest room as well. The *halle des marchandises* was considerably less spacious at 5 by 5 metres, supplemented by an open platform measuring 35 square metres. There was a metal water tank, supplied from a hand operated well. No doubt the diesel railcar was a particularly welcome alternative to steam on this section of the railway.

The station buildings were sold after the closure of the railway. There are road improvements nearby, but they exist in good condition in 1999. The *BV* is a private house, but there is now no sign of the outside WCs and the well has been covered over. The *remise* has also been uprated to a home, though the large door on its northern side continues to hint at its origin. The *halle* is now perilously close to the encroaching road. The original station fence which extended around it has gone, but most of the open platform survives.

The former railway left the station parallel to the road, crossing the southward- bound D87 135 metres from the station. It proceeded between road and river for a further ¾ kilometre, before running beside the D631 for about ¼ kilometre. Then road and rail part for just over 100 metres. The site is marked more or less clearly because a gravel dump was established here after the closure of the railway.

Road, rail and river accompanied each for another 300 metres. At the halt, named after the church of St Syriaque,[59] the railway turned off slightly left and the river sweeps away to the south. The railway forged westwards across fields, bypassing the hamlet of la Masquière. This is at the eastern end of the tourist line. To the north, the D631 climbs up on to an escarpment. Original plans envisaged following the road up to the small town of Giroussens, but the slopes were too steep, even for a tramway. The route actually taken avoided all settlement for more than two kilometres. Half a kilometre from St Syriaque is the hamlet of Les Martels, to the south of the railway. The request stop was moved to this road junction to serve this slightly larger community.

To the west, the verdant terrain presented the railway with problems. It is always at risk of flooding after rain, since on this section the railway grade corresponds with the spring-line. As the trackbed becomes waterlogged, ballast slips into quicksand patches of the the sub-roadbed and so must constantly be renewed. Another problem was landslip, again due to subterranean water. It is known as the Garrigole, derived from the local word *garrigue* meaning scrub. To avoid the worst pockets of marsh, the line follows curves of radius 250 metres, 120, 100 and 150 metres.

The Garrigole was always tricky. On its inaugural run on 2nd April, 1925, a trusty old Decauville 0-6-2 tank (TVT No. 2) derailed here, 3.6 kilometres from La Ramière. On 28th April, less than a month later, this was the scene of the most notable accident in the entire history of the line, the odd collision with livestock or unwary motorist excepted. In early evening, the pony truck of the very same Decauville derailed at the entry to St Sulpice station. This resulted in one of its spring supports breaking. As there were no spares available, the resourceful driver replaced it with a wooden prop and the train set out back towards Graulhet. Because they were an hour and a half late, the station master phoned ahead to warn his counterpart at Graulhet about the mishap.

All was well until the fateful spot on the Garrigole section was reached, a little before nine o'clock. This time, no less than six wheels left the rails, because of course there was no springing on one side of the pony truck. The driver, fireman and guard tried to ease the locomotive back on to the track. The jack just slipped into the soft ground of the embankment, and an attempt to use a U-shaped iron as a lever ended when this broke. They sent the guard, on foot, to La Ramière to summon help. He telephoned Graulhet but no one answered. The station master at Graulhet had left his post! Mindful of the six stranded passengers, the guard trudged up to Giroussens to hire a car to get them home.

Meanwhile, the wife of one of the passengers, anxious because he was so late, also hired a car and came out from Graulhet to meet him. She picked up the station master at Briatexte, and a solitary passenger waiting for the train. They drove through to St Lieux, only to be told that the train had passed through. The station master, aware of previous difficulties, suggested that they checked the Garrigole on their way home. There they found the stranded train.

When the travellers returned to Graulhet, they alerted the Manager who arranged for a breakdown train to tow the missing one home, which it did at a quarter to eight next morning. An investigation concluded that the guard, driver and fireman had behaved properly throughout. The derailment at St Sulpice which had started the trouble had not been caused by carelessness. The bend into the station needed repacking. The second derailment was entirely beyond their control. The staff at Graulhet, on the other hand, were formally cautioned; firstly, they had not taken any steps to warn the families of the passengers that the train was late, secondly they did not ensure that the station was manned all evening.

Nothing so serious ever occurred here again; the crew no doubt always took care to come prepared with suitable re-railing gear. There was one consolation for the hard pressed steam engine. The area offered a reliable watering point, fed by a perpetual spring.

The quicksands of the Garrigole lead down to a riverside that is liable to flooding; the best place for a town was on a hill. Just past the worst of the Garrigole is the halt for Giroussens, on the high ground. As might be expected,

Giroussens has been a settlement for centuries.[60] Just to the east of the junction with the country road which winds up to the village proper was the shelter, the old *BV* from the station at La Ramière. There was no siding. No goods traffic was expected or was ever generated.

Four hundred metres on, the line crossed the country road known as the Chemin de Salles which led to a ferry across the River Agout. The railway passed overhead on a viaduct which survived the closure of the line. It was the most costly work of engineering on the entire line. By the time it was complete, the bill came to 540,000 francs, more than a fifth of the total expenditure on the line, equipment and rolling stock included. The local earth is friable and the river has dug a deep channel. It is also liable to spectacular flooding and so it had to be strongly built - although the trackbed is 19 metres above the Agout, the line has, on at least one occasion, actually been submerged. The construction was masonry faced with brick. A total of 132 metres long, the four central arches, span of each 22 metres, were flanked to each side by one span six metres wide. Three of the piers were built in the river itself, the others into the rock of the river bank. At the top, the stonework projected 30 centimetres each side to give a permanent way 3.3 metres wide, guarded by a metal railing. Above each pillar there was a refuge alcove.

When the Tramways closed, the bridge reverted to the Department and took on a new lease of life as a road bridge. In 1974, it was announced that the trackbed was to be resurfaced, but that is another story. Once over the bridge, the railway rejoined the original ferry path, crossed it, and the two ran side by side. There was no official stop for Port de Salles on the west bank of the river. Half a kilometre further on, the railway crossed the D48 on the edge of the village of St Lieux.[61]

Permanent way across the viaduct. The view, taken in the late 20th century, is largely unchanged except that the railway is now 50 centimetre rather than 60 centimetre gauge.
Malcolm Wright

VIADUC SUR L'AGOUT

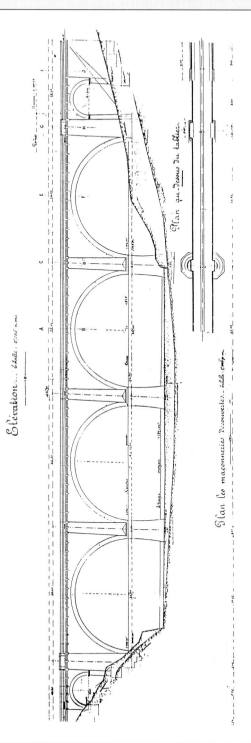

Élévation... échelle 0'005 p.m.

Plan des maçonneries nouvelles. échelle 0'005 p.m.

Plan au dessous du tablier.

Plan of viaduct at Salles.

The track turned away from the road into the station built on a generous plot to the south of the high street. At the planning stage, there were unduly high hopes for the small railway. The steady flow of merchandise into the goods yard, and passengers into the waiting room, were expected by the members of the commune to keep a full-time employee busy. The Board of the TVT did not share the optimistic mood. Expecting only light traffic, they proposed part-time service and the locking of the premises on a Sunday. M. de Belcastel, *Député* of Tarn,[62] pronounced in favour of the people of St Lieux and a full-time member of staff was employed. The commune put forward 3,000 francs towards construction, as did Giroussens.

The station consisted of a through line, a passing loop and a short spur which could accomodate perhaps three wagons. Buildings consisted of a waiting room cum office measuring 5.55 by 3.7 metres joined to a *halle* 4.35 by 5.05 metres in extent, opening on to a platform of vanishingly small proportions. The 'shed of convenience' which even the most modest station would usually provide was absent. Travellers had to remember to make themselves comfortable before leaving home or use the wasteland south of the station.

The hopes which had attended the construction of the line were already evaporating. St Lieux station was more modest than had originally been expected, and further cuts were in the pipeline. After only four months of operation, the three daily services each way were reduced to two. The station mistress was sacked in 1931 as was her colleague at La Ramière. This was part of the desperate retrenchment practised as traditional custom dried up and new business failed to materialise. The station yard and buildings, like the viaduct, have survived, the complete tale is told in a subsequent chapter.

Leaving the station to the west, the line crossed a stream over a culvert 1.5 metres wide. It went round a sharp curve radius 50 metres then one of 100 metres radius before joining the D38 (GC 38) on St Lieux High Street to cross the village on rails sunk into the surface of the road. Just outside the built-up area, less than half a kilometre from the station, road and rail part company for nearly two kilometres. The road follows rather difficult terrain close to the river while the railway passes to the south. It was here that a quarry was purchased to provide ballast during construction of the route. A temporary spur brought the ballast out.

St Lieux High Street.   *J. Daffis/ACOVA*

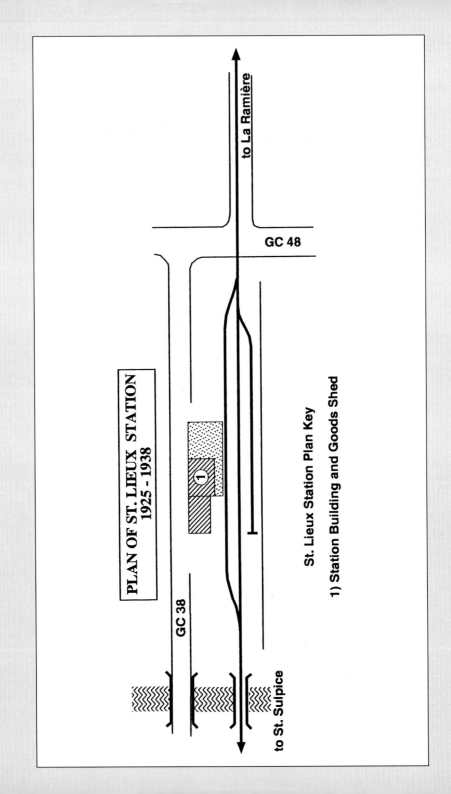

PLAN OF ST. LIEUX STATION
1925 - 1938

to La Ramière

GC 48

GC 38

to St. Sulpice

St. Lieux Station Plan Key

1) Station Building and Goods Shed

Beyond a stream, crossed by a 2 metre bridge, road and rail met at the junction with a side road. Here the train halted for La Mouline which never had a passenger shelter. For the next 600 metres, the railway ran on track on the south verge of the road but all trace of this has since been swallowed up by road widening. The railway then crossed to the north side of the road describing a curve of radius 100 metres and ran for a kilometre between road and river. In 1999, the river is eroding the bank, completely obliterating some of the former trackbed and even threatening the road.

To the west of La Viguerie farm, the main line railway coming east from St Sulpice crosses the river. To pass under the main line, a metal bridge, span 4 metres, had to be let into the main line embankment to accommodate the narrow gauge railway. The bridge is named after the landmark across the river, the church of St Vast.[63]

When the route was first planned, this railway crossing must have created diplomatic problems; the stretch of main line involved belonged to the Compagnie du Midi. The Tramway was crossing under to reach a competitor, the Paris-Orléans. The *Préfet* must have used all his influence to ensure co-operation on the project. The *Préfet*, as a representative of Central Government would have great influence on the *grand réseaux*. Today, the scene is one of rural tranquility, perhaps a fisherman down in the river, an infrequent train passing on the St Vast bridge, a glimpse of the ancient chapel on the far bank.

Once it had passed under the main line, the track climbed back up to the level of the D38. This it did up a gradient of 1.5 per cent over 313 metres which ended in a curve of radius 400 metres. For the next ½ kilometre, it ran along the north verge of the road, crossing one stream on an independent culvert 1.5 metres long, and negotiating no bend sharper than radius 340 metres. Road widening has swallowed up all traces.

The railway then moved on to the road bed for the next kilometre, road and rail entering St Sulpice together. Constrained by the river Tarn and a main *route nationale* to the west, the town has expanded eastwards swallowing up many fields which used to witness the railway, and making it difficult to savour any atmosphere. The railway kept to the northern side of the D38 until the stop for St Sulpice Ville in Place du Marché. The town was an original *bastide*, and the original market place would have been at the centre of the town. When the church was built on the site in the 15th century, the market place was moved to it present site to the east of the original town. It stops short of the Old Town, laid out on a grid plan, but the triple towers of the church of St Sulpice can be seen rising out of the Old Town centre, like brick hats.

At the far end of the Place du Marché was the *Monument aux Morts*, a few metres from the track. The railway crossed over to the left side of the street as it crossed the junction with the D630 from Lavaur. Some tight bends had to be negotiated. So tight was the bend at this point that the railway had to purchase land from the commune, and demolish the wash house standing there, to provide a passage. A curve of 40 metres radius was thus brought up to the minimum of 50. Once over the crossing, the railway followed the Avenue de la Gare to the main line station, then jointly owned by the Paris-Orléans and the Midi.

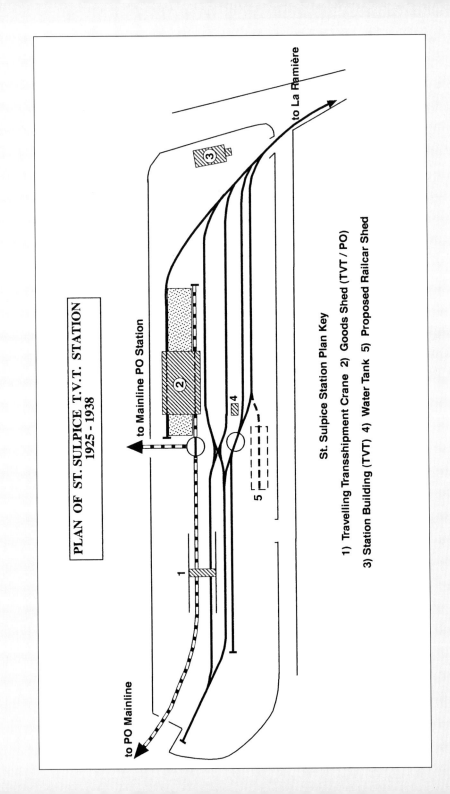

PLAN OF ST. SULPICE T.V.T. STATION
1925 - 1938

to PO Mainline

to Mainline PO Station

to La Ramière

St. Sulpice Station Plan Key

1) Travelling Transshipment Crane 2) Goods Shed (TVT / PO)

3) Station Building (TVT) 4) Water Tank 5) Proposed Railcar Shed

Station Road, St Sulpice, about 1928. *J. Daffis/AGOVA*

This part of the route has changed the least. To the right is a park, with a tourist information centre and Syndicat d'Initiative, to the left, the school building of the 1920s is recognisable. At the bottom of the road can be seen now as ever the old *BV* of the Paris-Orléans.

The narrow gauge station lay alongside the main station, requiring a fairly sharp turn to the left of radius no more than 50 metres. It was built on an independent plot off Avenue de la Gare. In essence, the TVT station plan consisted of two parallel passing loops turning sharply off the track which ended in a headshunt parallel to the main line at the north of the station. The passing loops each ended in a crossover and crossed over again to form a further passing loop and siding. At the extreme west of the station yard the track ended in a headshunt. The narrow gauge *BV* was sited parallel to the Avenue de la Gare, opposite that of the Paris-Orléans. It measured a fairly respectable 8.7 by 7.8 metres. The ground floor consisted of a waiting room, office and shop while upstairs was a four room flat for the station master. A second shop was built on facing the main line, while to the east were the WCs.

The line ended north of the *halle de transbordement* in a siding while a main line siding ran to its south. The enclosed area of the shed measured 4.2 by 4.6 metres; canopies extending on both sides over the rails brought the total area under cover to 17.2 by 13 metres. As a move in the direction of modernisation, a gantry straddled the main line and narrow gauge sidings, to lessen the labour of transhipment. There was a manual turntable to take wagons up a 'vertical' spur to further main line sidings.

TVT Timetable 15th May, 1930

This was the last timetable that was provided by rail alone. The services are described in two groups, odd and even. Even numbers are return trips. services 7 to 10 have been withdrawn as have 13, 14 and 17 to 20.

Service No.	1	3	5		2	4	6
	6.30	12.50	17.10	Graulhet	10.13	15.23	19.48
	7.13	13.43	18.03	Laboutarié	9.20	14.30	18.55

Service No.	11	31	15		12	36	16
		SO				SO	
	5.40	9.30	16.30	Graulhet	11.05	17.43	20.40
	6.38 arr.	10.30 arr.	17.38 arr.	La Ramière	10.07 dep.	16.30 dep.	19.42 dep.
	6.43 dep.		17.33 dep.	La Ramière	10.02 arr.		19.37 arr.
	7.25		18.15	St Sulpice	9.20		18.55

Service No.	21		23		22		24
	6.40	10.35	17.35	La Ramière	10.05	16.25	19.40
	7.05	11.00	18.00	Lavaur	9.40	16.00	19.25

TVT Timetable 1st May, 1931

This timetable was provided jointly by bus, train and railcar. The services are described in two groups, odd and even. The even numbers are return trips. The buses are much quicker than the trains they replaced.

Service No.	1	3	5		2	4	6
	Bus	Bus	Bus		Bus	Bus	Bus
	6.45	13.30	18.00	Graulhet	10.00	15.15	19.30
	7.15	14.00	18.30	Laboutarié	9.30	14.45	19.00

Service No.	11	31	15		12	36	16
	Bus	Train	Bus		Bus	Train	Bus
		SO				SO	
	6.15	9.30	17.00	Graulhet	10.00	17.34	20.00
	6.45 arr.	10.30 arr.	17.30 arr.	La Ramière	9.30 dep.	16.30 dep.	19.30 dep.
	6.49 dep.		17.34 dep.	La Ramière	9.26 arr.		19.26 arr.
	7.15		18.00	St Sulpice	9.00		19.00

Service No.	21		23		22		24
	Railcar		Railcar		Railcar		Railcar
	6.45	10.35	17.35	La Ramière	10.05	16.25	19.28
	7.05	11.00	18.00	Lavaur	9.40	16.00	19.08

At the eastern side of the station yard, parallel sidings led to the water tower supporting a metal tank and to a turntable. One instrument of modernisation proposed had been the railcar but the thrifty Directors had ordered one which could only be driven from the front. A turntable, ordered from Établissements Viset,[64] was needed to manoeuvre it into position for return journeys. Too late, it was realised that at 4 metres, the turntable which they had ordered was too small. They requested an upgrade to 6.5 metres, but Viset insisted on being paid at least for the one that had been made. They opted to take the undersized one and thus it was all but impossible to use the railcar on this line.

An engine shed was planned but never built, turning out of the southern passing loop. In all, the station plan would have made more sense if the planned extension to Salvagnac had been built. As it was, some of the sidings were redundant. At the close of the railway, the station plot was sold and has become private property. The site of the *Bâtiment Voyageurs*, parallel to the road, is now occupied by a larger building. Modern St Sulpice has doubled in population, with corresponding growth, and many traces of the railway have been obliterated. This branch of TVT territory has benefited from the vast growth of Toulouse, and particularly from the opening of the A68 *Autoroute*. Giroussens has become the upmarket preserve of rich weekenders and artists. St Lieux is growing in size and prosperity and St Sulpice itself, especially the school, is cheerily bursting out wherever it can.

Germain Olivet was the last driver on the St Sulpice line. He served in World War I, and then drove steam engines until the closure of the network. His job took him through to Laboutarié, but someone else drove the railcar on the Lavaur route. The job of engine driver was a prestigious one in local communities where the choice of employment was limited. Regulated by the *Conseil Général*, it conferred the same privileges enjoyed by an employee of the *Département* in matters of leave and pensions. Lunch was normally eaten at a local inn, nothing less being acceptable to an employee of his status. When the railway closed, M. Olivet took a job as a foreman at a farm near Mézens, 5 kilometres from St Sulpice. His daughter still lives there, though he eventually moved back to an eventide home in St Sulpice. He much regretted the passing of the little train.

M. Germain Olivet, former engine driver in 1994.
Marthe Lacaze

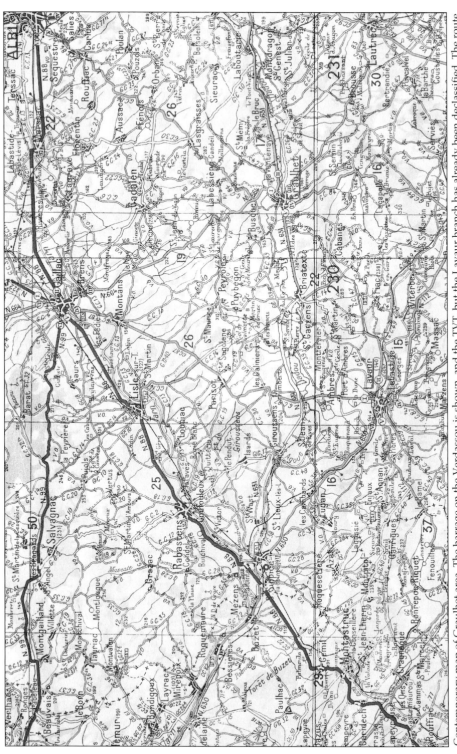

Contemporary map of Graulhet area. The barrage on the Verdassou is shown, and the TVT, but the Lavaur branch has already been declassified. The route to Salvagnac can be traced though there is no indication that anything permanent was built.

Cartes Michelin 1935

The Proposed Line To Salvagnac

The Salvagnac branch was being planned in 1913, with debate over the merits and otherwise of the projected route. In 1921, a track from St Sulpice station to the halt at La Pointe was, it appears, agreed, and the rural part of the route redesigned to reduce gradients. The line proposal given here might well have undergone further modification if the project had not been shelved by the late 1920s.

Origin of *Points Kilométriques* (*pk*) St Sulpice Station. Line to follow Avenue Auguste Milhes, then pass under main line using a specially constructed bridge, cross a field, follow GC11 for 100 metres, cross another field then follow N88 to La Pointe, total deviation from existing roads of 927 metres. Halt for La Pointe *pk* 1.324. Follow D28 (GC28) with deviation of 200 metres to Mézens halt *pk* 1.920. Important viaduct, i.e. more than 10 metres long, out of Mézens, deviation of 159 metres. Follow D28 to Condel *pk* 5.630. Deviations of 296 metres, otherwise follow D28 to Grazac station *pk* 8.150. Deviation of 445 metres. Follow D28 to Passé halt *pk* 10.617. Deviations 375 metres, 544 metres otherwise follow D2 to Raust halt *pk* 12.875. Deviation 3.947 m, picked up D2 to Salvagnac station *pk* 17.420.

A narrow gauge extension north of St Sulpice was considered for a number of reasons. Situated at the confluence of the Agout and the Tarn, the town enjoys excellent communication up both valleys. It was settled by ancient Gauls, and then by the Romans, who have left faint traces and then by the *Comté* of Toulouse which has left the town an ancient catacomb. It was reinvented as a *bastide* in the middle ages. A railway town by the 19th century, it became a junction between the rival PO and Midi in the twentieth. There were problems. In the east, St Sulpice is constrained by the River Agout, to the west by the mighty Tarn. Alternative centres of communication throng the banks of the Tarn; one roughly every 8 kilometres. At the time, the inhabitants of the route did not regard St Sulpice, for all its potential advantages, as an important trade or social centre. To take a small example, the post town for Mézens, two kilometres from St Sulpice, is in fact Rabastens, eight kilometres away. These factors are not so obvious now. In recent years, St Sulpice, with excellent road and rail communication has outstripped other towns, the population rising from 2,400 to 4,300 whereas that of Rabastens has, if anything, fallen.

The plan was, of course, not entirely practical, more to use the narrow gauge railway in its classic role, that of opening up a remote area. With about 1,600 inhabitants, Salvagnac was, and is, the largest village in the isolated upper Tescou valley; a line of communication southward was a welcome addition to the main road leading east-west. Since the D999 (then the N99) had been created 100 years before, transport had not substantially improved. The most accessible main line stations were Montauban 30 kilometres west along the Tescou valley or Gaillac and Villemur over the watershed; the area had never benefited from the growth in secondary railways.

We can see politics at work. The neighbouring department of Haute Garonne had initiated a substantial network, over 500 kilometres of secondary railways, some of which extended into Tarn. Tarn had only sponsored 200 kilometres.

Though this was a respectable total compared to many *Départements*, Lot and Garonne having only 130 kilometres of secondary railways, Aveyron virtually nothing, it was felt that proposals should at least be put forward for the Salvagnac area.

What is less easy to understand is why the planned railway should stop short of the valley and the main road. Two kilometres up a tributary of the Tescou, Salvagnac should not have been the terminus. If there was a case for building the railway at all, there was one for taking the railway as far as the D999, especially as the authorities wanted to link as many communities as possible to the rail network. We can only assume that politics once again and personalities demanded the prestige of the terminus for the town.

According to the agreement existing before World War I, the proposed line had the status of *utilité publique*. The State was to provide a fixed proportion of the costs of building, namely 17,000 francs, and shareholders were to raise capital of 885,000 francs. A route was mapped out and locomotives and rolling stock were planned. In 1913, seven 10 tonne wagons and 10 tipper trucks of Belgian manufacture were ordered. So far it has been impossible to find out which Belgian manufacturer was involved.

After the war, the whole network was regraded to the status of *VFIL*[65] and serious studies were undertaken of construction costs. They were shown to be at least three times higher than original estimates. On 15th October, 1921, the representative of Central Government, the Ministre des Travaux Publiques recommended that the Salvagnac project be postponed, and that the first part of the line, the branch to St Sulpice should proceed. This was confirmed by the company at a meeting on 16th September, 1922.

The day of the Salvagnac branch never came but two plans exist, one pre-war in which the minimum gradient permissible was 2.5 per cent, and a post-war one which reduced this to 2 per cent. It is worth remembering that on the existing railway, in the town of Graulhet, gradients exceeded 5 per cent.

Alternative studies exist for the route out of St Sulpice where crossing the main line was to prove a particular problem. The original plan would have required considerable construction work. The narrow gauge line was to run up a gradient alongside the main line to the south-west of the station. After 700 metres enough height would have been gained to take the railway over the main line at a point shortly before it divides *en route* for Toulouse and Montauban respectively. The narrow gauge line would have made the crossing by a 25 metre metal viaduct and then joined the N88 along a side road. The PO granted wayleave in March 1913 and the Directors of the TVT retired to do their sums.

They concluded that it would be cheaper to pass under the main line instead. At the eastern side of the town, the line was embanked so that it could cross the Agout. At this point, the standard gauge railway was five metres above the trackbed of the proposed narrow gauge. Girders encased in concrete could be inserted to form a bridge 3.7 metres wide, high enough for the passage of the *petit train* but without disturbing the ballast above. We cannot be sure of the enthusiasm with which the PO greeted the new scheme, but in December 1914 it received authorisation from the Central Government Ministries involved. As World War I had begun, no immediate action was taken.

The new plan meant that the TVT had to cross the town to reach the site of the proposed bridge. The plan was for the Salvagnac train to come up the Avenue de la Gare, and branch off at Square Pradel in front of the local school. It would then follow the course of a stream under the Rustau bridge until it reached the eastern bank of the Agout, which it would follow north to the bridge under the main line. This proposal was opposed by those who thought that there were already too many trains on Avenue de la Gare, the route for trains coming in from La Ramière. Furthermore they wanted the stream bed for a new road. Siting the railway along the side of the existing Square Pradel likewise met with opposition, this time from townsfolk who objected to road widening, especially when it was close to a school.

The main road leaving St Sulpice to the north was the D630 (then the GC86) which offered the advantage of a ready made bridge under the main line railway. The TVT was discouraged from using this main road. Busy at the best of times, it was particularly so on market days. In the end, it was decided that the railway would follow the stream bed; by this time, it was built over and known as Avenue Auguste Milhes, under the main line, and behind another school, the École St Charles, to the edge of town and as far as the neighbouring village of La Pointe, now a part of modern St Sulpice.

Neither of the plans was realised. Some earth was moved at the site of the planned bridge under the main line, but the bridge was never constructed, and no trace remains of preliminary work. It was impossible for trains to run through from St Sulpice to Salvagnac.

Although nothing ever escaped St Sulpice, work may have started to the north. No less an authority than Henri Domengie claimed that there were construction trains running somewhere. M. Germain Olivet, former engine driver, confirmed that work was done, though he could not remember where. It is unlikely that both were mistaken; official records note that some money was spent. This would have been an isolated stretch, but the practical difficulties are not as great as they would be for main line. The original selling point of 60 centimetre gauge track was that it was easy to lay and take up again and that portable rolling stock was available. Equipment could have been transported by road beyond the railway bridge so that a start could be made and backers up in Salvagnac encouraged. A fair proportion of the cost of the project was spent before the Salvagnac branch was put into official limbo.

The planned route was to have followed the east bank of the Tarn for 200 metres. It would then have described a wide bend to the left, to meet the intersection of the D28 with the road to La Pointe, crossed over the latter, and followed the D28 (GC 28) for 100 metres. It then turned off to the right in a bend of 100 metres radius. Over 300 metres of open country, it would have joined the N88 where a side road led off to La Pointe a couple of hundred metres to the south. The village halt was to have been at this crossroads. The railway was then to run along the right of the main road.

Today, this stretch of the N88 has been vastly upgraded. The Directors of the TVT agonised over the crossing of 10 metres of main line track. By the 1920s, with growing road traffic, following the roadbed of the N88 would have been impractical. Plans would surely have been further modified.

Within 100 metres of the halt, the N88 crossed the River Tarn and about 50 metres further on, turned to the right northward bound. The railway was to share the road bridge with this road. The plan even demanded that the railway weave its way from the right hand side to the left of the bridge. The D128 (GC28) turned off to the left on the far side of the bridge. The railway also turned on the north bank, and crossed the D128 about a hundred metres from the junction. Now began the climb out of the Tarn valley. The route to the village of Mézens then followed the road, but slightly to the north on an independent trackbed. The railway would probably have rejoined the road just before the bridge over the Passé river which flows south to join the Tarn.

At Mézens, with a population then of 300, and two kilometres from St Sulpice, the D28 turns north off the D128. A halt with shelter was planned for the village but no sidings as the planners did not understand the importance of freight. The halt would have been sited close to the road junction, if usual company policy was followed. There was potential for goods traffic.[66]

Old M. Bonnet and the founding fathers of the TVT had amply provided for freight on the first section of the railway. Each stop had its siding. Their successors had not pursued this side of operations with sufficient vigour. In 1902, there were 52,000 passenger trips, while just under 20,000 tonnes of goods were carried. In 1911, ticket sales were up 280 per cent, freight a mere 50. In the days of decline, freight fell away first. All too typically, at Mézens, and at the other halts along the way, the planned route to Salvagnac lacked facilities for this vital side of operations. Alternatively, the cynical might suggest that, as the railway was planned around subsidies, a commercial study of the rewards for investing in sidings and other provisions for freight was never attempted.

It would have been costly to take the railway out of the Tarn valley. A viaduct was needed to take the railway out of Mézens. The village lay snugly between the D28 and the little River Passé, bounded to the south by the D128 coming in from the west bank of the Tarn and to the north by the D35. We can assume that the station was intended to be near the D28. The gradient up to Grazac exceeded the maximium of 2.5 per cent and a route therefore would have required extensive engineering. The distance given between Condel and Grazac station in the plans deposited with County Administration in Albi is 2.52 kilometres. This is consistent with a route that, with modest deviations, kept to the D28. The D28 ascended and then descended a ridge (with a gradient of 20 per cent in places) on leaving the village, hence the necessity for a separate route. It is understood that the viaduct would have been of the order of 50 metres and a total of 135 metres permanent way would have to be created. It might have been built to a design similar to that of the Salles viaduct.

Road and rail were planned to run close together into the next village, Condel, 3½ kilometres further on. The western slopes are wooded and present a fairly uniform slope. The eastern side of the valley, though as a rule lower, is less uniform, with more gradients. The road and settlement are here to the west and that was the planned course of the railway. Consistent with normal policy, the planned halt and shelter would have been at the crossroads of the D28 and the D18 (the GC18) which connects with Rabastens to the east.

To the north of Condel the D28 tackled steep gradients, therefore road and railway were to part company for nearly 300 metres. Road and rail would reunite, crossing the next stream together and come to the crossroads with the D12 which leads to the village of Grazac up a gradients that exceeded 14 per cent in places. It was not intended to take the railway to the village, rather to site the station near the crossroads over a kilometre away.

This was a relatively important commune with over 800 inhabitants. A station was intended, though the Directors of the TVT never produced a final plan. A plan along the lines of St Lieux would probably have been envisaged, the buildings consisting of an enlarged version of the shelter conjoined to the goods shed, and a goods siding, passing place and water tower. We can assume that, as with St Lieux, local politics would have been an important influence on the final plan.

Two and a half kilometres further again, the railway would have reached the junction with the D2 (GC2) There was to be a halt without a shelter to be simply called Passé. We are in remote and rugged country, near the watershed between the Passé river and the Tescou to the north. Road and rail would have crossed a tributary of the Passé just beyond the halt, then the railway was to leave the road for 375 metres to avoid a gradient that exceeded 14 per cent. The hamlet of Raust was perched on a hill; the railway would have more or less followed the D2 to the crossroads about a kilometre to the east of the hamlet. The halt was to have a shelter, no doubt to the plan of shelters on the St Sulpice line.

From Raust to Salvagnac is three kilometres as the crow flies. By road it is twice as far. The proposed railway was to run through four kilometres of embankment and cutting before picking up the D2 once more a little to the east of Salvagnac, the whole journey from St Sulpice would have been a matter of 17½ kilometres.

A station was planned. There was, of course, no pre-existing station, and so the terminus would probably have followed the pattern of La Ramière with a turning triangle, station building, engine shed, water tower, sidings and perhaps a larger goods shed.[67]

A public service was never to be. The Government decision to postpone the project in favour of the line to St Sulpice, ratified on 15th October, 1921, was the official death sentence. Unofficial interest did not completely subside until 1932, when closure faced the whole Chemin de Fer à Voie Étroite et Tramways à Vapeur du Tarn.

This route would make an agreeable excursion for the modern visitor. The countryside is pleasant, away from the urbanising influence of the motorway, and on the edge of the celebrated Côtes de Gaillac. There are chateaux to admire at Mézens, Salvagnac and St Urcisse, and venerable churches such as the secluded Notre Dame de Grâce below Grazac.

Taken at Laboutarié. To the left is the *BV*, inside the station railings. To the other side, with the hurricane lamp, is the wooden shelter with waiting passengers. Just above the fore-shortened *fourgon* can be seen the roof of M. Bonnet's house. We apologise for the state of the photograph but the view is unique!   *J. Daffis/ACOVA*

A view in 1993, the trains have long gone, as has the wooden shelter. The small *BV* was demolished when the road was widened, but M. Bonnet's house still stands.   *M.D. Wright*

Chapter Six

Locomotives and Rolling Stock
of the Tramways à Vapeur du Tarn

Locomotives of the TVT

The character of the line was expressed in its locomotives and rolling stock. Acquisitions were heavily influenced by the personalities and motives of the Directors, by technical advance, and by local politics. Purchases coincided with planned extensions to the network, with some gestures towards modernisation and efficiency. A number of phases of acquisition can be recognised. Locomotives and rolling stock were bought for the opening of the line in 1885, and then to service the extension to Lavaur opened in 1903. Purchases were made when the line to St Sulpice and Salvagnac gained official recognition in 1913.[68] Lastly, there were deliveries when the line to St Sulpice opened in 1925. Outside these main purchases, War Surplus stock was acquired because it was cheap and the railway in great need. The lorry arrived as an attempt to compete on the roads with road transport and in the final years of decline some stock came from the defunct Tramway de Réalmont.

According to the *Statuts de la Société*, the company logo, that is, the initials STT (Société des Tramways du Tarn) on a shield, was to appear above the smokebox door of the locomotives.[69] The carriages and, later on, the railcar were, to have the complete company name, Compagnie des Chemins de Fer et Tramways à Vapeur de Tarn, painted on the side. Photographs[70] suggest that this intention was not carried out. Witnesses remember that the locomotives were mid olive green with borders in red. The company initials and the engine number followed the standard French practice and appeared on the buffer beam. Unusually, the early locomotives were named. These were engraved brass plates with inset lettering and were mounted on the water tanks.

The width of the bodywork of locomotives and rolling stock was to be 1.8 metres, but making allowances for projections, there was an absolute limit of 2.03 metres. Locomotives were limited to 2.6 metres in height, though cabs and chimneys were permitted to be slightly taller. No freight was to be piled above a height of 2.4 metres because a load of that height on gauge this narrow would be top-heavy.

From the start, the buffing arrangement was of the standard centre type. The buffing plate was cut away at the sides to avoid fouling the couplings on the very tight radii of the street tramway bends. Coupling was effected by a screw link coupling on either side of the centre buffing plate. The centre buffing plate additionally was spring loaded with a volute spring. This ensured a flexible but very secure coupling arrangement. All locomotives, carriages and brake vans were equipped with Soulerin vacuum brakes as did, in theory, one in every two of the freight wagons. The others were through-piped for vacuum, and all were equipped with manual shunting brakes. Only the railcar was to have brakes operated by compressed air.

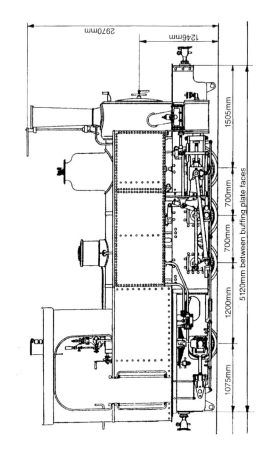

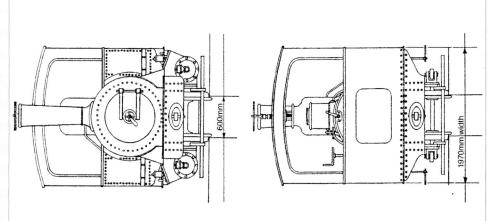

Drawing of *Decauville* 0-6-2T as supplied to the TVT in 1895. Though this was ordered from Decauville, there is reason to believe that it was in fact made by Weidknecht. It is not apparent on the drawing, but the frames splayed out at an angle underneath the cab. This can be seen on the photograph of the model of a Type 10 locomotive.

© *Malcolm Wright 1995*

The Decauville 0-6-2T

After M. Bonnet had visited the Paris Exhibition and talked to Paul Decauville, the Société des Établissements Decauville Aîné[71] became the official supplier to the TVT, providing three 0-6-2T engines known as Type No. 10. Each locomotive weighed 10 tonnes unloaded and 13 tonnes in working order. The tractive effort was 2.4 tonnes. The total wheelbase was 2.6 metres.

The locomotives had three driving axles but the pony truck was of an unusual radial design supported only from the rear and the outside. The frames were widened below the cab to accommodate the swing of the pony truck wheelset within the frames. Heavy springing from above, and a relatively long axle box served to prevent the wheels from unseating. The rear hinges and pivot points were of substantial, but simple, design. So good was this pony truck design in what must have been very rigorous operating conditions that the Decauville company used it unmodified for at least 30 years. An attractive feature of the engines was the steam dome housing. The Tarn engines differed from the catalogue illustration in that the domes were made of brass with a distinctive trumpet top. It is not known whether the domes were painted or polished. Coal, or more usually briquettes, was carried piled on the water tank tops and in the cab. As well as a warning whistle, the engines carried a bell mounted on the cab front. This was probably a more acceptable warning in towns when the locomotives would be passing within a metre or so of some bedroom windows!

The locomotives were modified during their lifetime by the provision of better weather protection for the crew. One engine may have had a cab front with large round spectacles. The other locomotives had the front cab cutout filled in and two rectangular openings formed for a lookout. It is possible that the rear cab opening was enclosed too. Certainly, the cab side doors and rear were equipped with tarpaulins which were rolled and taped at the top for storage.

A few locomotives of Type 10 ordered from Decauville in the period were in fact made by Établissements Weidknecht, notably the ones supplied to the Tramways de Royan.[72] Photographs of the locomotives supplied to Tarn show that they were all but identical to the ones made by Decauville except that the water tanks were rounded at the base and had a double slide bar. This suggests that they were also made by Weidknecht but were plated by the Decauville Company. This evidence appears to be countered by the fact that they appear in the Decauville works list. However, according to M. Duton, a Decauville should have single bars and a rounded top to the water tank.

The only surviving locomotive of this type which is on public view and in operation, is at the Musée des Transports de Pithiviers.[73] The preserved engine has been modified by the addition of a spark arresting chimney to be nearly identical to a Royan engine, probably done because the museum owns several of their coaches. This preserved engine was originally supplied to Aubineau and Company, Aisne, northern France and has the double slide bar characteristic of 'true' Decauvilles.

Extract from Decauville catalogue 1908. This illustration shows a typical 0-6-2T type '10' locomotive. However, the Tarn locomotives had a longer frame extension at the front than is suggested by this engraving. There was great variety in the steam dome covers also.

Raymond Duton

A mixed train headed by *Réalmontaise* No. 203 at Laboutarié station including a Carde carriage waiting to set off for Graulhet.

J. Daffis/ACOVA

Decauville 0-6-2T No. 203 in Graulhet station. This is an excellent view of details of the front of the locomotive. The cab front and rear differ from the drawing in that a spectacle plate has been fitted to weather proof the cab. At least one engine had round spectacles.   *J. Daffis/ACOVA*

Side view of Decauville 0-6-2T No. 203 on the turntable is being turned. A pile of coal can be seen in the left cab bunker. The tallow cups have been removed from the cylinders which suggests that some form of modern cylinder lubrication has been added to the engine.   *J. Daffis/ACOVA*

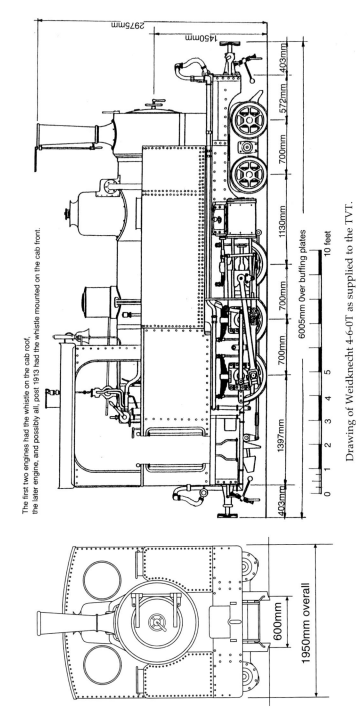

The first two engines had the whistle on the cab roof,
the later engine, and possibly all, post 1913 had the whistle mounted on the cab front.

2975mm

1450mm

403mm

572mm

700mm

1130mm

700mm

700mm

1397mm

403mm

6005mm 0ver buffing plates

10 feet

0 1 2 3 4 5

600mm

1950mm overall

Drawing of Weidknecht 4-6-0T as supplied to the TVT.

Locomotives Nos. 1-3 continued to sport their original maker's numbers, also used as a running number, on a plaque above the smoke box. They were also named, *Graulhétoise* (No. 205), *Réalmontoise* (No. 203), and *Montdragonne*, No. 204. One can understand why M. Bonnet wanted to name locomotives 'the Maid of Graulhet' and 'the Maid of Montdragon' because these were towns they served, but to name one after Réalmont was provocative because that town was served by a rival tramway.

From the start, the locomotives were slightly disappointing. They could in theory pull 40 tonnes up a gradient of 4 per cent at a speed of 6 kilometres per hour, but were unable to pull anything like this weight up the approach to Laboutarié station where the locomotive encountered first a 30 metre radius curve and then a rising gradient in excess of 4 per cent. The radius was later ameliorated to 50 metres, but nothing could be done about the gradient because of the route. In 300 metres, the Tramway had to drop from the level of the Midi main line station yard to one where it could pass below to make use of the bridge. This gave a practical weight limit to any train of 28 tonnes going up and 36 tonnes down towards Graulhet. Though the rolling stock was small-scale, this meant that only two carriages, one wagon and a brake van could come in to the station, and an extra wagon could leave.

The Weidknecht 4-6-0T

When the Lavaur extension was built, two new locomotives were ordered, this time from Weidknecht. They had three driving wheels and a front bogie. Overall dimensions were fairly similar, except for the longer wheelbase, and they were heavier. Although in theory both the 4-6-0T and the 0-6-2T delivered the same power, the Director was assured that the actual output of the Weidknecht locomotives was better. As we have seen, the gradient approaching Laboutarié station had imposed limits on train length. The only hope of tackling the 5 per cent gradients found in Graulhet near to the river crossing, had seemed to lie in using two locomotives. There was a plan to station a banker on a short spur on the main road opposite the Hôtel Clavel. Needless to say, the *maire* would not give his consent to this plan. The Weidknecht 4-6-0Ts were able to cope alone, unless the trains was exceptionally long.

Relatively few of the Weidknecht 4-6-0T locomotives were built, as they were really too heavy for industrial use; six served the summer traffic on the Chemins de Fer de Calvados,[74] where they proved very successful. The only problem with locomotives of this type is that they have to be turned because their track holding is usually better forwards than in reverse. Some locomotives of this type were supplied to the 60 centimetre gauge system in Morocco. It is possible that a Weidknecht from the TVT found its way abroad after the line was closed, but no surviving example is known for certain, within France at least.

The first two locomotives were delivered in February 1903. The works numbers were 698 and 699, TVT numbers 4 and 5. They were not given names; now that the line was coming under the influence of local politicians, it was likely that the old desire to give locomotives names was suppressed in favour of a less controversial but duller system.

LE TARN ILLUSTRÉ
446. GRAULHET — La Gare

View of Weidknecht 4-6-0T in Graulhet station. A train consisting of a box van and two Carde type carriages is waiting, at the station before setting off for Lavaur. The fuel is going to be briquettes. A bell has been added to the locomotive.
J. Daffis/ACOVA

Phototypie Tarnaise, Poux, Albi

The engines, empty, weighed 11 tonnes and in working order 14.25 tonnes. The tractive effort was 2.4 tonnes and the total wheelbase 3.23 metres. The better performance of the Weidknecht 4-6-0Ts will have been due to the greater weight available for adhesion. They were very attractive locomotives with generous and well weatherproofed cabs for the crew. Like the Decauville 0-6-2Ts, they sported an attractive steam dome casing in brass and likewise were provided with a warning bell.

In 1913, when the extension to St Sulpice and Salvagnac was planned, it was agreed that four more locomotives would be needed, and these were ordered from Weidknecht. Another 4-6-0T, identical to Nos. 4 and 5, was delivered on 6th August. The works number for this engine is not known. The outbreak of war in 1914 put further plans into abeyance. The post-war extension was to go no further than St Sulpice, and so it was decided that only one more locomotive would be required. Weidknecht was no longer able to supply them and so the Board of the TVT returned to Decauville who offered them a new model, the 2-6-0T based on the 0-6-0T model developed for the Army just before the war. The 0-6-0T was designed for poorly laid track under testing conditions; the Army must have been satisfied with it, because 350 were supplied, a comparatively large number.

The 2-6-0T (construction No. 3502) was a longer, heavier beast than its warrior brother. The tractive effort of this type was 2.5 tonnes, the total wheel base 2.8 metres and it weighed 14.5 tonnes in working order. The 2-6-0T was a much more modern looking locomotive than its predecessors and with its rounded cab it looked considerably more like the surviving Decauville engines that one sees today. Trials on 2nd April, 1925 were satisfactory; one assumes that in practice the tractive effort of the locomotive approximated at least to theory. It was able to use the newly installed turntable at St Sulpice. The locomotive was not, however, to see much service. Given the weight and the shorter wheelbase of this locomotive, it tended to spread the track which, given the low maintenance that the line was receiving at this period, doubtless caused operational problems.

As we have seen, the TVT, in common with other narrow gauge railways, was in economic difficulty by 1930. Perhaps this explains why only five locomotives of this model were supplied to operators in France, of which none survive. According to Decauville records, a similar model, weighing 17.5 tonnes empty, may have been supplied to the 60 cm gauge railway of Kotiéou at Pichétchai, China. Possibly it has survived.

No more steam locomotives were ever purchased. In the same month, however, as the 2-6-0T was delivered, so was a petrol powered railcar. M. Valièch had entered serious discussions with the agent for La Société des Automobiles Berliet[75] the previous March, and the Prefect had approved the purchase on 10th May. The design was derived from the type A 60 B developed in 1922 which Berliet had supplied to the suburban railways of Rabat in Morocco. The TVT was not alone in turning to railcars using the relatively new technology of the internal combustion engine. Most secondary systems were to acquire a few; the advances which had been made in such vehicles could not be ignored. The *Cahier des Charges*, laid down by Central Government in 1894,

Locomotive de 8 tonnes à vide

(10 t. 500 en marche)

Voie de 600 ᵐ/ₘ (et au-dessus)

POIDS ET DIMENSIONS PRINCIPALES		
Poids	à vide..................	8ᵗ 000
	en charge.............	10ᵗ 500
Gabarit sans tampon	Longueur..............	4ᵐ350
	Largeur...............	1ᵐ620
	Hauteur...............	2ᵐ600

MACHINE	
Distribution système Walschaert.	
Diamètre des cylindres...................	215 ᵐ/ₘ
Course des pistons.......................	280 »
Diamètre des roues au roulement........	600 »
Effort de traction $\dfrac{0,65\ p.\ d.^{\mathit{t}}.l}{D}$	1752 k.

CHAUDIÈRE	
Surface de grille...........................	0ᵐ²36
Surface de chauffe	du foyer..............	2ᵐ²30
	des tubes.............	15ᵐ²05
	totale	17ᵐ²35
Tubes à fumée	Nombre..............	74
	Diamètre.............	36/40
	Longueur entre plaques tubulaires.............	1ᵐ800
Volume d'eau dans la chaudière.........	625 litres
Volume de vapeur dans la chaudière.....	245 litres
Diamètre moyen du corps cylindrique......	0ᵐ736
Timbre de la chaudière..................	12 k. 500
2 soupapes de sûreté de 44 ᵐ/ₘ de diamètre.	

CHASSIS, ROULEMENT, FREIN	
Longueur du châssis sans tampon........	4ᵐ212
Ecartement intérieur des longerons.......	0ᵐ488
Nombre d'essieux couplés.................	3
Empattement entre essieux...............	0ᵐ700
Empattement total des essieux..........	1ᵐ400
Ecartement des bandages.................	0ᵐ550
Largeur des bandages...................	0ᵐ092
Frein à vis à 4 sabots.	

APPROVISIONNEMENTS	
Volume d'eau dans les soutes.............	1150 litres
Charbon dans les soutes..................	600 kilos

Vitesses en kilomètres à l'heure	Admission	Effort de traction	Charges nettes en tonnes remorquées sur rampes de :									
			0	5	10	15	20	25	30	35	40	50
8	0.61	1979	169	108	79	62	49	41	35	30	26	19
12	0.40	1618	135	87	63	48	38	32	27	22	19	14
17	0.28	1326	109	69	50	38	30	24	20	17	14	10

Le rayon minimum des courbes à employer est de 20 mètres.

Decauville 0-6-0T, 8 tonnes weight. This design was produced pre-1913 for the military campaigns in Morocco, and had an important effect on post-war design. The distinctive shape of the water tank gave it a low centre of gravity, and the tyres of the centre wheels are without flanges, in order to give extra flexibility on tight bends.   *ACOVA*

Locomotive de 12 tonnes env. à vide

à 3 essieux couplés et bissel à l'avant

Voie de 0 m. 60

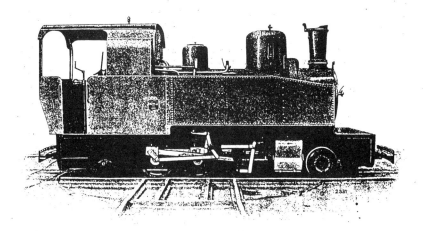

Cette locomotive peut être employée dans les grandes Entreprises de travaux publics, dans l'industrie et en particulier dans les sucreries, utilisant de la voie en rails de 12 k⁰ˢ et même, en cas de nécessité, de la voie en rails de 9 k. 500 p. m.

La chaudière, en tôle d'acier, est du modèle avec boîte à feu à berceau cylindrique armaturée au moyen de tirants verticaux ; la grille est droite et disposée pour brûler du charbon, le foyer est en cuivre rouge avec ciel incliné légèrement vers l'arrière ; la boîte à fumée est munie d'une grille pour arrêter les flammèches. Le foyer allongé donne une très grande surface de chauffe permettant de brûler du bois.

L'alimentation de la chaudière se fait au moyen de deux injecteurs Ré Starting N° 5 du type aspirant.

L'approvisionnement en eau est assuré par deux caisses à eau placées sur le tablier à droite et à gauche de la chaudière.

L'approvisionnement en combustible est assuré par deux caisses à combustible placées sur le tablier dans le prolongement des deux caisses à eau.

N° 74   **DECAUVILLE**   Réf. 1181

Extract from the Decauville catalogue showing the 2-6-0T design based on the 0-6-0T seen opposite.   *ACOVA*

Decauville 2-6-0T. This was a publicity photograph arranged by the Decauville works. In the view of Roger Bailly, this is almost certainly the locomotive supplied to the TVT. In the catalogue of 1905 Decauville recommended it for industrial use, such as in the sugar industry, running on rails weight 12 kilogrammes per metre or even of 9.5 kilogrammes (it is hard to take this claim seriously!). The boiler, in steel plate, has a firebox on a cylindrical spring mounting with vertical stays. It burns coal and the firebox is fitted with a spark arrester. The boiler is fed by injectors. Water is carried in tanks on either side of the boiler. The rear extensions of the tanks carry the fuel.   *Roger Bailly*

Specifications of the Locomotives of the TVT

Builder	Decauville*	Weidnecht†#	Decauville§	Berliet¶
Type	0-6-2T	4-6-0T	2-6-0T	Bogie Railcar
Length of passenger compartment (railcar only)				8.84m
Overall width	1.97m	1.95m	1.97m	2.03m
Area of grate	0.56m²	0.565m²	0.6m²	
Heating surface of tubes	24.59m²	24.92m²	21.25m²	
Cylinder diameter	0.25m	0.25m	0.25m	
Stroke of pistons	0.32m	0.32m	0.32m	
Diameter of driving and coupled wheels	0.65m	0.65m	0.65m	0.6m
Diameter of pony truck/ uncoupled wheels	0.5m	0.45m	0.5m	0.45m
Rigid wheelbase	1.4m	1.4m	1.4m	
Bogie wheelbase		0.7m		1.2m
Total wheelbase	2.6m	3.23m	2.8m	
Distance between bogies				5.1m
Unladen weight in tonnes	10	11	11	9 approx.
Working/fully laden weight in tonnes	13	14.25	14.5	12 approx.
Capacity of water tanks in litres	1,400	1,450	1,450	
Fuel capacity	0.7 cu.m.	0.75 cu.m.	800 kg	
Tractive effort in tonnes	2.4	2.4	2.5	
Tractive effort in horsepower				30/40

Notes

*   Three Decauville 0-6-0T models, maker's Nos. 203-205 delivered 1st May, 1895.
†   Two Weidnecht 4-6-0T models, maker's Nos. 698 and 699, delivered 28th February, 1903. STT Nos. 4, 5.
#   One Weidnecht 4-6-0T model, maker's number unknown, delivered 6th August, 1913. STT No. 6.
§   One Decauville 2-6-0T model, maker's No. 3502, delivered 2nd January, 1925. STT No. 7.
¶   One Berliet railcar, type A60C, petrol motor, delivered January 1925.

still strangled steam railways. The speed limit, for instance, was 15 kilometres per hour. The Berliet railcar was capable of 30 kilometres per hour, a theoretical doubling of output and a boon to impatient passengers.

It was not, however, speed or convenience which appealed to the Board. It was to save money. With 30 passengers' capacity, a relatively good petrol consumption and power to cope with gradients of 5.5 per cent, the railcar was bought for economy. It cost 106,000 francs. Simply paying off the capital cost of the railcar would have required about 50,000 fare paying passengers[76] or the entire profits for all traffic in a reasonable year. In a word, the railcar should have been seen as an investment rather than an economy and the TVT should have made every effort to attract passengers. There is no evidence that this was so, rather to the contrary. The railcar was specified for little-used services. La Ramière and Lavaur were the only stations where it could conveniently be turned since it was too long for the turntable at St Sulpice and they could not bring themselves to invest in a larger one.

The railcar was put fairly speedily into use, after trials early in February 1925. It appears to have been satisfactory. It climbed and descended the Col d'Ambres, towing a trailer (a superannuated brakevan). It could accommodate a maximum of 30 passengers. On 7th October, the transmission shaft broke and the railcar was out of action for a fortnight, but this was put down to careless driving rather than a mechanical fault.

The design of the railcar showed both its rail and road origins. The underframe, mounted on two bogie trucks rolling on diminutive wheels, was like a conventional narrow gauge wagon. The couplings were standard. The engine, a water cooled Berliet Z 30/40 hp four-cylinder petrol motor, was at the front, beside the driver's cab. It was electrically started. Joined to the engine was a bronze multi-plate clutch. The output was by a Cardan shaft (universal joint) to a transmission box at the centre of the car. From this box, Cardan shafts were taken to the power bogies. Power transmission to the axles was mechanical, by bevel gears running in oil baths. Power take-offs from the engine powered a generator for lighting and ignition. They also powered a compressor to provide air for braking using the Westinghouse system, and for an air-operated whistle. In the driver's cab, pedals controlled clutch and acceleration. Gear selection was by hand, there being four ratios plus reverse. There was a driver's brake valve and also a screwdown parking brake.

Although we can admire the comfort and convenience of the railcar compared with the antiquated TVT rolling stock, it was itself already dated. The design was safe rather than innovative, the engine a trifle underpowered. While precious momentum was being lost, motor vehicle technology continued to progress. Bureaucracy also weighed more heavily on the railways; a bus driver could collect fares, doing away with the need for a conductor as well, but the railcar was obliged at all times to have a two-man crew. By 1931, the railcar cost 5.25 francs per kilometre to run compared to 2.61 francs for a bus. Railcar services disappeared on 1st August that year. So much for economy.

Above: Berliet railcar. This was the manufacturer's photograph of the railcar supplied to the TVT in 1925. A number of models based on this design were built but most of them had a driver's cab at each end.

Fondation Berliet

Left: Cab interior of Berliet railcar.

ACOVA

Carriages and Wagons

When the tramway opened in 1895, it had the four coaches and 20 wagons, as stipulated by the *Cahier des Charges*, for a railway of this nature. The provision of continuous braking through the train was required. To this effect, the locomotives were fitted with a vacuum ejector and all the stock was either through-piped or braked. All passenger stock and *fourgons*[78] were fitted with brake actuators and the make-up of trains ensured that at least 50 per cent of the goods stock had them. Provision had to be made for night running. The locomotives, vans and *fourgons* were provided with lamp irons, essential as much freight was transported at night to avoid scheduling problems.

The first two coaches supplied by Decauville, Nos. 1 and 2, had a capacity of 40 combined first and second class, eight seats in first, 20 in second and standing room for six on the open platform at each end. The coaches were 9.7 metres long over the buffing plates. They had steel girder frames with rod truss bars. Attached to the underframe was the Soulerin vacuum brake system. The bogies had a wheelbase of 0.85 metres and were set at 6 metre centres. The bogies were interesting, of a plate frame variety. The axle boxes were sprung with leaf springs and the bolster was carried either by a rubber shock absorber or a cased volute spring. Unfortunately, no drawing survives of the bogie.

Generally the coaches show a very American influence. Entry is from end balconies with drop down plates over the couplings. The roof was of a complex shape. Construction of the body was of tongued and grooved boarding with a tumble home. Detailing was with raised mouldings. Lettering on the coaches to denote class and ownership was in raised applied characters, gilded. The early coaches were finished in varnished wood with painted roofs.

Coaches Nos. 3 and 4 were of identical construction except that they had a capacity of 42 passengers, all second class, consisting of 30 seats and space for 12 more on the open platforms. There is evidence of tongue and groove construction of carriage bodies but some certainly were finished with a smooth outer skin. There were 12 windows on each side. There is no evidence that these windows could be opened, but there were ventilators on the windows opening on to the platforms at front and rear. Seating was provided on two benches with their backs to the windows which ran the length of each carriage. First class seats offered sprung upholstery, but second class passengers had to make do with wooden slats. Lighting of all four coaches was by Schallis & Thomas petroleum lamps. These standards were probably acceptable in the late 19th century. Rail travel was a novelty, and so perhaps people did not mind being deprived of a view. The marvel of artificial lighting, however smelly, was probably accepted in the same way. To be able to sit down at all was probably a relief to agricultural and industrial labourers but perhaps they were not so comfortable with having to stare at each other for the duration of a trip. A photograph of a crowded carriage shows men and women sitting in stiff opposing rows. The eyes of many passengers are modestly downcast to the floor, which did not add to the amentity of the journey.

The rest of the rolling stock can be broken into two classes, goods stock and *fourgons*. From photographs of the trains, it would seem that the *fourgon* was the

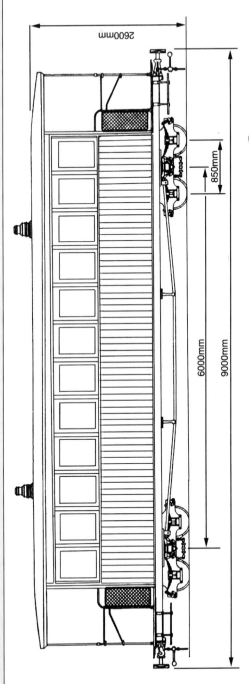

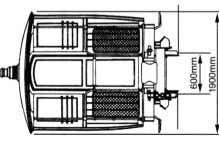

2600mm

850mm

6000mm

9000mm

600mm

1900mm

Decauville carriage 1895. These carriages were supplied to the TPT in Loiret, the CFC in Calvados and the TVT. They followed the same *Cahier* rules as the Carde coaches but they have 12 windows per side and two ventilators. The number of places given, 40, is that of a mixed first/second class carriage.

Second class Decauville coach. Although the quality of the photograph is not as good as we should like, it is included for its historical interest. The legend on the side refers to the Lavaur line which was not open in 1895. This means that the carriage may be one of the last to be supplied. Alternatively, it has been renamed; we know that all the rolling stock was in due course re-numbered.

J. Daffis/ACOVA

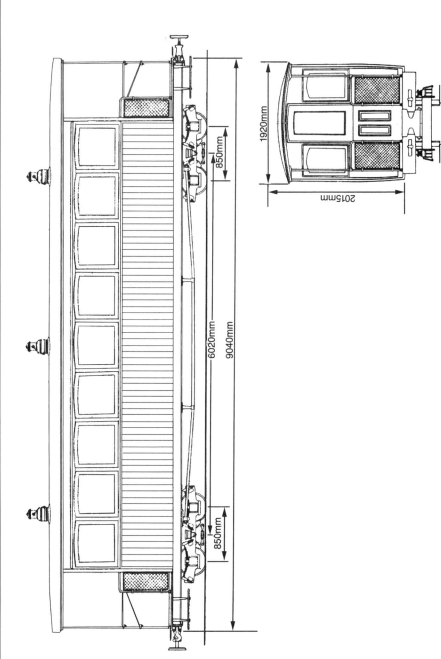

Carde carriage 1903.

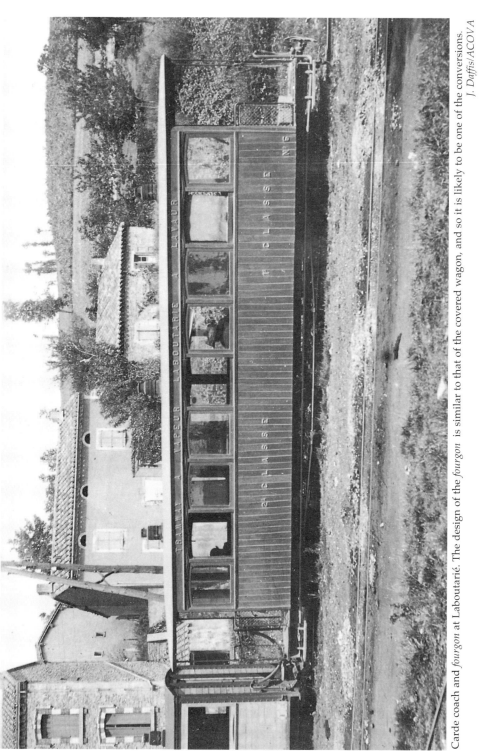

Carde coach and *fourgon* at Laboutarié. The design of the *fourgon* is similar to that of the covered wagon, and so it is likely to be one of the conversions.
J. Daffis/ACOVA

Carde coach mounted on a wagon, photographed in Bordeaux on its way to the TVT.

J. Daffis/ACOVA

Carde coaches on a mixed train headed by a Decauville.   *J. Daffis/ACOVA*

last vehicle in a passenger-only train but ran next to the locomotive in a mixed train, the goods stock being carried last, behind the carriages.

The first two *fourgons*, system Nos. 1 and 2, Decauville type G, were 4 metres long. They ran on a four wheel underframe made of wood. The wheel base was 1.8 metres long. The wheel-sets were plain spoked. The body was built of wood with external wood framing. One central sliding door was fitted.The roof was broken with a birdcage lookout and this end of the wagon had a dog-box. As before mentioned, one of the four-wheel *fourgons*, it is not known whether it was 1 or 2, was used as a trailer by the railcar on the Lavaur route. There are no surviving illustrations of this van in use on the line.

The later two *fourgons* Nos. 3 and 4, supplied by Carde of Bordeaux[79] on running gear almost certainly supplied by Decauville, ran on shorter underframes of identical construction to the coaches. They were 8.32 metres over the buffing plates. The distance between the bogie centres was 4.98 metres and the bogies were of the same wheel base as the coaches, but the axle boxes were sprung with volute springs not leaf springs. The construction of the body was of an external angle iron frame inset with tongued and grooved boards. There was an end balcony at one end, and a sliding door. The guard's lookout was a drop light at the open end. At the other end of the van was a dog box. They were vacuum-braked. Another version of *fourgon* was later introduced.

Six 10 tonne open wagons (Class A) were supplied by Decauville in 1895. They had steel underframes, and bodies of wood braced externally with riveted steel angle frame. The top plank of the wagon was protected with a steel angle rubbing strip. They were 7.82 metres long over the buffing plates. The bogies were identical to the ones on *fourgons* 3 and 4. Their centres were 4.5 metres apart. They were designed to carry freight of relatively high density such as coal.

Ten 6 tonne open wagons (Class B) and two covered wagons (Class C) were supplied by Decauville. They were of identical construction to the Class A open wagons but were 9.82 metres over the buffing plates. Every second wagon was fitted with Soulerin brakes, like the Decauville carriages, and all were equipped with a hand operated brakewheel.

For the opening of the Lavaur section, initially it was agreed to increase passenger capacity to 350 and freight to 350 tonnes. But this clause was modified on 6th May, 1902, to 452 places for passengers and 280 tonnes of freight. To bring the existing stock up to strength, three new combined first and second class carriages were ordered, taking 40 passengers each, and four second class carriages, capacity 42. The new order went to Carde who supplied them in 1903. The mixed carriages were numbered 5 to 7 and the second class 8 to 11. The specifications for the carriages remained the same as Nos. 1 and 2 for the first/second class and 3 and 4 for the second class, but a number of small changes can be noted. The new chassis were slightly longer, and the unladen weight of the carriages was slightly increased. Nine slightly larger windows per side replaced the 12 on the Decauville carriages, and droplights replaced the ventilators at each end of the original coaches. Lighting was provided by three petrol lamps rather than two as formerly. The coaches added 188 places to existing capacity.

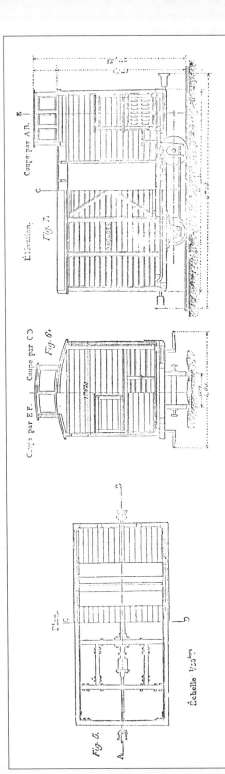

Coupe par AB.

Élévation.

Fig. 7.

Coupe par CD

Fig. 6.

Coupe par EF.

BAGAGES

Fig. 5.

Plan.

Échelle 1/25.

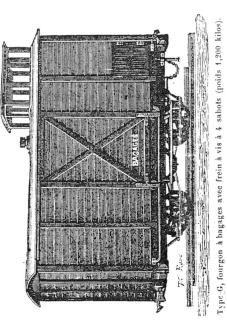

BAGAGES

T. Kirs.

Type G, fourgon à bagages avec frein à vis à 4 sabots (poids 4,200 kilos).

Brake van 1895. This was the standard Decauville design of the period and fits the description given by TVT records.

Jim Hawkesworth

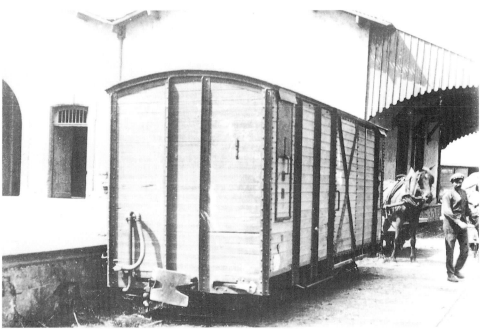

Box van at Laboutarié. As well as a good view of the coupling and brake pipe detail in the foreground, the photograph shows a horse from the Réalmont tramway. *J. Daffis/ACOVA*

Open box van. *J. Daffis/ACOVA*

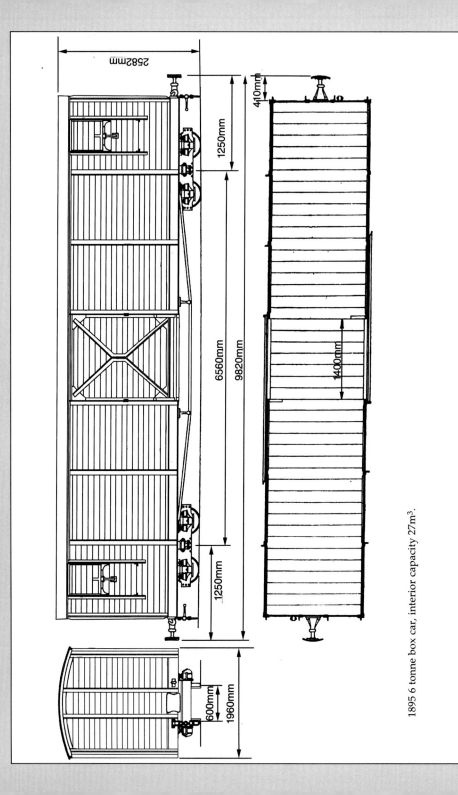

1895 6 tonne box car, interior capacity 27m³.

6 tonne box car, probably at Graulhet, with the open platform of a carriage visible to the left. A wagon number has been crudely stencilled onto the side.

J. Daffis/ACOVA

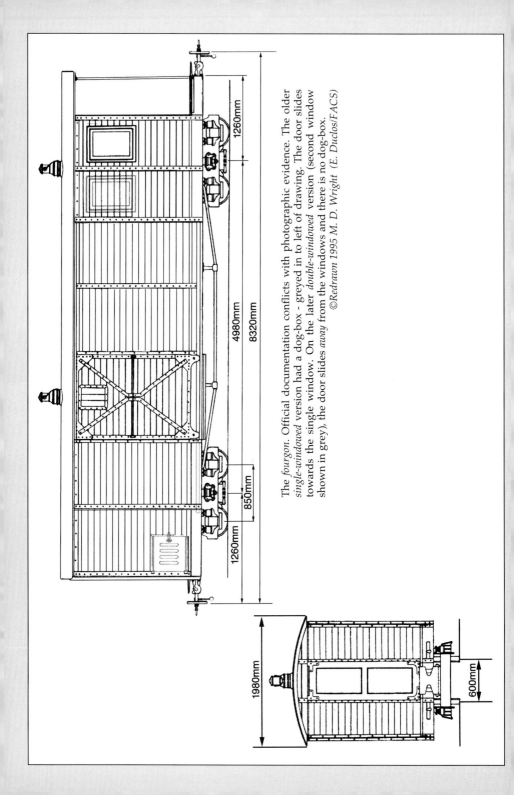

The *fourgon*. Official documentation conflicts with photographic evidence. The older *single-windowed* version had a dog-box - greyed in to left of drawing. The door slides towards the single window. On the later *double-windowed* version (second window shown in grey), the door slides *away* from the windows and there is no dog-box.

©*Redrawn 1995 M. D. Wright (E. Duclos/FACS)*

Box car at Laboutarié, with Carde coach visible to the right. For some reason the window covers have been removed from both sides of the wagon.

J. Daffis/ACOVA

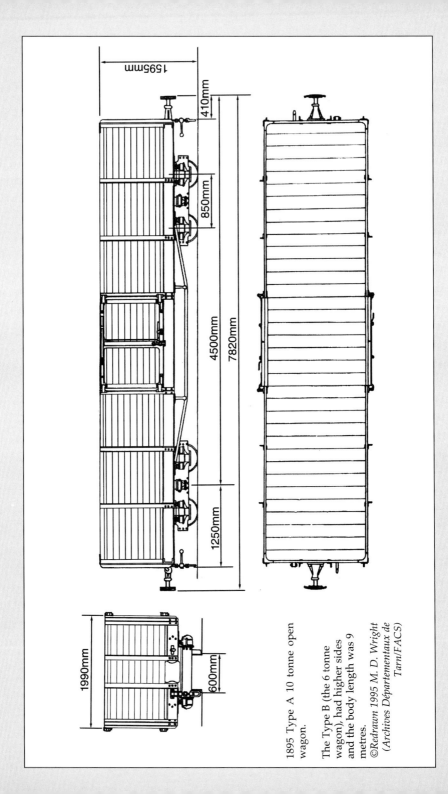

1595mm

410mm

850mm

4500mm

7820mm

1250mm

1990mm

600mm

1895 Type A 10 tonne open wagon.

The Type B (the 6 tonne wagon), had higher sides and the body length was 9 metres.

©Redrawn 1995 M. D. Wright (Archives Départementaux de Tarn/FACS)

With the supply of new rolling stock, an opportunity to increase passenger comfort was lost. Over the years since the opening of the railway, upholstery and a bit of decoration were coming into every French home. Bare wooden slatted seats would be less and less acceptable as the 20th century advanced. Another persisting source of discomfort was the arrangement of the benches. Perfect strangers were pressed up against each other on the tortuous journey, and there was no way to avoid eye contact with the row opposite. More modern transport, with benches arranged in rows, gives more support to passengers and provides them with a window rather than looking at each other, one extra comfort supplied by the arrival of the motor bus.

Six new covered wagons were ordered, Nos. 3 to 8. In addition, five open wagons, Nos. 7 to 11 with sides 0.99 metres high, were supplied, and four platform wagons, Nos. 1 to 4, with sides of 0.33 metres. All were of the standard length, 7.8 metres and were designed for a standard load of 10 tonnes. The bogies were identical to the rest of the goods stock. The bodies were also constructed by Carde.

Days before the new line was due to open, the *Ingénieur du Contrôle*[80] wrote to request a change to the system of naming. The *fourgons* were to be FF 1 to 4, numbered according to the time of acquisition. Covered wagons were to be C, or Cfm if they only had handbrakes. A handbrake is known in French as *frein à main*, whereas a vacuum brake is *frein à vide*. The other wagons were to be known as T (*tombereau*) for high sided wagons or P (*plat*) for flatcars, with the letters fm added as before where applicable. All wagons with vacuum brakes were to be suffixed with the letters fv to avoid confusion ('f' could be confused for *frein*, brake, or *fourgon*)

It is not clear if the request was rigorously enforced. This was days before the grand party with the Government Minister, Camille Pelletan, and the trainloads of celebrants. The original stock probably continued to be called A, B etc. To the best of our knowledge, the new stock had probably already been numbered with the flat wagons known as 'D' and the new *fourgon* as 'F'. If the wagon in question was one of the newer delivery, in most cases, the appropriate letters were added to the existing number to indicate whether it was fitted with vacuum brakes or not.

In 1910, stock was again renumbered and reclassified. We can assume that the *Ingénieur du Contrôle* at the time had belatedly insisted on compliance with his original request. 'C' for covered, 'P' for flat wagons, and 'T' for wagons with high sides was the accepted code for all stock, original or not. The wagons fitted with a vacuum brake were known as 'CF', 'PF' and 'TF'. All four *fourgons* were 'FF'. Numbering was according to the date of acquisition, so for example the first box wagon fitted with air brakes was CF2, and ones acquired in 1903 were CF3 to CF5. This system of numbering survived to the closure of the line.

Although there is no official record, it was probably during this period that a flat wagon converted into a tanker was purchased. At Graulhet the river was becoming unacceptably polluted and a municipal water supply was not installed until 1929. Water in quantity was needed to supply steam engines at Graulhet station.

In 1913, M. de Valièch of the TVT concluded negotiations between the PO and the Departmental authorities over the rail link with St Sulpice. New orders were placed in anticipation of the growth in traffic. Requirements for the enlarged line were originally set at three new locomotives, passenger places for 694, and

The station yard at Laboutarié. There is a good view of a *wagon tombereau* and a platform wagon with low sides.
J. Daffis/ACOVA

At least some of the open wagons had 'gable' ends so that they could be covered with tarpaulins during bad weather.
J. Daffis/ACOVA

freight capacity of 460 tonnes, that is five new first and second class coaches, a second-only coach and 18 ten tonne freight wagons. What was actually delivered consisted of one locomotive, four box wagons Nos. 9 to 12, 10 open wagons, numbered 22 to 31, and four flat wagons Nos. 5 to 8. All the wagons of this delivery were vacuum-braked and their overall length was 7.8 metres.

The new rolling stock delivered was all for freight which should have helped redress the balance in favour of goods traffic. War came soon after delivery and there was general disruption, thus it is hard to assess results; no attempt was made to modernise the design, and so the new wagons did not make the impact they should. The new wagons were no safer or more labour-saving for the operators. They were built to exactly the same specifications as before, except that the bogie wheelbase was increased by half a centimetre.

During the Great War, much civil rolling stock was requisitioned for military purposes; even though our railway was more successful than most in having its property returned, this must have shortened its working life. The TVT complained that the leather industry in Graulhet was pivotal to the war effort and it appears that wagons were soon returned to the network. In 1916, carriages 1 to 4, that is the two first/second class carriages and two second class built by Decauville in 1895, were sent to a munitions factory in Bergerac.[81]

In 1922, as we have seen, the long delayed extension was finally put into effect, at the expense of the Salvagnac line. The official rolling stock requirements were reduced to two extra carriages which were duly supplied by Decauville in early 1925. They were similar to the earlier Decauville carriages.[82] They were numbered 12, which was a combined first and second class carriage, and 13, second only. According to the rules of the *Cahier*, 90 tonnes' capacity of freight wagons were required. One hundred and sixty tonnes' worth had been supplied before the war. It was hard to argue for more.

The *Cahier des Charges*, however, demanded that there should be two new *fourgons*. In 1922 two box wagons which had been supplied in 1903 were sent back to Carde to be converted. They retained their numbering in spite of their new rôle although it is not now certain exactly which (they were in the series CF3 to CF5).

In 1926, the TVT showed another flicker of initiative. It purchased six ex-US Army open wagons of the Pershing type from the dealers Maison Parel. Although used by the Allied armies during the Great War, they were constructed in the USA.[83] In 1932, observing the success of road transport, the railway purchased a delivery lorry, a Ford BBF, and built it a garage in Graulhet station.

In January 1938, M. Cazals executed the melancholy task of selling all the rolling stock to pay the company's debts. In theory, the company retained a part interest in them but the *Département* had underwritten construction and operations to such an extent, that it took all the scant proceeds of the sale. The sale records also provide evidence of a number of service vehicles acquired at varying times. There were four trucks probably used for carrying rail with some form of lifting gear on at least one of them. There was a tanker for carrying water, as previously mentioned. There were two side-dump trucks, two skips and a set of bolster wagons. No further details have survived.[84]

Some of the stock as well as the locomotives were sold for use on forestry lines in the then French colonies of Congo and Gabon.

Coaches and Wagons on the TVT

	Brake	Original No.	Final No.	Length m.	Total length m.	Bogie *	Weight unladen t.	Payload
Decauville 1895								
1st/2nd class coach	y	1 and 2	1 and 2	8.88	9.7	6.00	4.1	40 pass.
2nd class coach	y	3 and 4	3 and 4	8.88	9.7	6.00	4.1	42 pass.
Guard's van	y	D1 and D2	FF1 and FF2	4.15	4.82		1.65	3t.
Box wagon	n	C1	C1	9.15	9.82	6.5	4.2	6t.
Box wagon	y	C2	CF2	9.15	9.82	6.5	4.2	6t.
10 tonne wagon	y	A1 to A3	TF1 to TF3	7.00	7.82	4.5	3.4	10t.
10 tonne wagon	n	A4 to A6	T4 to T6	7.00	7.82	4.5	3.4	10t.
6 tonne wagon	y	B4 to B8	TF9 to TF11, TF7, TF16	9.06	9.82	6.5	3.7	6t.
6 tonne wagon	n	B7 to B11	T8, T12 to T16	9.06	9.82	6.5	3.7	6t.
Carde 1903								
1st/2nd class coach	y	5 to 7	5to 7	9.04	9.74	6.02	5	40 pass.
2nd class coach	y	8 to 11	8 to 11	9.04	9.74	6.02	5	42 pass.
Guard's van	y	FFV3 and FFV4	FFV3 and FFV4	6.88	7.68	4.98	5.02	10t.
Box wagon	y	AFV3 to AFV5	CF3 to CFV5	7.00	7.80	4.48	4.64	10t.
Box wagon	n	AFM6 to AFM8	C6 to C8	7.00	7.80	4.48	4.64	10t.
Open wagon†	y	BFV7 to BFV9	TF17 to TF19	7.00	7.80	4.48	3.7	10t.
Open wagon†	n	BFM10 and BFM 11	T20 and T21	7.00	7.80	4.48	3.7	10t.
Platform#	y	DF1 and DF2	PF1 and PF2	7.00	7.80	4.48	3.37	10t.
Platform#	n	DF3 and DF4	P3, P4	7.00	7.80	4.48	3.37	10t.
Belgium 1913								
Box wagon	y		CF9 to CF12	7.00	7.80	4.48	4.64	10t.
Open wagon	y		TF22 to TF31	7.00	7.80	4.48	4.64	10t.
Platform	y		PF5 to PF8	7.00	7.80	4.48	3.37	10t.
Supplied 1926								
Decauville coach	y		12	8.88	9.7	6.00	4.1	40 pass.
Decauville coach	y		13	8.88	9.7	6.00	4.1	42 pass.
Guard's van	y		CF3 and CF4 rebuilt	7.00	7.80	4.48	4.64	10t.
Supplied 1926								
Pershing§			T32 to T37	5.8	7.15	4.58	4.25	10t.

Also supplied
1 tanker, 2 tipper wagons, 2 small skips, 4 breakdown trains, 2 small platforms.

Notes
*   The distance between bogies, as measured from back axle of front bogie to front axle of rear one, is given for each class of wagon. Measurements within the bogie tended to be consistent. Nearly all axles were 0.85m apart (except the Belgian wagons supplied in 1913 - 0.855m apart, and the Pershings, supplied 1926 - axles 0.92m apart).
†   Sides of the open wagons, both with and without vacuum brakes were 0.99 metres high.
\#   Sides of the platform wagons, both with and without vacuum brakes were 0.33 metres high.
§   Sides of the Pershing ex-military second-hand wagons were 1.1 metres high.

Chapter Seven

Return of the Rails

The steam tramways of Tarn were closed in 1937. Few were surprised or upset by the closure; the little railway seemed to have lost the affection as well as the custom of the local people. Perhaps this was the saddest aspect of its demise. The story of its successor, the Tarn Tourist Railway, Chemin de Fer Touristique du Tarn (CFTT), that is the tourist railway of Tarn, is therefore a heartening one.

Origin of *Points Kilométriques* is the western end of St Lieux station. St Lieux *BV pk* 0.013. Railway joins public road (D38) *pk* 0.068, crosses D48 Dépot-Musée *pk* 0.143. *Arrêt facultatif* Le Port *pk* 0.712. *Arrêt facultatif* Salles *pk* 0.924. *Halte-Évitement* Giroussens *pk* 1.483. *Halte* Lascazes *pk* 2.152. *Dépot de rails pk* 2.273. *Halte Évitement* Les Martels *pk* 2.721 and provisional terminus. The planned terminus is La Masquière *pk* 3.566. On the days of service, trains are considerably more frequent than in the days of the TVT, hence a number of *haltes évitements*, i.e. passing places. Running is controlled by radio. The driver of each locomotive is in constant contact with St Lieux station headquarters.

A few comments are needed about the relationship of the original Tramway with its successor. When the lines were closed, the TVT was in debt to the *Département*,[85] for the majority of the cost of construction of the St Sulpice line. The value of rolling stock, buildings and so on was estimated at just over a million francs. The company in turn demanded compensation of 3.15 million francs for being obliged to close the line before the termination of the concession.[86] As mentioned in the previous chapter, locomotives and rolling stock were sold in January 1939. An agreement was reached in May 1939 whereby the TVT kept what remained of portable stock and buildings. The *Département*[87] took the trackbed which they had provided, while the bridge at Briatexte and the St Lieux viaduct came into the possession of the *Département*. The TVT continued to hold on to the concession and a substantial proportion of debt.

At the end of World War II, nothing remained really but the name though this did not cease to exist until 1949. What little that there was of value was ceded to the local authority in consideration of outstanding debts. In this case, the local authority was Graulhet, which is a canton. The assets were the station yard and buildings. As France rebuilt herself after the war, the roadside sections of the railway were absorbed by engineering improvements or by housing. The trestle bridge over the Dadou at Briatexte was dismantled; as before mentioned, a workman was killed. The Agout viaduct continued in use as a road while the trackbed between La Ramière and St Lieux remained intact because there was no reason to disturb it.

For 30 years, the right of way slumbered, unremarked. By the 1960s, in France as a whole, a move to conserve what remained of the once vast network of secondary railways was begun. Small, therefore relatively easily handled by amateurs, and often situated in remote therefore charming countryside, they had

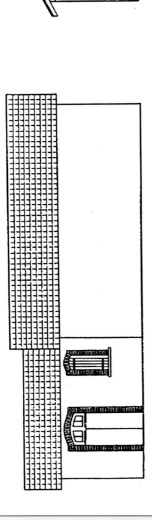

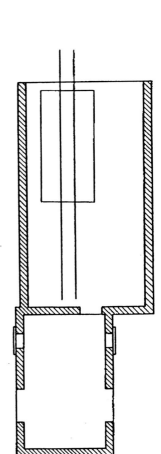

SAINT-LIEUX-LES-LAVAUR

Batiment-Voyageurs
Ateliers avec voie sur fosse

The sales and ticket office is to the left. The building to the right is the workshop with line running over the inspection pit.

GARE DE SAINT-LIEUX-LES-LAVAUR

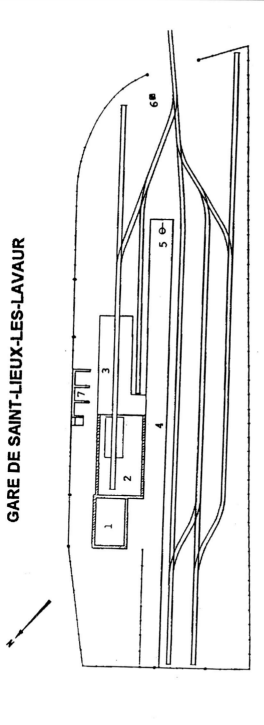

St Lieux, the modern station 1993. The external dimensions of the *BV* (1) have not been changed, but the old *halle* has been extended. Double doors have been inserted on the eastern side to admit locomotives. A track runs into the building as it is now used as a workshop (2) Cleaning takes place outside (3) in an area served by parallel sidings, the northern one ending in a headshunt - modern additions. Coal bunkers (7) have been built against the northern fence. The platform (4) has been extended, with a water pump (5) at the eastern end. The main line comes in at the eastern end, past an old-fashioned semaphore signal (6). This is a *carré d'arrêt* and when the red and white chequer board faces the oncoming train, it means STOP. This is prevent a train entering the section of single line between the station and the first passing loop. A turnout to the right serves the workshop and maintenance facilities. Turnouts serve parallel loops, linked at the far end by crossovers to allow locomotives to be released from their trains.   The original station plan was far simpler, consisting merely of a through line, passing loop and siding.

J. Daffis/CFTT

a natural appeal. The first lines to attract the interest of enthusiasts were the ones which had struggled into the 1960s. W.J.K. Davies, writing then, claimed that there were over 1,200 kilometres of surviving secondary railways. In the Preview to *French Minor Railways* the author claims that there were still 800 miles of secondary railway in France. The network would have been diminishing rapidly even as the book was being written. FACS (Federation des Amis des Chemins de fer Secondaires) was an early expression of the new interest and confidence stirring in France. The Society Journal has been in official existence since 1957 and there was plenty of activity before. Preservation groups in alliance with FACS, Réseaux Touristiques Fédérés, run a number of preserved railways. The Musée des Transports de Pithiviers has already been mentioned. The Chemin de Fer de la Baie de Somme, 30 kilometres from Boulogne, is the nearest to Britain, and is the subject of another Oakwood Press book, *Railways of the Baie de Somme.*

Among the regional branches of FACS was the group at Toulouse. This was formed when the last surviving local *petit train* was under threat.[88] Over the years, however, the nostalgic mood of group meetings was transformed into a more active one as members witnessed the rebirth of narrow gauge lines in other parts of France.

Sceptics were surprised at the success of such enterprises. A typical railway, run by amateurs, was soon attracting fare-paying passengers of all sorts. These included visitors and tourists, middle-aged people wanting to relive youthful experiences, and young people wanting to sample a bygone way of life. The senior administration of Paris, well represented in enthusiasts' groups, smiled upon these enterprises, and so organisations as diverse as the French education system, local authority tourist boards and conservationists came to support the efforts of railway lovers.

By the beginning of the 1970s, the Toulouse branch of FACS was determined to reopen a railway. It had to be narrow gauge. For a start, narrow gauge lines could be run as a manageable unit, serving communities within a well-defined district. Former stretches of main line on the other hand are just part of a country-wide system and so running a derelict section of main line has all the charm of playing with a dismembered limb. When restoring a narrow gauge line, there is to some extent a chance to breathe life back into an entity. At first there was also a practical advantage; as narrow gauge railways closed all over France, second-hand stock was fairly easy to obtain.

The Toulouse group had to find a system to restore. Haute Garonne[89] had formerly been the centre of an important and interesting metre gauge system; no doubt a reason why interest was still so lively. The VFDM,[90] connecting Toulouse with Castres had been partly electrified and trains ran at speeds similar to those of the main line. This network and others depended heavily on suburban passenger traffic which fell away during the 1930s. Some lines survived the war to be closed soon after and the rights of way were immediately swallowed up by the city of Toulouse as it expanded. Rural tramways that had been built alongside country roads had disappeared as these were widened. To purchase the land to build a railway from scratch would be far too costly. What the group needed was the permanent way of a narrow gauge railway that still belonged to the local authorities, preferably with some sort of existing station.

Although the theoretical possibilities were enormous, there having once been 1,056 kilometres of secondary railway in the Midi-Pyrénées region,[91] there were not many sites actually available. For obvious reasons, such survivals tended to be remote. Most of the volunteers, and the fare-paying public, were based in Toulouse and a railway would need to be within easy reach.

St Sulpice, the former terminus of the TVT, is 30 kilometres from Toulouse. Within the town the line has completely vanished, but the part of the route which survives is only a few kilometres to the east where the main road climbs fairly steeply up to the village of Giroussens while the railway kept to the valley of the Agout. Station buildings with public access survived in the village of St Lieux. Eastwards the trackbed forges its way through three kilometres of woods and water meadows before joining the D631. The section of the track which had proved hardest to build, the spectacular viaduct over the Agout, contributes to the charm of the route. They needed a site for a station; one such still existed at St Lieux, and the mood of the commune was encouraging. The group agreed that they had found the railway that they wanted to reopen and went to seek permission from the authorities concerned. The commune of St Lieux which owned the station land and buildings was one authority, the neighbouring commune of Giroussens another, but the *Département* would have an interest as well. It would grant the necessary planning permission, grant permission to use public roads, and be expected to support the enterprise in various ways such as publicity and grants.

In January 1975, the group received official permission to proceed. Although not readmitting the railway to the class of *chemins de fer d'intérêt publique* the station buildings and wayleave through the *communes* of St Lieux and Giroussens were granted to the group.[92] The *Département* was favourable to the establishment of a new tourist attraction and the local inhabitants enthusiastic. As was described earlier, absolutely nothing remained of the original track and rolling stock. The Toulouse group started looking for 60 centimetre material at a reasonable price. There was nothing available, either new or second-hand, that the group could afford. Many of the original suppliers[93] had completely disappeared. Equally, there was no local 60 centimetre material. World War II had depleted stocks and rival conservation groups were collecting what remained. Material that had gone to the former colonies would be too costly to ship back to France. After a year, the group had found nothing.

In the autumn of 1974, the *Département* announced its intention of tarring over the roadbed of the viaduct at Salles unless the group made a start. This was in use for road vehicles and the *Département* was under pressure to modernise the decaying layer of ballast. If the group delayed, they would have to rip up a tar-macadam road before they could lay their track. At almost the same time, there were moves within the commune of St Lieux to demolish the station. By a fortunate coincidence, the Salins du Midi was just abandoning its narrow gauge railway system.[94] An application from the Toulouse volunteers was favourably received and rails, locomotives and rolling stock were offered for a small sum including delivery. Further cash would be needed for tools, construction and repairs. What was on offer was a 50 centimetre gauge system but as the need was urgent, the material basically sound and the projected costs within reasonable limits, it was decided to abandon plans for 60 centimetre.

A Crochat heads a train back towards the viaduct, in a scene dominated by the timeless view of Giroussens.   *ACOVA*

Crochat on the scenic route.   *ACOVA/F. Saussède*

Fifty centimetre gauge as used by the Salins du Midi was standard for industry, agriculture and mineral extraction. Fortunately, as it would turn out for the nascent railway, there were potteries, mines, ironworks within and beyond France which had also used this gauge. It was, however, almost unknown in France for a passenger railway to run on this gauge. The 10 kilometre Lac d'Artouste line[95] was one exception, but this had originally been an industrial railway.

Once they had decided to accept the offer from the Salins, and change to 50 cm, an appeal was circulated among all FACS members in the area, as far north as Lot and as far south as Aude. The target sum was raised and the new railway launched officially on 31st January, 1975. The group associated with the launch published their constitution in the FACS Review and took the name ACOVA (Association pour la Conservation Occitane de Véhicules Anciens). With this choice of name, the group were able to keep their remit quite broad; as well as running a railway they were declaring their intention of preserving almost anything worthwhile on wheels. The derelict station yard was handed over to a cleaning squad.

On the very day that the Association was formed, 300 metres of portable track arrived at St Lieux station. This was accompanied by a 7 hp Heim Lilliput locotractor, which ran on paraffin, five small trucks, seven turnouts, and rail for the section of the route which lay along the public road. The wagons acquired from the Salins du Midi were converted into carriages by the Association, each with a capacity of six passengers. The carriage design was known to the tourist fraternity as a 'smack bottom' because the suspension was so basic! On the other hand, as a relatively simple design for a wagon conversion, it had already proved its worth on another tourist railway.[97] A tub wagon from the Salins was kept, unconverted, because of its historic interest. It can be discharged from below. The first two Crochat locomotives (Nos. 8 and 10 on the Salins) arrived on 16th May and were numbered 2 and 3 on the new system. Produced by the Établissements Henri Crochat in 1919, these locotractors run on diesel with an interesting electrical transmission. Able to run with equal readiness in forwards or reverse gear, they have a distinctive profile. They are described in more detail later in the chapter.

The first train ran on 25th May. The diminutive Heim locotractor left the station, pulling five dumpy carriages with 30 passengers aboard. The line officially opened on Sunday 6th July because that was the day of the *fête locale*,[98] and a good attendance was assured. Crowds arrived, and were transported along the 920 metres of track in coaches, wagons, dump trucks, anything. Among the visitors were many who remembered the old line, foremost among them M. Cloup. He said that it wasn't quite the same without a steam locomotive, but he did admit that he was enjoying himself! It was a small reminder of the opening celebrations.

In that first year, trains ran every day until 31st August and there were 6,500 fare-paying passengers. Two locotractors provided motive power. When both failed on the same day, a car towed the train. The CFTT decided to expand.

Gradually the original supply of material was repaired and brought into use, and Association members started to look for further locomotives, rail and

Locotractor with 'smack bottom' coaches. RACO (CFTT No. 5) locotractor pulls a rake of coaches. The photograph will have been taken after July 1976, the date of acquisition of the first RACO. *ACOVA*

Crochat locotractors. This picture was taken after 1985; the Couillet 0-6-0 has joined the engine park. *ACOVA/P. Romani*

rolling stock. Volunteers continued the job of restoration and tracklaying and in what was a relatively short period, 1½ kilometres of track including sidings and spurs was laid. By 1976, the line extended to the temporary terminus of Salles on the far side of the viaduct, one kilometre away. The first steam engine arrived in June that year, a Decauville 0-4-0 tank locomotive Type Progrès, Works No. 1087. Older inhabitants of St Lieux were said to be reminded of the old Decauville 2-6-0 tank which plied the line in the days of the TVT. Unfortunately, it was not, and still is not in running order. It came originally from the Forges d'Audincourt, which was to be the source of two further Progrès locomotives. With this and other acquisitions, the Association began its collection of historic material from sources within and outside France. In 1979, the first of two Baguley coaches was air-freighted from England. Even before the Association officially started, members have acted as *fouineurs*, honorary scouts who sought railway relics far and wide.[99]

Public response was altogether good. At peak times, a train would leave every 20 minutes. As the track and therefore journey times extended, departures became a little less frequent - every 30 minutes. Level crossing gates and pedestrian access were constructed, and a beginning was made to landscaping the area. It was no longer possible to house all the material which the Association had acquired in the station yard and original *halle à marchandises* even when this was extended. Open ground to the west of the main road (D48) was rented to the Association for conversion into a depot. One minor acquisition which proved a great encouragement, was a station bell. It gave proceedings a professional tone.

Although the trains were small and light, 7 kilogramme rail for the track soon proved inadequate. The Association acquired some heavier 15 kilogramme/metre rail from the Houillères des Bassins du Centre et du Midi.[100] Unlike the 7 kilogramme prefabricated rail, this had to be pinned to oak sleepers laid on ballast. Progress was slow. By 1978, the terminus was Giroussens (Giroussens Road, to be accurate) but Les Martels, 2.7 kilometres away, was not reached until 1989.

There were a number of reasons why, after an initial flying start, progress on the line slowed down. For a start, the line was open in that first year every day between 1st July and 31st August. There were no paid staff, and so Association members were devoting all their time just to keeping the trains running. In addition, even the 15 kilogramme railway track had turned out to be too light. In 1978, it was decided to upgrade the entire line. At this time rail weighing 25 kilogrammes per metre became available from the Chemin de Fer des Landes at Sabres.[101] This was another tourist line.

The years from 1978 to 1981 were therefore spent in the disheartening task of ripping up work already completed, and replacing it. Heroic feats of muscular endeavour were achieved, particularly before the society acquired modern contractor's machinery. Not only did Society members have to rip up their own track but also on occasion, they had themselves to go up and reclaim in person the second-hand track required. Rail came from the Mines de Carmaux,[102] north of Albi. There were further rails to be salvaged from the Salins du Midi. Villeneuve-lès-Maguelonne on the coast south of Montpellier was the site of

Train on the village street. Following the traditions of the rural tramway, No. 3 has just crossed the D48 and is making its way along the lane that leads to Salles.

ACOVA

another salt refinery which had been linked to a main line siding by a 50 centimetre gauge railway similar to the original. A particular three days in the pouring rain, rescuing derelict track, and carrying it to the waiting transport, will never be forgotten by the participants. Small wonder that the volunteers felt that progress was slow.

History was to some extent repeating itself. The former TVT had been obliged to keep upgrading its track, sometimes with second-hand rail, as experience proved that heavier rail was more satisfactory.

The next problem was the terrain. East of the Giroussens Road halt, the permanent way enters a wood, ominously named La Garrigole (*garrigue* is scrubland). Over the 40 years since the closure of the original line, nature had been busy and obstacles ranged from sturdy trees to oozing quagmires. Compared with the open terrain encountered so far, it was as though a bad fairy had created a thorn hedge. As well as hacking their way through the vegetation, volunteers had to renew embankments and the drainage system before the track could be relaid. In 1979, it was decided that the railway should only open on Sundays and public holidays. The duties of running the railway were overwhelming the volunteers, and maintenance work during the summer had been impossible.

By 1982, the re-engineered line had crossed the Garrigole. Now a well-established attraction, the Association faced the problem of storage. A variety of locomotives (one steam, and 13 diesel or petrol) and rolling stock, much painfully reconstructed by volunteers, had been amassed and far exceeded the capacity of the original shelter.

Originally, the old goods shed had been earmarked as the engine/carriage shed, and was extended. The overflow was established on a field about a hundred metres from the station but of course outdoor storage was unsuitable for the stock, much of it of historic interest and all of value. The Association were given the chance to buy the site, and an industrial hangar was put up between 1982 and 1983, providing 250 square metres of covered space. The former engine shed at the station was converted into the central workshop.

This all took time, but it also gave the railway a proper depot and workshop. Now the CFTT resumed its onward march. In 1985, the track extended two kilometres and by 1988, a further half kilometre.

In 1984, the Association acquired steam traction in the form of an 0-6-0T Couillet locomotive originally from the Sucrerie de Maizy, Aisne.[103] Manufacturer's number 1560, and built in 1910, this was a more powerful locomotive than the little Decauville 0-4-0T already in use. Better still, it worked! The original gauge was 60 centimetres, and so it had to be adapted to track of 50 cm, a mildly ironic twist. Association literature was proudly amended to show carriages being hauled by steam.

The provisional terminus was 2.8 kilometres from St Lieux, just beyond Les Martels. The next goal is La Masquière, on a slight detour from the original track of the Tarn Tramway, making the tourist railway a very respectable 3½ kilometres long. To level the track and build a platform at the terminus is a professional job requiring a bulldozer. For all practical purposes, La Masquière is the end of the line as the original tramway then followed the main road and the right of way is lost.

Decauville on the scenic route. CFTT No. 3 pulls a train through the Garrigole. The enchanting woodland concealed many unpleasant surprises for construction parties.　　ACOVA/J. Daffis

Decauville 0-6-0T Type Progrès Nos. 1087, 1132 and 1111, CFTT Nos. 2 to 4, these were always 50 centimetre gauge and outside framed. They are interesting representatives of a successful design.　　ACOVA

Steaming up in St Lieux station, Decauville 1132 (system No. 3) heads a crowded train.
ACOVA/J.Daffis

St Lieux station 1993. There is a good view of the workshop/former *halle* and the modest proportions of the *BV*. In the foreground is a Decauville coach and a Baguley conversion.
Malcolm Wright

St Lieux station in 1999 showing workshop and rolling stock.					*Malcolm Wright*

Decauville 0-4-0T Type Progrès No. 1132. The design shows the influence of the 0-6-0T military locomotive.					*Malcolm Wright*

To take a trip on the modern CFTT, start from St Lieux station. The railway, still wholly run by amateurs, is open on Sundays and public holidays from Easter to October, and everyday during the first fortnight of August. Rail lovers can take the SNCF to St Sulpice station and walk or cycle. Coming by car or coach, St Sulpice is 30 kilometres north-east of Toulouse on Route Nationale 88 and the A68. Turn towards the town centre then take the D38 eastward into St Lieux. Coming from Graulhet in the other direction, follow the D631 through Briatexte as far as Giroussens. A turning off to the left at the western side of Giroussens takes you over the river to St Lieux. Turn off to the right into the village just before the level crossing. There is ample parking. The station is easy to find, to the south of the High Street.

The *BV* of the former railway is still recognisable from the outside, though the *Halle* has been extended. Open the *BV* door with the fanlight above, and changes are apparent. Instead of a waiting room, there is now a shop. Travellers buy tickets and find out the time of the next train. Trains start at 2.30 pm. Between then and 5.30, trains run every hour, more frequently on busy days. Anyone who arrives after 5.30 on a chilly afternoon, may find that there is no 6.30 service, which runs if there are 15 passengers or more (*train facultatif*).[104] The 2.30 train was originally also optional but for two years there was consistent demand, and so it was added to the schedule. If the weather is fine, the picnic park nearby makes a good outdoor waiting room. If it is cold, visitors make for the local cafeteria.

The train may be pulled by one of the steam locomotives. The 0-6-0T Couillet is being refitted and so the service in Spring 2001 will be handled by Decauville 0-4-0Ts No. 1111 and 1132. The Schöma is used at busy, or very quiet times, with the Ruston in reserve. Crochat No. 8 may perform light duties.

The passengers take their seats. The station bell sounds and the train sets off along the platform, past the water tower and through the station gates into the street. As before mentioned, this is close to the junction with the D48. The level crossing has been recently relaid in 30 kilogramme track, one of the few works on the railway not carried out by members of ACOVA. The line carries on, more or less in the middle of the street, past the houses at the crossroads. From a window on one side, an old lady may wave. On the other, a family are relaxing behind a trellis. Passengers can savour the atmosphere that was once created by a rural tramway, passing through the heart of a village, a rare experience today.

Less than 200 metres from the station, the railway swings off to the left before resuming its path eastwards along the side of the road. We pass the depot and museum (La Garenne) off to the left. We are now in open country, following the old road down to the river. In the time of the TVT, the railway would have taken the middle of the road. With the growth of road traffic, the track has been routed to the north side.

Almost opposite Giroussens, perched on its defensive escarpment, the railway reaches the hamlet of Le Port. This is an *arrêt facultatif*. As most visitors will be taking the train back to St Lieux with its car and coach park, this is really only useful to local people, using the service as they might have used the old Tramway. Immediately after the hamlet is the viaduct. The view has changed

General view of workshops and engine shed at La Garenne in 1999. The new museum will be to the right.   *Malcolm Wright*

A close-up view of the engine shed at La Garenne in 1999.   *Malcolm Wright*

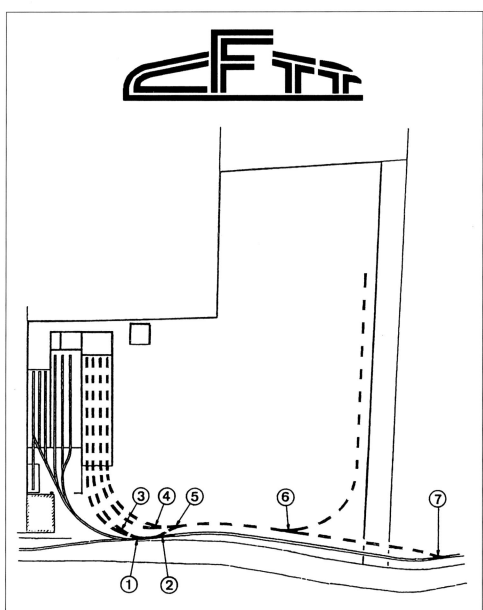

The depot and museum at La Garenne is the modeller's dream because of its wealth of stock. At the base is the lane, at bottom left, a private house. The plan shows the new museum building, with new sidings (shown as a broken line); seven new turnouts are envisaged. New houses are being built around the CFTT grounds.   *ACOVA*

little since the 1920s. Far below the wooded banks, the river flows through field and pasture while the 17th century village of Giroussens still dominates the hill above. It is hard to believe that in flood the tranquil river can rise above the bridge, as it did during the floods of 1930. It damaged the western-most arch, but don't worry, regular repairs take place, the last in 1999.

As on the west side, there is an *arrêt facultatif*, the Chemin de Salles, on the far side. The railway follows the *Chemin* for a few yards, before the road forks right to serve the farms dotted about the fields to the south. We make our way west, climbing steadily, as the TVT once did. On the plaine de Salles, riders on horseback from the Centre Equestre nearby may be glimpsed. Roughly half a kilometre further on, the railway crosses the Chemin de Giroussens,[105] site of the original TVT halt and passenger shelter. One hundred metres further on is the Halte de Giroussens, a passing place. On our day, the returning train had to wait, and so we sailed through.

Passengers enjoy the next stage of the journey through tranquil woodland. This is the marshy Garrigole which caused such problems during construction. The gradient is 1.5 per cent overall and the whole area is one of small watercourses. Just before the bridge over the largest of these is the Halte de Lascazes established for the convenience of steam trains which need to take in water. The *Chef de Train* gives visitors a technical and historical briefing. The Halte de Lascazes may be the place where steam trains halted to take water in the days of the TVT, water being difficult to obtain at La Ramière station.

Soon after, the railway comes back into more open country, with an artificial lake to the side of the line. The line crosses a country road with the hamlet of Les Martels visible to the south and the Halte-Evitement des Martels just beyond. The Halte-Evitement des Martels is both a Halt and a passing place. Tourists stop here to enjoy the public garden. In the days of the Tarn Tramway, this was a request stop. The modern train halts and the locomotive runs round to the front. A *parc floral* and mini-zoo have been created at this end of the line, established since the creation of the CFTT as a complementary attraction.

At present (2000), the track has not yet reached its planned terminus. The planned route veers left, away from the track of the former TVT. This used to continue past the hamlet and chapel of St Cyriaque and then along the D631. On the return journey, future trains will be able to pull into a museum sited beside the depot. In 1996, the site of the depot was extended. There is a new siding with third rail to accommodate 60 cm stock.

From 6,500 in 1975, passenger numbers have grown. In 1993, 12,000 people travelled on the railway, but numbers increased in the next two seasons by an astonishing 50 per cent. In 1997, numbers were up to 20,000. They were affected by repair works on the viaduct, but have since soared to 24,000. Many come in organised groups, especially school parties in the summer term. This sort of custom is very welcome and the Association has been to some trouble to attract them, but schools make their visits on weekdays during the term. This can be problem for a railway still run by volunteers.

The Association may have limited itself by only using volunteer labour. In defence it could be argued that this is a small railway running on a narrow gauge and so the network should stay small. With scant funds, the collection of rolling stock has a serendipitous quality that could easily be swamped by money. The line can only be open at holiday times. This contributes to the atmosphere, and makes for good neighbourly relations with the folk of St Lieux. In addition, all the amateurs are professionals in some other field and in itself this adds to their style. They have, they feel, managed to preserve more than just a railway.

Locomotives And Rolling Stock

As observed before, an essential difference between the TVT and its successor, is that the present line is 50 centimetre gauge. The aim of the enthusiasts and their backers who built the CFTT was to reconstruct a piece of the past, and to serve its public by entertaining and informing them. Attending to local transport needs which was the main aim of the original railway is now a secondary consideration. The stock consists of purchases from industrial concerns whch were closing down or modernising, material which was at first cheap, but as public interest in railway heritage has grown, so has the asking price. The second important source of material has been the Association's own workshops, staffed by volunteers, producing mainly coaches for the summer visitor traffic and vehicles for track maintenance.

Firmly in the first category are the railway's steam locomotives, numbered 1 to 5. One and Three are classed as *Monuments Historiques*.[106] Number 1 is an outside framed 0-6-0T Couillet, Maker's No. 1576, date of manufacture 1910, acquired in 1985, ten years after the railway started running. Ten tonnes empty and 12 tonnes in working order, it was originally used for hauling sugar beet.

Locomotives Nos. 2 to 4 are Decauville 0-4-0T steam engines, Type Progrès, outside framed. Originally designed for 50 cm gauge, the nominal weight is 5 tonnes, 6.75 tonnes in working order. Number 2 came in June 1976, in the railway's second season. The maker's number was 1087, date of manufacture 1930 and the original purchaser had been the Forges d'Audincourt. It came from a scrap dealer, only the chassis, running gear, tanks and boiler surviving. Although it was just a shell, it was felt that a member of the Decauville family had returned to the line after many years. The original intention had been to restore it, and in 1995, work began. In November 1987, another Progrès class, built in 1947, maker's No. 1132, and also from the Forges d'Audincourt, was bought from a collector. It was in far better condition and restoration was completed in 1992. The Couillet could be withdrawn for a refit.

Some years before the CFTT opened, the Forges d'Audincourt had sold yet another Progrès class (manufacturer's No. 1111). It was then sold on to the Chemin de Fer de l'Odière, Loir-et-Cher. This was on the private estate of a member of the Guinness family. When he died, a new owner took over the estate but put the railway into store. The locomotive waited in a shed until 1991 when news reached the CFTT. Negotiations began, and in 1995, the small locomotive was brought to St Lieux. The locomotive was almost intact, but she underwent a complete overhaul and was fitted with a new boiler. Decauville

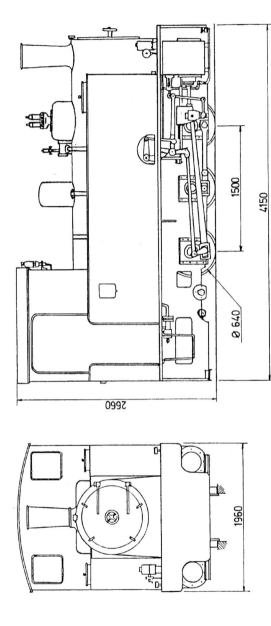

COUILLET 030T № 1576 - 1910

Couillet 0-6-0T No. 1576, built in 1910, CFTT No. 1, this locomotive shows the adaptations needed when regauging.

ACOVA

Heating surface of tubes	15.64m²
Diameter of cylinders	0.28m
Stroke of piston	0.32m
Tractive effort	3.25 @ 75%
Fuel capacity	0.3 tonnes
Capacity of water tanks	1,200 litres
Unladen weight in tonnes	10 tonnes
Weight in working order	12 tonnes

4150

1500

Ø 640

2660

1960

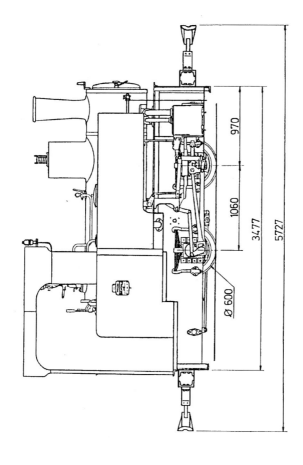

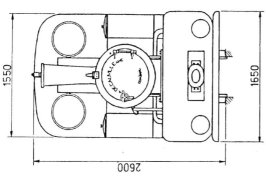

DECAUVILLE type "PROGRÈS"

Heating surface of tubes	$10.44m^2$
Diameter of cylinders	0.175m
Stroke of piston	0.25m
Top speed	17 km/h
Maximum load at top speed	72 tonnes
Tractive effort	1.036 tonnes
Fuel capacity	0.3 tonnes
Capacity of water tanks	1,000 litres
Unladen weight in tonnes	5 tonnes
Weight in working order	6.75 tonnes

2600

1550

1650

970

1060

3477

5727

Ø 600

Locomotive de 3 t. 250 à vide
(4 t. 250 en marche)

Voie de 500 m/m.

POIDS ET DIMENSIONS PRINCIPALES

Poids	à vide......................	3ᵗ 250
	en charge..................	4ᵗ 250
Gabarit sans tampon	Longueur....................	2ᵐ920
	Largeur.....................	1ᵐ520
	Hauteur.....................	2ᵐ465

CHAUDIÈRE

Surface de grille............................		0ᵐ³29
Surface de chauffe	du foyer......................	1ᵐ²38
	des tubes..................	4ᵐ²42
	totale........................	5ᵐ²80
Tubes à fumée	Nombre.....................	48
	Diamètre..................	36/40
	Longueur entre plaques tubulaires.....................	0ᵐ850
Volume d'eau dans la chaudière............		280 litres
Volume de vapeur dans la chaudière........		90 litres
Diamètre moyen du corps cylindrique......		0ᵐ650
Timbre de la chaudière......................		12 kilos
2 soupapes de sûreté de 36 ᵐ/ₘ de diamètre..		

MACHINE

Distribution système Walschaer.

Diamètre des cylindres.....................	135 ᵐ/ₘ
Course des pistons.........................	200 »
Diamètre des roues au roulement..........	500 »
Effort de traction $\dfrac{0{,}65 \cdot p \cdot d^2}{D}$	568 k,

CHASSIS, ROULEMENT, FREIN

Longueur du châssis sans tampon..........	2ᵐ750
Ecartement intérieur des longerons........	0ᵐ800
Nombre d'essieux couplés..................	2
Empattement total des essieux.............	0ᵐ850
Ecartement des bandages (voie de 0ᵐ500)...	0ᵐ415
Largeur des bandages.....................	0ᵐ080
Frein à vis à 2 sabots.	

APPROVISIONNEMENTS

Volume d'eau dans les soutes..............	480 litres
Charbon dans les soutes	100 kilos

Vitesses en kilomètres à l'heure	Admission	Effort de traction	Charges nettes en tonnes remorquées sur rampes de :									
			0	5	10	15	20	25	30	35	40	50
9	0,95	606	50,5	32,5	23,5	18	14,5	11,5	10	8,5	7	5,5
12	0,70	551	42,5	29,5	21	16	12,5	10,5	8,5	7,5	6,5	4,5
17	0,50	482	40	28	19	13,5	10,5	8,5	7	6	5	3,5

Nota :
   Le rayon minimum des courbes à employer est de 10 mètres.
   Si le train se trouve à la fois dans une rampe et dans une courbe de faible rayon, la résistance du train au passage de la rampe se trouve augmentée de la résistance due au passage de la courbe.
   Cette dernière correspond à peu près à la résistance résultant du passage dans une rampe supplémentaire de 10 ᵐ/ₘ par mètre.

Exemple :
   Pour déterminer la charge remorquée par une locomotive 3ᵗ 250 ayant à gravir une rampe de 15 ᵐ/ₘ par mètre en courbe de 20 mètres de rayon, il faudra l'assimiler à une locomotive ayant à gravir une rampe de 25 ᵐ/ₘ par mètre en partie droite.

Page from the Decauville catalogue showing 0-4-0T, Type 1, new style, weight 3.25 tonnes. The Type 1 was designed for quarries and agricultural work.

1111 is further distinguished from her sisters by a plaque which reads *Honneur au vin, honneur au charbon.*[107] In July 1998, she joined her sister for service on the line.

The most exciting of all recent acquisitions is Decauville Type 1 0-4-0 tank locomotive, maker's No. 288, date 1898. This was one of three, delivered to the Higgison International Nickel Corporation to exploit a mine in New Caledonia. When the mine closed in about 1920, she was transferred to the Guériom mine where she was regauged to 50 cm though her two companion Decauvilles were not. In 1946, when this mine also closed, Nos. 287, 288 and 632 escaped being scrapped because it was too costly and difficult to bring them off the mountain. Instead they were abandoned in the jungle. In 1996, all three were rescued by air, thanks to the French Air Force.

No. 287 is on display in Noumea, New Caledonia but 288, name *Recope*, with a gauge of 50 cm, seemed ideal for the CFTT. After lengthy negotiations, she was loaded into a container and arrived in France in 1998, the only example in Europe of a fascinating and historic prototype. This was the workhorse which really made Decauville famous, the prime mover in engineering and industrial concerns the world over. She is to be steam engine No. 5, the 'little flower' on account of her size, a diminutive 3.25 tonnes.

On arrival, she was put together for her photo-call, but currently (2000), she awaits the go-ahead for a complete rebuild, as befits a *Monument Historique*. Her chassis and valve gear are in relatively good order, as are her wheels, but the platework, notably the water tanks and boiler, have suffered tremendously. A tide-mark was visible because she stood in water for nearly 50 years. No-one will want to forget that we owe her to the good-will of New Caledonia, and her place in the industrial heritage of both countries.

The first locomotive to see service on the line was a Lilliput locotractor built by Heim in 1955. As noted elsewhere, it was in the first shipment to be dumped at St Lieux station on the day that the Society came into being, 31st January, 1975. (The name is inspired by Jonathan Swift's book *Gulliver's Travels*.) With a 7 hp petrol engine, the locotractor provided all the motive power that first year.

In May 1976, the first two Crochat locotractors arrived from the Salins du Midi. They are important historic relics. During World War I, the Éts Henri Crochat were commissioned to design a petrol-driven locomotive. Steam locomotives emit steam, naturally, and sparks, making them good targets for enemy artillery. The Type 14L 4-60 was developed. A modified version of this design was sold to the Salins du Midi in 1919. Six survived to be inherited by the CFTT. Of these, No. 2 (ex-No. 8) is in working order. No. 8 is in working order, two have been withdrawn from service, two await restoration and one has been used for spares.

In the original design, an 30 hp petrol motor drove a generator of 110v. This was compound, consisting of a shunt coil and a series one. Through a controller which made the connections as necessary, this generator supplied the electric traction motors mounted in each bogie. When the petrol engine stopped, the generator was switched into the other, shunt, mode so that the current generating by the still moving coils did not burn it out. The bogie motors could be permanently connected because the shunt effectively cut them off. There was

'Lilliput' Locotractor. This small petrol driven locotractor was the first locomotive on the CFTT.

ACOVA

Engine	Bernard 7 hp petrol W112 (4-stroke)
Starter	Manual handle
Transmission	Chain
Brakes	Pedal, 4 brake shoes
Top speed	8 km/h
Maximum load at top speed	19.2 tonnes
Weight in working order	1 tonne

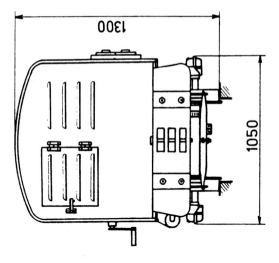

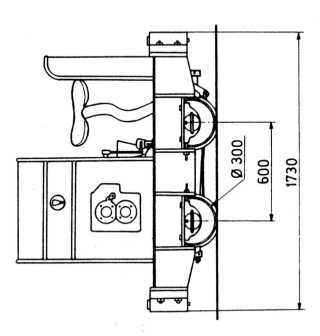

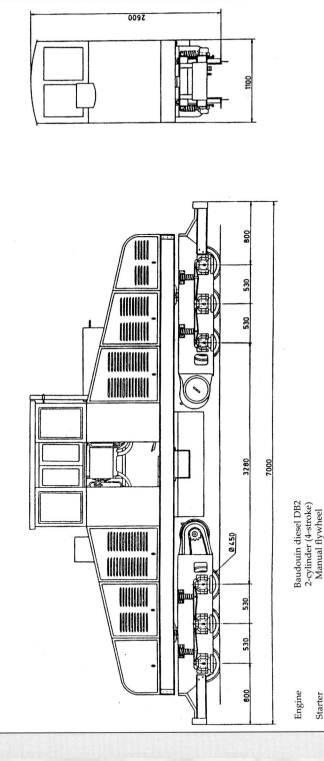

Engine	Baudouin diesel DB2
	2-cylinder (4-stroke)
Starter	Manual flywheel
Transmission	Electric
Brakes	Compressed air and coil
Maximum load at top speed	90 tonnes
Capacity of tanks	650 litres
Unladen weight	5 tonnes
Weight in working order	6 tonnes

The Crochat has six speed positions, a top speed exceeding 50 kph is possible. Fuel capacity for the original Crochat was 350 litres giving, acording to the claims of the manufacturers, a remarkable 10 hours' running.

Crochat SL6 50. This version was mounted on 6 axles and was designed for 50 centimetre gauge. A 60 centimetre gauge, 4 axle version also existed.

ACOVA

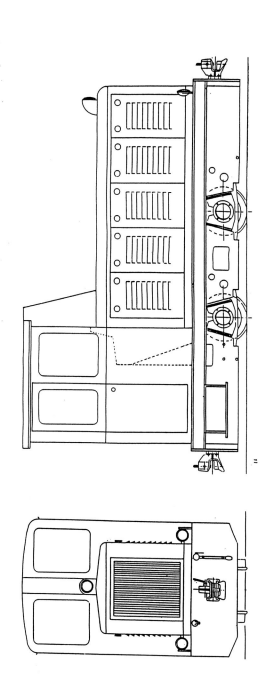

Shöma type CFL 60 DCL reconstructed by the CFTT.

SCHÖMA type CFL 60 DCL - Reconstruction CFTT 1998

no gear box as such; but to move into a higher speed, the driver increased the flow of fuel to the petrol motor by one notch. As the motor speeded up, so did the generator, increasing the power supplied. There were six such 'notches' plus a seventh, stop, position which put the current through the shunt, and position zero which was 'rest'. The generator is air cooled, with a fan mounted on the transmission rod.

The system was known as Crochat Collardeau. As there were two centres of traction, it was perhaps more tolerant of rough track than a close coupled engine. It had compressed air brakes and also an early example of 'resistance' or regenerative braking. With its armoured body and double fronted design, it was a monument to the problems of the time, and interesting to compare with the 'Tin Turtle' produced by Simplex in the same period. Of the 200 Type 14L 4-6-0 locomotives that Crochat produced for the French army, one has survived to be preserved.

The CFTT locotractors act as tributes both to a fascinating design and to the tragic waste of the war. The original 30 hp petrol motor has been replaced by a variable speed diesel one, Baudouin Type DB 2, with a restrictor. The rest of the machine is virtually the same, still requiring 650 litres of water (more than one-tenth of its 6 tonne weight) for the cooling system. Their characteristic shape appears in the railway's logo.

These Crochats are not the only survivors. Fifteen of Type 14L50 went to Morocco, and the design was also used in railcars. A two-axle model survives at Pithiviers as do the bases of two bogie railcars.[108] Établissements Crochat also used the *pétroleo-électrique* system in two designs for military use on standard gauge, the 22L2N and 44L4N.[109]

The main back-up locomotive is No. 10, a Ruston LFT 50 hp diesel supplied in 1965 to the Usines Von Roll de Gerlafingen, a steelworks in Switzerland, which supplied other locomotives to the CFTT. Its top speed is 19.6 km/h, rather faster than most of the other locomotives in the engine shed. The Ruston came to the railway in 1981. Its partner is a Schöma 6 cylinder 90 hp diesel type D 916-6. It has been rebuilt, with a new, more powerful motor, new bodywork, side panels, brakes and control panel. It is affectionately known as 'Monster'.

Secondary backup is provided by a locotractor built in 1981 . This was built by Établissements Patry[110] for use in the galleries of the Chaux des Paviers, Indre-et-Loire south of Tours. It uses a 50 hp Deutz diesel engine adapted to produce the minimum of diesel fumes; essential for the enclosed workplace for which it was originally designed. It ran on 60 centimetre gauge rail and had to be adapted. It is ideal for hauling track maintenance trains. In the shed are a Decauville locotractor, a Weitz type 'France' and a 37 hp LKM. This Lokomotivbau 'Karl Marx' originated in a brickworks near Erfurt in the former East Germany but came via an enthusiast in Kessel. It has been re-gauged from 60 cm but does provide the system with another historic machine.

The engine shed has a number of other locotractors of interest rescued from mines and industrial works. This is to be expected because ACOVA is dedicated to preserving old vehicles. Many have been restored to working order, but as most are quite small, delivering less than 20 hp, they are not used for hauling

LKM Type Ns 2F.

full length tourist trains. A pantograph locomotive has also been restored. Made by Sociedad Metalurgica Duro Felguera (SMDF) in Asturias, maker's No. 1067, date 1962, it used to work in the Berga mines. It was then transferred to the mines of Figols, also in Catalonia, where it was given larger wheels and the motors replaced by one made by Siemens. Weighing six tonnes and designed for 50 centimetre gauge it worked off 220 volts. Its height including catenary is 1.8 metres. In 1986, the mine replaced the railway with a conveyor belt, and in 1993, the CFTT acquired the locomotive. Some of the catenary system was also salvaged; perhaps the CFTT plans to build an electrified branch!

The passenger coaches have all had to be regauged or completely rebuilt, many in the Society's workshops. Most of the second-hand material would originally have been used for freight handling, but the principal need of the CFTT is for passenger stock. The five carriages which were used on the first trains, Nos. 31 to 35, were built on the chassis of old salt wagons formerly in use at the Salins du Midi. They were small, only seating six, with minimal springing. When the railway was less than a kilometre long, this mattered relatively little.

Coaches Nos. 41 and 43, maker's Nos. 3238 and 3237, were built by Baguley in 1947 as toast rack coaches for service at Butlin's Holiday Camps. They ran first on the two foot gauge railway at Clacton-on-Sea, Essex and then at Meirion Hill, North Wales. They seated thirty-two. Both were adapted for 50 centimetre gauge by Alan Keef Ltd. One was flown to Toulouse in 1977, the other in 1981 and transported on to St Lieux.[111]

Coaches Nos. 51 to 54 are enclosed, and are complete reconstructions using materials from the Houillères de Carmaux.[102] Two are third class, with wooden seats, one second class, but the first class carriage has velvet upholstered armchairs and panelled ceiling.

Another carriage has been rebuilt from five small wagons and recently put into service. The bogies were acquired from the Lac d'Artouste line near the Spanish border in Pyrénées Atlantiques. The new carriage, No. 45, offers seating for 32 and is partially enclosed. A similar one is under construction.

A number of wagons have been welcomed for their historic interest. Originating on diverse systems and railway gauges, most of them do not run. They include eight tub wagons from the Mines de Plomb de Peyrebrune built for 50 centimetre gauge. The lead mines were about six kilometres west of Réalmont and, in the 1890s, Monsieur Bonnet had proposed to extend the TVT eastwards to take advantage of their mineral traffic. The Administrator of the Mines had issued a counter-proposal and that part of the project was shelved, as described in the chapter on the early TVT. It is interesting to note that the Société des Mines de Dadou had a strong tradition of self-sufficiency; they made these wagons. The six large ones (system Nos. 201 to 206) and a smaller one are side opening. The eighth opens from the front.

The Houillères de Carmaux mentioned above also supplied a tipper wagon with a wooden body. Also from the *département* of Tarn, the collection boasts a tipper wagon and flat wagon with a backboard made by Établissements Popineau. They were formerly used by the plâtrerie de Marssac, west of Albi. Four Decauville tipper wagons came from the Four à Chaux de Ronel.[112]

LOCOTRACTEUR A ESSENCE " FRANCE " 20
20 chevaux
JULES WEITZ

S.421

TRACTEUR A ESSENCE POUR TRAVAUX PUBLICS ET USINES
Poids maximum en service lesté : 3.700 kg.
A 3 vitesses en marche avant et marche arrière

VITESSES en km./h. env.		Force de traction	TONNAGES REMORQUÉS SUR RAMPE DE :					
			en palier env.	1 % env.	2 % env.	3 % env.	4 % env.	5 % env.
Série normale	3	920 kg.	82	41	26	18,7	14,3	11,4
	6	546 kg.	48	23	14	9,6	7	5,2
	9	327 kg.	28	12	6,8	4,7	2,7	1,7
Série accélérée	5	920 kg.	82	41	26	18,7	14,3	11,4
	9	460 kg.	40	19	11	7,5	5,3	3,8
	15	278 kg.	23	10	5,3	3	1,7	0,9

A Weitz type 'France' was acquired in 1996 and restored to working order in 1998. This illustration is an extract from the Jules Weitz catalogue.   *J. Daffis/ACOVA*

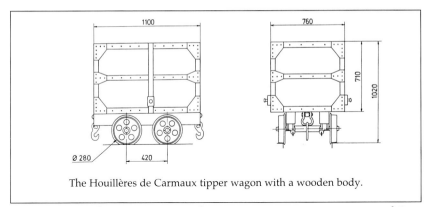

The Houillères de Carmaux tipper wagon with a wooden body.

Retired from the Sablière de Larchant is a Popineau tipper wagon, while a Popineau chassis can be seen under another tipper from the Sablière de Poligny. Popineau provided the Maraîcher Lambert with a vegetable wagon. Consisting of a large raised tray, the wagon was suitable for sorting produce without having to stoop. All these businesses were in Seine-et-Marne, east of Paris and not far from the Popineau factory.

Under a slatted flat wagon rescued from the Faïencerie de Sarreguemines, Marne, can be seen bogies constructed from British War Department parts. Marne was an area of trench warfare in World War I, and after the war much peaceful use was made of Army Surplus material.

A number of interesting wagons have come from the Carbones de Berga.[113] Two were designed to transport coal. The others reflect other aspects of coal mining, for example the transport of explosives, and track and pit maintenance. There is even a *chargeur* (ex-CB 5) worked on compressed air for filling the tipper wagons with coal or spoil.

The Association has been able to put some of its collection to practical use. Since 1976, they have used a weed-spray mounted on a Decauville chassis, and a portable generator. Since 1991, they have had a high pressure cleaning wagon. Of the chassis in the shed, five once carried rail mounted cranes. Some were for workshop use or as trailers. There are also three hand cars. A John Deere mechanical shovel and smaller equipment such as a pneumatic drill help maintain the line.

Since 1982, the Association has housed its rolling stock in a hangar built just to the west of St Lieux but an indoor museum has been planned. In the early 1990s an application was approved to turn La Garenne, site of the dépôt, into an exhibition building of the order of 2,000 square metres. By 1999, the museum had not yet been built, but the laying of sidings for the exhibits had begun.

Visitors, it is hoped, will soon be invited to admire the display of historic railway material which has been gathered. At present, the tally stands at four steam locomotives, 18 locotractors, two inspection cars, the pantograph electric locomotive and two powered by battery. The total of passenger coaches now stands at nine and there are about 70 wagons. Of the wagons and locomotives, some await restoration in the depot. Others see occasional service. Some were for a different gauge and it is perhaps not right to convert them all. They deserve a museum building.

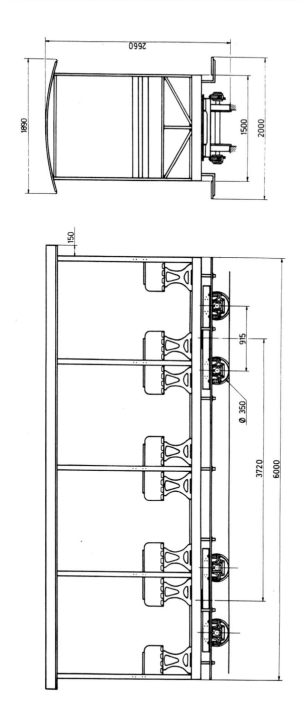

BALADEUSE à BOGIES n° 43

Coach No. 43

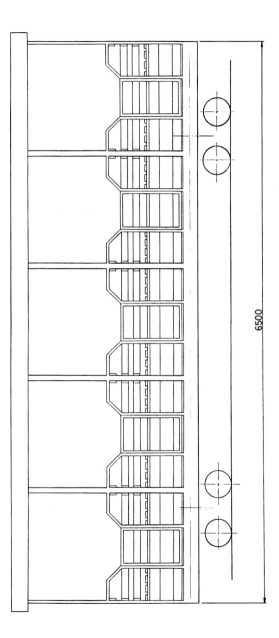

6500

BALADEUSE à BOGIES n° 45

Coach No. 45

CFTT Stock List 2000

No.	Type	Builder	Works No.	Built	Origin	Acquired
Steam Locomotives						
1	0-6-0T	Couillet	1576	1910	Sucriere de Maizy (Aisne)	1985
2	0-4-0T	Decauville	1087	1931	Forges d'Audincourt (Doubs)	1976
3	0-4-0T	Decauville	1132	1947	Forges d'Audincourt (Doubs)	1987
4	0-4-0T	Decauville	1111	1929	Forges d'Audincourt (Doubs)	1995
5	0-4-0T	Decauville	288	1898	International Nickel Corp.	1998

No.	Type	Builder	Works No.	Built	Origin	Acquired
Locotracteurs						
1	Lilliput	Heim	315LL	1955	Salins du Midi (Aude)	1975
2	5L6.50	Crochat	?	1918	Salins du Midi (Aude) No. 8	1975
3	CACL JW 15	Weitz	?	1948	SNCF Artouste (Pyrénées-Atlantiques)	1982
4	TE	Campagne	?	1915	Etablissements Potz (Ambérieu, Ain)	1976
5	16 PS	Raco	1939	1948	Usines Von Roll de Gerlafingen (Suisse)	1976
6	KDL S1	Ruhrthaler	1329	1934	M. Delamont (Tarn et Garonne)	1977
7	16 PS	Raco	1304	1946	Usines Von Roll de Gerlafingen (Suisse)	1978
8	5L6.50	Crochat	?	1918	Salins du Midi (Aude) No. 3	1978
9	5L6.50	Crochat	?	1918	Salins du Midi (Aude) No. 11	1978
10	LFT	Ruston	518189	1965	Usines Von Roll de Gerlafingen (Suisse)	1981
11	5L6.50	Crochat	?	1918	Salins du Midi (Aude) No. 4	1982
12	5L6.50	Crochat	?	1918	Salins du Midi (Aude) No. 5	1982
13	HDD	Heim	773	1960	Quarry near Troyes.	2000
14	P3	Patry	10	1981	Usine des Chaux de Paviers	1991
15	3 tonnes	Decauville	696	1939	Mines de Pessens (Aveyron)	1991
16	GK 9 B	Deutz	56610	1956(?)	Pechiney Manosque (Alpes Hte Provence)	1992
17	CFL60DC L	Schöma	4199	1978	Mines de Figols (Catalonia) No. 3	1993
18	Lilliput	Heim/Paltry	324	1961	Mine du Burg (Tarn)	1996
19	France	Weitz	982	?	Mine in Aveyron	1996
20	Lilliput	Heim/Paltry	334	1961	Mine du Burg (Tarn)	1996
21	Lilliput	Heim/Paltry	?	1961	Mine du Burg (Tarn)	1996
22	NS2F	VEB/LKM 'Karl Marx'	248894	1957	Höngeda Brickworks	1996

No.	Type	Builder	Works No.	Built	Origin	Acquired
Battery Locomotives						
E1		Genty	1	1958	Dynamiterie Nitrochimie (Seine et Marne)	1986
E2		Vetra	?	1935	Dynamiterie Nitrochimie (Seine et Marne)	1986

No.	Type	Builder	Works No.	Built	Origin	Acquired
Electric Locomotives						
4	Dufel 1000	SMDF	1067	1962	Mines de Figols (Catalonia)	1993

No.	Type	Builder	Works No.	Built	Origin	Acquired
Draisines						
D2		Brial	1	1990	CFTT	1990

Carriages					
No.	Type	No. of seats	Builder	Date in service	Notes
31	4 wheel open coach	6	CFTT	1975	Chassis ex-Salins du Midi, rebuilt, handbraked.
41	Open bogie coach	32	CFTT	1975	Reconstruction of Baguley coach No. 3238 of 1947, imported 1977. Handbraked
42	Open bogie coach	32	CFTT	1978	Decauville type KE, 'in house' design.
43	Open bogie coach	32	CFTT/ASPE	1984	Rebuild of Baguley coach No. 3237 of 1947, imported 1981.
44	Open bogie coach	32	CFTT/ASPE	1984	Decauville type KE, 'in house' design.

No.	Type	No. of seats	Builder	Date in service	Notes
45	Bogie coach	30	CFTT/ASPE	1994	A conversion of ex-Artouste Railway bogies.
46	Bogie coach	30	CFTT/ASPE		As above, but under construction
51	Enclosed 4 wheel coach	10	Hôpital de Jour (Carmaux, Tarn)	1991 1991	Gerone-Palomas type. Miners transport from Carmaux. 3rd class.
52	Enclosed 4 wheel coach	10	CFTT/Lugan	1994	Miners transport from Carmaux. 2nd class.
	Enclosed bogie coach	28	GIGAGR		Replica of Carde coach as used on TVT. Under construction
53	Enclosed 4 wheel coach	10	CFTT/Lugan	1996	3rd class carriage
54	Enclosed 4 wheel coach	10	CFTT/Lugan	1998	1st class carriage

Wagons

Type	Builder	Notes
Tarn - Peyrebrune Mines		
Tub wagons	In house	6 examples. Metal, discharges sideways
Tub wagon small	In house	Metal, discharges sideways
Small wagon	In house	Lipped for discharge
Tarn - Carmaux Coalmines		
Wagon	?	Wooden body, tipper, ex- 57cm gauge
Tarn - Marssac Plasterworks		
Tipper	Popineau	
Flat	Popineau	
Tarn - Ronel Limeworks		
Tippers	Decauville	4 examples.
Aude - Salins du Midi		
Wagon		Empties through base, wooden body.
Artouste Railway		
Well wagon	Pétolat	
Gard - Alès Coalmines		
Large tipper wagon		Metal body.
Marne - Vitry le François		
Flat		Leaf springs, WD bogies.
Seine et Marne - Larchant Sandpit		
Tipper	Kowalski	
Tipper	Popineau/Vizet	
Seine et Marne - Poligny Sandpit		
Tipper	Chassis Popineau, body, Pétolat	
Seine et Marne - Lambert		
Trailer	Popineau	For horticultural use.
Alpes de Haute Provence - Pechiney Enterprises		
Mineral wagon		Empties by tipping, 60 cm gauge.
Catalonia, Spain - Berga Coal Mines		
Large wagon	Workshops at Figols	Pegaso type. Capacity 1,750 litres, No. CB 357
Bogie		2 examples. Pivoted bogie wagons for rails.
Flat		2 examples. Wagons for pit props.
Flat		Made entirely of wood.
Dynamite		2 examples, Metal chassis, wooden body.
Workshop wagon	Workshops at Figols	Adaptation of Decauville chassis.
Tank wagon	Workshops at Figols	Large mineral wagon converted for transport of hydraulic fluid.
Transporter		For carrying coal waste. Operates on compressed air.
Small wagon	Decauville	From Sant Josep mine.
Guard's van	GIGAGR	In the style of the TVT. Under construction.

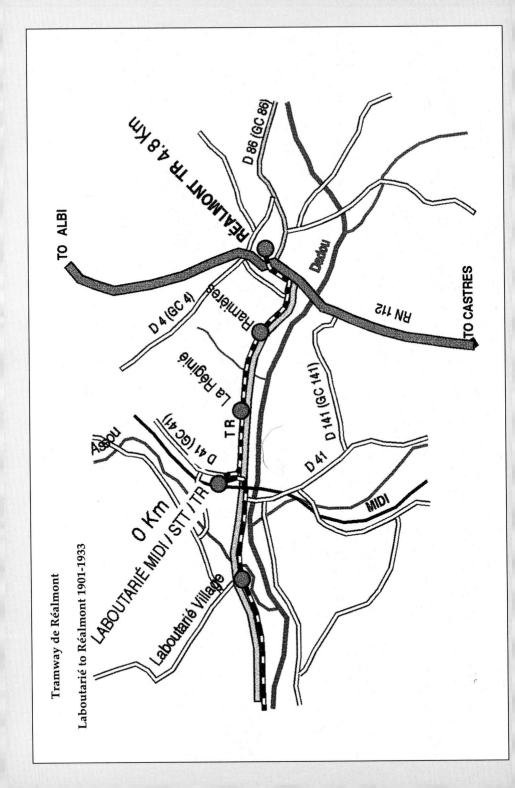

Tramway de Réalmont

Laboutarié to Réalmont 1901-1933

Chapter Eight

Réalmont Tramway

The Tramway de Réalmont shared the same facilities at Laboutarié, and in many important ways it compared and contrasted with the TVT, and so this history is incomplete without that of its smaller rival. It is also of interest to social historians because for two-thirds of its existence, it was run by a woman.

Laboutarié to Réalmont opened to goods and passenger traffic October 1901. Officially closed 19th May, 1933. Origin of *Pointes Kilométriques* is Laboutarié main line station, though most distances are approximate. From goods yard of Laboutarié Midi main line station followed D41 (GC41) for 300 metres, then D631 (GC86) eastwards on northern side of road. At 1.7 kilometres, *Halte Garage* of La Réginié. At 3.5 kilometres, *Halte Garage* of Ramières (turnout and spur to allow passing) At 4 kilometres, joined N112; kept on northern side of road. Followed main road (Avenue de Castres) into town; made right turn into Rue Porche to *Gare-Dépot* of Réalmont *pk* 4.833. Apart from the station, all track was sunk into the metal of the road.

The population of Réalmont in 1999 was about 2,600, static for a century. It was once a more important town, always enjoying good communication westwards along the valley of the Dadou and one of the largest towns on the N112 between Albi and Castres. As well as livestock, wine was important, and a further source of wealth were the lead mines of Peyrebrune to the east. In 1900 Réalmont was a market centre with over 3,000 inhabitants with associated rural industries such as sawmills and flourmilling. It felt itself a rival of Graulhet, then a town of 6,000.

As we have seen, the towns vied with each other to attract the railway line from Albi to Castres when this was proposed in the 1860s. The railway was built to the east of Laboutarié in an attempt to please both and in reality serving neither. The Ponts Et Chaussées put into effect feasibility studies for branch lines linking both towns to the main line. In the case of Réalmont, these took place in 1884 and 1885. In both cases it was concluded that likely traffic would not justify the expenditure involved in building a standard gauge branch line.

In 1895, the narrow gauge link from to the Graulhet to the main line was opened. Partly reassured by the success of the project, partly in a spirit of rivalry, local people determined to build a line of their own. At that time, there was serious prospecting for coal around Montdragon, Laboutarié, Réalmont and as far north as Lombers; concessions were on the verge of being granted. We know now that, far from developing into a new Carmaux-type industrial complex, this interest died away, but it might have concentrated minds at the time.

In 1898, backed by his Municipal Council, the Mayor of Réalmont forwarded a proposal for an electric-powered branch line to the town. Unfortunately, we do not have more details about this fascinating idea. The backers of the project were Auguste Benoît, a local landlord and Paul Viguier, a merchant. Once these gentlemen had done their sums, they decided against electric traction in favour of horse power. A 60 cm gauge railway was, like its rival, to leave Laboutarié station, join the GC 86 (now the D631), but follow it westwards for roughly four kilometres then join the N112 running into Réalmont.

1ᶠ10

Nombre de places assises : 32

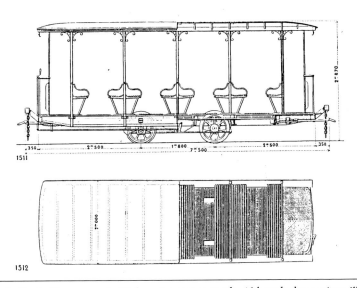

Carriage similar to Tramways de Réalmont summer coach. Although the carriage illustrated was designed for metre gauge, and has four passenger compartments rather than three, thus offering seating for 32 rather than 24, this gives an overall picture of the TR version. The axles are set close together, to ensure that the rigid wheelbase was as short as possible. The design of the chassis with wheel tops projecting into the passenger compartment, the rudimentary seating and the canopy are similar as is the brake lever. At 2 m including running board, the overall width of the vehicle, at 1.75 m was similar though the track gauge was different. There were a number of important differences. The Réalmont coach, at about 5.7 m was considerably shorter than the one here. The chassis frames were straight, not cut away at the end. There were two small lamp holders at each end above the platforms. The most obvious difference was in the curtains of striped canvas which screened each passenger compartment on the TR coach. Thin metal supports running up the back of each seat were reinforced with retaining strips to hold the curtains. The canopy supported a scalloped valance in matching striped material.

Jim Hawkesworth

Horse drawn. The quality of this illustration is not good, but it is included because of its interest. In this side view of the larger of the all-weather coaches, the windows are all open. In theory, there was room for 16 seated and 14 standing. If the carriage had been filled to capacity, it would be very crowded! *Archives Départementales de Tarn*

As the N112 was a *Route Nationale*, the *Département* had to seek the concession from Paris, and then were free to award it to whoever they thought fit. There was not much suspense, however. Anxious not to ruffle local feathers, the *Conseil Général* at Albi agreed in 1899 to award the concession to Benoît and Viguier. Benoît bought a house to be converted into the *Gare-Dépôt* at Réalmont, late in 1900. Viguier retired, leaving Benoît as his agent and so on 6th July, 1901, a Convention of Retrocession was signed by the Prefect and Benoît. The concessionaire would undertake all the construction at his own expense, but would not be charged for using the highway. In plain English, the project was approved.

A *Cahier des Charges* had been approved that June. It specified the details of the concession, the route, the 60 centimetre track, the dimensions of the rolling stock (width to be limited to 2 metres, height to 2.6 metres) the minimum permissible radius of a curve and the maximum gradient. It contrasted with what had been initially allowed to the frugal M. Bonnet of the TVT. The general limits of 100 metres radius and gradient of 3 per cent were to be waived at the stations, especially at the entrance to Laboutarié where a curve of 13 metres radius was encountered. The rails were to be steel, 15 kilograms in weight per metre, laid on sleepers of creosoted pine. There were to be two garages (or small depots). Trains could not consist of more than two carriages, nor be more than 25 metres in length. The speed of this horse-drawn enterprise was not to exceed 16 kilometres per hour! Traction was to be provided by six horses. The *matériel remorque*[114] was to include carriages with a total capacity of 60, and freight wagons which could carry up to 20 tonnes. The guidelines for tariffs and fares followed standard rules.

M. Benoît formally agreed to the specifications and undertook to run the line at his own risk, without subsidy and also agreed to contribute to a repairs fund up to a maximum of 2,000 francs. Two days later, the Department formally approved his application and the *Cahier des Charges*. A Council resolution, *décret*, of 8th July, 1901 officially pronounced the line to be of *utilité publique*. Construction was completed in three months and the line was opened late in 1901. The staff consisted of M. Benoît, one ostler, two drivers and two part-time labourers.

In December 1902, the Compagnie du Tramway de Réalmont à Laboutarié was formed, taking over the concession, with M. Benoît as Director. He had contributed three-quarters of the capital of the new company, total 72,500 francs, the rest coming from 13 other shareholders. M. Taussac, formerly a policeman, was employed as an adminstrator and station master. There was also an ostler, two drivers and labourers hired as the occasion demanded. One assumes that the job descriptions were to satisfy the French love of titles. In fact, everyone had to pitch in and contribute to whatever task was on hand.

Blowing his horn. The larger all-weather coach is seen here. The horses are looking up Réalmont High Street, ready to set off.   *J. Daffis/ACOVA*

At the depot the other side of the same vehicle and passengers pose outside the Réalmont depot/station which is to the right of the photograph. There are puddles on the road, and a good display of period costume.   *J. Daffis/ACOVA*

Passenger services were set at seven round trips daily. This was probably a maximum; the main reason for the journey to Laboutarié station would be to catch a main line train, so the tramway timetable was set accordingly. In 1902, the first complete year of operation, 36,237 passengers were carried and 1,163 tonnes of freight. Freight trains were fitted in between scheduled services. There were also several tonnes of express deliveries.

M. Benoît was vigorous in registering protests, the main ones being against rival carriers; in his opinion, the Midi, which ran the main line railway at Laboutarié was far too liberal in recognising them. There were arguments too with the TVT about the short stretch of public road that they shared and the possible damage that the relatively heavy steam locomotives might do to his track. At Réalmont, the municipal authorities complained in turn about the passengers and freight waiting in the high street. A number of hotels in the town made representation because travellers were using the bar-restaurant of the Hôtel Combelles (next to the depot) in preference to theirs. But on the whole, the tiny operation was a success, returning a profit at least until 1911. By now the workforce included a Director, Administrator, guard, two drivers as ever, a mechanic and a supervisor. The post of ostler had been dropped; obviously, the duty of caring for the horses was shared out among the others.

On the death of M. Benoît in 1910, the other shareholders elected his widow, Pauline née Carayon, as the new Director. Under the Code Napoléon, she would have inherited her husband's majority shareholding. Although France at the time was considered a patriarchal society, her authority was never challenged.[115] One historian unchivalrously points out that Mme Benoît had M. Taussac to help her; but as M. Taussac had been working in that capacity for years, it can fairly be said that Madame Benoît took on no less responsibility than her husband. The year after she took over, the period of the full flowering of secondary lines, the railway was at its best. 38,613 passengers were carried, 3,794 tonnes of goods and 216 tonnes *à grande vitesse*. *À grande vitesse*, literally at great speed, was the express service. Most goods were carried *à petite vitesse*, the standard service.

At the beginning of World War I, all traffic stopped, to begin again on a limited basis in 1916. By the end of the war, rolling stock and permanent way were very run down. In 1917, the Prefect in Albi agreed to a rise in fares and freight charges, but required repairs to the trackbed in return. These were not carried out. The time taken to cover the five kilometres to Laboutarié reached three-quarters of an hour, the original seven return services daily had been reduced to four and the morale of the staff slumped. M. Felix Gisclard the local Chemist, who had taken over as Administrator on the death of M. Taussac, used to come out and personally collect tickets from travellers. As we shall see, he was soon to be heavily financially committed.

In 1920, after much prompting, track repairs were started. Because the horses walked between the rails, the surface was so eroded that it constituted a hazard, but the vital work was not executed with much urgency. In the same year, the line was reclassified as an urban tramway. This must have caused some amusement especially as the language of the *cahier* became more florid. In practical terms, the railway became eligible for subsidy, which it soon requested. In 1923, some investment in rolling stock was carried out and the depot at Réalmont refurbished. There were five departures daily in each direction and journey times were reduced to the former half-hour. The cost of a single ticket was 60 centimes.[116] In three successive years, starting in 1926, tariff rises were authorised and substantial further investment in track and rolling stock was started. In 1926, the single fare was raised to 1.44 francs, to be increased in 1927 and 1928. This was an era of high inflation, but it can safely be assumed that as charges rose, so traffic was attracted away to road hauliers. The four daily services in each direction were cut to three. All orders that the company had submitted for new stock were in 1927 frozen, pending reorganisation and the number of staff, including the Director, reduced to four.

Then the fortunes of the company seemed about to turn. High hopes were pinned on the locotractor which was to replace the horses. 40,200 francs were spent on the new engine, 38,000 on track improvement . Of this, just over 12,000 francs went on heavier grade rail, 3,350 on new turntables and just under 12,000 on surveys, labour, and repairs to the existing track. M. Gisclard paid 45,000 francs out of his own pocket. In 1929, a subsidy was requested from the Department, and one was granted, amounting to 4,380 francs per year, to be reviewed in 1934.

The last gamble failed. This small, late attempt to automate, possibly partly inspired by the purchase of a railcar in 1925 by the TVT, created new problems. By 1929, after less than two years of service, the locotractor was off the road and passengers were ferried to the mainline in a Peugeot charabanc with 15 seats. Freight was horse-drawn once more. The locotractor came back into service on New Year's Day 1930 but broke down again on 15th March to end its days in a corner of the depot at Réalmont. Its place was taken first of all by a rented lorry but on April Fool's Day, the tractor was permanently replaced by a Ford bus, offering 12 seats. Freight transport went back to the horses. The bus was destroyed by fire in November that year, to be replaced by a second-hand Unic. It was noted that the Unic was 'comfortable'. One has to assume that the Ford was not.

Passenger transport was now committed to the road. Freight traffic also continued to fall. In March 1932, driven by mounting losses, M. Gisclard asked the Department to buy back the Tramway. The response of the Authorities was to stop the subsidy and offer the running of the Tramway to the TVT. Mr Gisclard was to recoup his investment in the company by selling the stock.

The TVT nominated STED buses of Toulouse to run the service which they did from 1st July to 31st December of that year. In that time they had manged to make a loss of 20,000 francs. The Department had to pay, but confided the service to another contractor at a fixed subsidy.[117] The Tramway was declared *déclassé*, officially closed, on 19th May, 1933. This came into effect on 12th March, 1934. The sale of all the stock, second-hand rails and the depot at Réalmont brought in 40,000 francs. M. Gisclard was returned most of his money in November 1935. As before mentioned, he had put more than 45,000 francs of his own into the enterprise, about the cost of the entire refurbishments.

The horses were sold and probably finished their working lives on neighbouring farms. There is no further mention of Madame Benoît, the Director and major shareholder, but Germain Olivet remembers her vaguely. In 1930, she would have been 85 years old.

Description of the line and Proposed Extension

The line started, as we have seen, at the main line station of Laboutarié on the western side of the standard gauge line. At this end of the line, there was no depot or building of any sort which belonged to the Tramway; passengers had to use Midi facilities or wait in the rain. A spur took passengers to the *Bâtiment des Voyageurs* of the Midi while another spur running north parallel to a spur from the TVT brought wagons to the freight transhipment platform and shed. A turnout took wagons on to the TVT siding, to make loading possible.To the east, a short spur led to a turnout linking the railway to another TVT siding. M. Benoît insisted that sidings of their own were unnecessary because the wagons were horse drawn; horses could simply be unhitched and led round to the front of the train. Two turntables were bought at the same time as the locotractor for use at either terminus but there is no evidence as to where exactly they were installed, if they ever were.

These spurs united and crossed a spur of the TVT to travel down the western side of the GC41 (now D41) passing within a few feet of M. Bonnet's house. The line then crossed and recrossed the line of the TVT, before making a sharp left turn and climbing a gradient in excess of 4 per cent to join the GC86 (D631) 300 metres from the station.

Before leaving the station, it is worth commenting on how little the two small railways had to do with each other. What little tracksharing there was seems to have been accompanied by persistent bickering. Moreover, Réalmont track was crossed in two places by the TVT, by its most easterly siding at the station entrance, and the passenger spur by the transhipment siding. Never mind that he probably made use of both of these, M. Benoît complained that the heavier stock of his rival would distort his rails and proposed to the Board of Control provision of a *sauterelle*[118] a form of drop crossover whereby the large machines of the TVT could cross on top of his line. Such a device was common on industrial narrow gauge railways but there is no evidence that this was ever in fact installed. Perhaps M. Benoît felt that verbal victory was enough.

It is a pity that the two railways could not have shared a spur up to the transhipment shed; the number of wagons involved in the Réalmont operation were always few because their system involved small and frequent trains. The employees of the Midi had to lift freight bound for Réalmont over intervening TVT trackage to the Réalmont siding; perhaps commonsense prevailed when the Directors were safely shut in their respective offices. It is also surprising that the two could not have shared a track up the D41, but technical difficulties, and the lack of signalling, also supervened. Freight and passengers were never encouraged to make the through journey from Graulhet to Réalmont, although that clearly would have been possible. By supporting each other the two networks might have survived longer.

The Tramway took the D631 (then the GC86) road eastwards, staying on the northern verge all the way. As the road was at least 7 metres wide, no objections were raised about the presence of a 60 cm gauge railway line. No bridges or culverts were widened. As the road was reasonably straight, the guidelines of the *Cahier* as regards gradients or bends could generally be met. Where requirements were infringed, the railway simply asked for dispensation rather

Waiting outside the depot. This is the only clear view of the depot/station which shows the larger of the all-weather coaches waiting outside the depot door. A siding ran down the street parallel to the depot wall. A turnout leads straight into the building and a short siding sufficient to take one coach. Two further sidings carry on the length of the building to accommodate other rolling stock. The horses have already been unhitched and led to their stables at the far end of the building. We apologise for the quality of this print. *J. Daffis/ACOVA*

Réalmont High Street looking south. *Louis Briand/Cart Club Tarnais*

than performing any actual engineering. The *Département* had specified *garages* along the way, that is, dumps for materials for remetalling the road, but these were never built, nor was the planned siding at La Réginié, although there was one further east at Ramières.

Road and railway followed the River Dadou upstream. Just over a kilometre from the main line, there is a junction with a country road going north to the hamlet of La Réginié. This was the site of the first *halte garage*. Nothing was ever constructed. The train simply stopped, and passengers would mount or dismount as necessary. If the horses needed watering, the driver would unhitch them and follow the people up the lane to the village.

Less than a kilometre from the halt, road and tramway crossed a stream and move away from the river. The second *halte garage*, Ramières, is sited just before the junction with a lane from the south. A spur led off the road so that the horses could be rested. Half a kilometre further on, the N 631 merges with the N112 from Castres, the railway kept to the northern side. The road climbs; the tramway gradient exceeded 3 per cent for 300 metres.

The tramway kept, as ever, to the north side of the road. Skirting the side of the hill, road and railway came into the town. A few suburban villas have been recently built, but otherwise the town has hardly changed. Development was originally to a gridplan and it is easy to find the junction with the Rue Porche on the High Street to the right, just short of the main square.

The Maison Puech which was bought by M. Benoît to be remodelled as a depot has been, if not demolished, competely altered. In the days of the tramway, the line made a sharp turn to the right as it crossed the High Street up the side street to a turnout. One spur led down the side road to the stables at the back of the depot building. The other led into the house which had been gutted to provide a depot and *remise*.[119] There is no firm evidence as to where the second turntable was situated. A headshunt, if one could use the term, led straight across the depot. The track led to a turnout ending in two parallel sidings for garaging the rolling stock. A door led into the courtyard of the adjacent Hôtel Combelles so that horses could use the drinking trough. There was no waiting room for the passengers, apart from the street and so the Hotel became a popular substitute. As previously mentioned, the other hostelries and *limonadiers* of the town complained and the *maire* moved to have the door bricked up. There is no evidence that this actually happened, and so we hope that horses and humans continued to enjoy refreshment.

After the closure, the site of the depot became a cinema, closed by 1999, though the adjacent building is still recognisably an inn. Authorities state that the complete building was demolished in the 1930s; we thought it more likely that it was given a 'makeover'. The back extension has been completely assimilated, doors have been enlarged, windows removed and the façade was given a noble pediment in keeping with its new function, but we believe that features remain of the original. The approach along the Route de Castres is recognisable, in 1999, with the street and houses in place, as they were in the old postcards.

The distance that a train would have covered between the main line at Laboutarié and the depot at Réalmont was 4.833 kilometres. The total track, including spurs and sidings that the Tramway possessed measured 5.11 kilometres. 277 metres of sidings, etc. is relatively little for a railway network,

Le Tarn — RÉALMONT
Avenue de Castres

Cliché Broumet

Réalmont, early 20th century, looking north and south.   *J. Daffis/ACOVA*

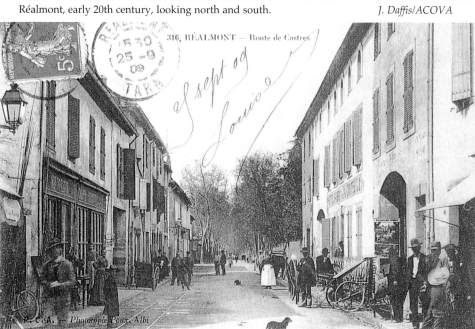

but, as before mentioned, most trains were horse-drawn and so the prime-movers needed no runarounds. They were merely unhitched and walked up to the head of the train. Proposed extensions were another story.

Originally, there were plans to take the tramway up Réalmont High Street, to serve the factories at the north of the town. This would have followed the D112 as it bore to the left, away from the central church, Notre Dame du Taur. At the time, Réalmont was a centre for industries such as flour milling. A quarter of the freight consisted of flour and cereal. At least one tenth was generated by the spinning of yarn, the saw mill and a small tannery. Plans for this extension were shelved in 1904; the Tramway invested instead in *l'araignée* of which more presently.

We might note in passing details of the *sauterelle* proposed by M. Benoît to protect his permanent way from bruising by the rolling stock of the TVT. It was to be a portable climbing turnout, length 0.8 metres, which was to be laid down over the rails of the actual turnout when wagons were to be manoeuvred. It would be bolted to the rails below and over it could pass the wagons of the *TVT*. Mr Bonnet agreed to this demand, and it was duly recorded by *le Contrôle*,[80] but there is no photograph of the device and quite possibly it was never actually used.

Trains and Rolling Stock

After the rejection of electricity, horses were chosen to provide motive power. There were a minimum of six retained by the company. Normally, a team of two would pull a train or, in the case of some heavier goods shipments, four. There is no sign of provision for horses at Laboutarié station. They were expected to make the round trip of 10 kilometres to the stables in Réalmont. Possibly the nearby farm helped out if necessary.

Passengers could only travel second class, or, as the Tramway preferred to put it, *classe unique.* There were three carriages. The 'summer coach' offered seating for 24 in three open compartments, providing two benches for four apiece facing each other. A running board and covered platforms at each end offered standing room for up to 12; in the days before the locotractor, the front platform had to be shared with the driver. Striped curtains with an attractive valance gave passengers, including those standing, some protection from summer rain. Being a comparatively short vehicle, as were they all, bogies were not considered necessary. The carriage was a four-wheeler, with axles mounted under the first and third compartments. As it was designed for horse traction, the brake consisted of a hand brakewheel operating wooden brake shoes.

No records exist for its dimensions but commonsense and photographic evidence suggest that it was built along the lines of the Decauville third class open carriage, as used on the Chemins de Fer de Calvados. This was 8.5 metres long and had five rather than three compartments. Proportionately, this suggests that our carriage was of the order of 5.7 metres long, width 1.75 and overall height probably 2.4 metres - 15 centimetres less than the bogie-mounted CFC coach.[120]

The larger of the two other 'all season' coaches had a theoretical capacity of 16 seated and standing room for another 14. Commonsense, photographic evidence, and the dimensions that were recorded all suggest that the coaches were built along the lines of the ones supplied by Carde to the TVT at around the same time. The seats were arranged as two benches seating eight, facing each other across a central corridor. The seats were of first class standard in that they were padded. The interior dimensions of the passenger compartment, which does not seem to have had side doors, were 1.5 metres wide, 1.85 metres high (at the lowest point, the side) and 3.65 metres long. An outside platform at both ends 90 centimetres long offered standing room and a place for the driver. The front platform had the lever for the hand-operated brake.[121]

The smaller coach was similar except that it was even shorter. The interior passenger compartment was only 2.1 metres long, each bench able to accommodate up to five seated passengers. The external platforms were 73 centimetres long, again with the brake lever operated from one end. Total standing room was for 12. Both carriages were, like the summer carriage, mounted directly on to a pair of axles which made their overall height 2.4 metres, slightly less than their bogie mounted equivalents. Lighting was provided from portable lanterns; ventilation additional to the draught which streamed through the open doorways could be obtained by opening the carriage windows. An average of 100 people travelled on these coaches every day, at least until the 1920s.

The tramway also possessed two *fourgons* which were probably used for express freight delivery; they are seldom mentioned except in official reports. They may have been too cumbersome for general use because they had to be manoevred to the rear of the train at the end of every journey; this being a railway with no passing loops. Small though they were, they weighed a quarter of a tonne with a maximum loading of up to one tonne. Tarpaulin hoods could be erected in bad weather. If they were permitted to be called *fourgons*, we can assume that they had hand-brakes.

There were two wagons with sides 0.9 metres high, overall length 3 metres and two platform wagons, i.e. with 'drop' sides that were 3.5 metres long. Exact figures are not given, but it can be inferred that the weight of each was about 1.7 tonnes and that each could carry up to 5 tonnes of freight. There were four of them in all and the *parc matériel* specified by the *cahier* was 20 tonnes. The wagons appear in Government statistics with the qualification: 6.7t. The abbreviation could mean *tonnes ortare* but it is reasonable to assume that it means maximum total weight in tonnes of loaded wagon in this context. This would give the wagon itself the weight of 1.7 tonnes. They would all have been fitted with the standard hand-operated brake. At its peak, the little railway was transporting about 10 tonnes of freight daily, hauled by teams of two to four horses.

One tramway vehicle for road use offered an interesting solution to the transhipment problem. Known as *l'araignée*, the spider, it was a flat wagon supporting a length of track on stubby wheels, with a drawbar at the front. At the depot, a wagon could be loaded on, up a ramp. Horses would then draw the wagon to its destination, usually a factory or processing works at the northern side of town. This device saved the Tramway from having to unload or store much freight. Space was at a premium within the depot and so, as mentioned before, the freight often ended up in a pile on the narrow High Street.

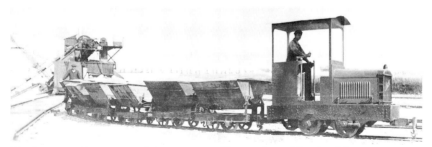

The locotractor is seen at work in a quarry, pulling a substantial train of tipper wagons on an industrial railway. The challenges would have been different to those faced at Réalmont. *Fondation Berliet*

The last big purchase of the Tramway was the locotractor purchased in 1927 from Automobiles Berliet in Lyon, the same supplier which had in 1925 charged the TVT over 100,000 francs for a railcar. The locotractor was, at 40,200 francs including delivery, a more modest purchase but was planned to achieve the same ends, efficiency and cost saving. It was designed for work in a quarry or agricultural use rather than as the prime mover of a tramway, which may explain why it gave satisfactory service for only a very limited period. Possibly, in spite of the good intentions behind the purchase of the turntables, they too were never installed, and with the lack of turning facilities, the chain drive required more maintenance than it received. When it broke down the second and final time, M. Gisclard had it checked by a professional and threatened Berliet with legal action, but there is no record that the manufacturers ever had to pay a sou.

The locotractor had a four-cylinder petrol motor with a disc clutch. It had a three-speed gearbox good for either forward or reverse. Power was transmitted to the front axle by a chain drive. Front and rear axles ran on ball bearings and the wheels were steel. The tractor could in theory pull 20 tonnes up the steepest gradient of the railway at 7.5 kilometres per hour, and develop a top speed of 14.

At the time of closure, the Tramway had some other property. A third platform wagon had joined the others, along with spares, a skid, a jack, hand cart and various tools. All these were sold off along with the depot to repay M. Gisclard who had invested substantially in the concern. The three platform wagons and some other stock were sold to the TVT for 9,000 francs, but as this too was on the verge of closing, they rusted away at Laboutarié station.

Souvenirs and railway documentation passed from Pauline Benoît to her sister's grandson, Michel Smeyers, and he donated these to the Archives Départementales at Albi. The railway, never independent of the road, has disappeared, the *Dépôt* has long since been sold and even the Hôtel Combelles has gone.

In conclusion, the reader might like to compare what the three railways carried. For the TVT and the Tramway de Réalmont, the figures are for 1911, the heyday of secondary railway systems. For the CFTT, they refer to 2000.

The manufacturer's photograph. The Réalmont locotractor poses for its maker. The overall impression is of simplicity. *Fondation Berliet*

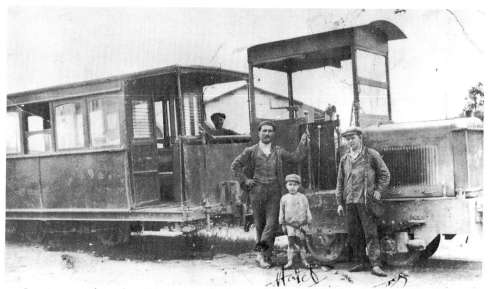

Locotractor with coach. In this photograph, the locotractor is pulling the larger of the all-weather coaches. *J. Daffis/ACOVA*

In the High Street, the new locotractor, and friends, pose proudly. The Réalmont depot is ahead. As well as providing a good view of the Berliet locotractor, the *fourgon* with tarpaulin hood can be seen to the left. We apolgise for the quality of the original of this valuable record.

J. Daffis/ACOVA

Network	TVT	Tr de R	CFTT
Length of network in kilometres	46.2	4.8	3.5

Nature of traffic			
Passengers	138,441	38,613	22,000
Raw materials, finished goods (in tonnes)	10,629	430	-
Coal	5,905	400	(1)
Oil and lubricants	4,060	510	(1)
Miscellaneous	2,685	142	some
Grain and flour (principal freight at Réalmont)	2,353	833	-
Construction materials	1,977	310	(1)
Wine and other alcohol	647	(2)	-
Foodstuffs	514	419	(3)
Iron and steel	312	350	(1)
Total in tonnes	29,082	3,794	(1)

Notes
(1) The CFTT carries virtually all its ballast, rail and fuel on the line but figures are not available.
(2) Small volume, included in 'miscellaneous'.
(3) Trains can be hired for celebrations. It is a well-respected French tradition that food and drink be carried on such trips!

View of a similar Berliet locotractor at work in a quarry. Here, its qualities of power and manoeuvrability would have come into their own.   *Fondation Berliet*

List of Appended Notes

Note 1. The Syndicat d'Initiative is the organisation which exists for every French town in order to promote local industry and tourism. It is usually housed in a public building such as the Town Hall. In the case of Graulhet, it is in the now redundant Public Shower Baths.
Note 2. The land-locked *département* of Tarn produced France's most celebrated sea-farer. Jean-François Galaup de La Pérouse was born at Albi in 1741 and died under mysterious circumstances on Vanikoro in the Pacific in 1788. Louis XVI wanted a national hero who could rival the exploits of Britain's Captain Cook. Lapérouse was the first European to send back reports of areas within southern America and Asia. Graulhet was considered home by two career Admirals. Taffanel de la Jonquière (1685-1752) was baptised at the local church of Notre Dame des Vignes. At the height of his career, he was the Governor-General of Canada, then an important and growing French colony. Admiral Jaurès (1823-89) has a tomb in the same church. He emerged creditably from the war with Prussia in 1870-1 and followed his military career with one in politics.
Note 3. Langue d'Oc was the language spoken in an area which extended from the Atlantic to the Mediterranean. The origin of the name is supposed to lie in the word 'yes' This was *oc* as opposed to *oil* which became the modern French *oui*. The language and literature of the Languedoc flourished up until the 13th century and was particularly noted for poetry and music. The language is more akin to Latin and Spanish than is modern French. To take one example, the word for water is *aiga*, which is nearer to the Latin *aqua* than the modern French word *eau*. The name Graulhet, which is pronounced something like 'Grow-yey' would be spelt according to conventional French as Grauillet. The language declined as the prestige of northern France grew. It survived as the local patois and a number of educated people continued to favour it. In the 16th century, for example, we hear of the Compte d'Aubijoux as patron to troubadours, Occitanian poet/musicians. In the 19th century, helped perhaps by travel and growing interest from abroad, the *Langue d'Oc* enjoyed a revival.

The name of Languedoc also exists in a geographical sense. It was given to the region administered by the Counts of Toulouse. By the 12th century, the area had shrunk but still constituted a powerful independent state. Although Languedoc was to be absorbed by force into the growing kingdom of France (*see note 7*), the name survived during the years of the French monarchy. It disappeared just after the Revolution when France was reclassified into *départements*. Haute Garonne, Tarn, Ariège, Aude and Hérault were all more-or-less within the ancient boundaries, as were parts of Aveyron, Lozère and Gard. The name was revived in the 1982 when the Mitterrand administration created *régions*, an administrative grouping of *départements* but, whether by accident or design, much of ancient Languedoc including Tarn and Toulouse, the traditional capital of the Languedoc, is in the Midi-Pyrénées region. The new Languedoc-Roussillon extends up to the Massif Central and incorporates the home of the French Basques.
Note 4. Gallia was originally a disparaging Latin term meaning 'land of strangers'. The Gauls, i.e. strangers, were the inhabitants. To the ancient Romans, civilisation was confined to central and southern Italy and to a few favoured areas such as Greece. Gaul was more or less everything else, including northern Italy. By the 1st century BC, as the area of Roman domination extended, Gaul was the territory bordered by the Atlantic, the Pyrenees, the Alps and the Rhine. Julius Caesar earned his place in history by conquering it. France was thus, in part, defined by foreigners.
Note 5. St Sernin (Saturninus to his contemporaries) lived in Toulouse in the 3rd century AD. He enraged pagan priests by building a little church beside their temple. In 250 AD he was tied to a bull at the top of the temple steps and his head was smashed as the animal was driven away. He has a fine tomb in Toulouse cathedral, resting on bulls of bronze. A distinguished successor to St Sernin, as Bishop of Toulouse, was St Hilaire (315 to 350 AD), St Projet was an early Bishop of Montpellier.
Note 6. *Comté* was literally the territory of the *comes* which is a Latin term from which the French *comte* and the English 'count' are derived. Although a *comes* was originally a

lifetime appointment, the office became hereditary. The *Comtes* of Toulouse, many called Raymond, were all related.

Note 7. Catharism, also known as the Albigensian heresy was a creed which came to southern France by the 12th century. Adherents could also be called Manichees after Mani who was born in Persia in the 3rd century. He was influenced by the ancient religions of Persia, Babylon and by the new religion of Christianity. Unlike Christians who believe that the universe is controlled by a supreme Creator God, the Manichees believe that God and the forces of good are opposed by independent and antagonistic powers of evil and chaos. Manichees survived in Turkestan until the 13th century and in Bosnia until the Islamic conquests of the 16th century.

Catharism was not a formal church but it had its spiritual leaders known as *parfaits*, the perfect ones, men and women who led ascetic lives, eschewing all pleasure which they believed was evil. Lay believers admired the *parfaits* and no doubt prayed with St Augustine (once himself a Manichee) to be themselves given purity from all vices . . . but not just yet! They did not acknowledge Roman Catholic authority and in 1208, Pope Innocent III ordered a crusade against them. The Capetian dynasty in the Ile-de-France used the crusade as a pretext to invade their neighbours. The entire Languedoc rallied to the defence of the Cathars; some of the local nobilty were active Cathars.

The campaign was ferocious. In 1229, Languedoc was formally annexed to France and was split into the provinces of Languedoc, Haut (Upper) Languedoc which included Tarn, and and a part of Guienne. In the remote eastern Pyrenees, the citadel of Montségur held out until 1244 when 200 *parfaits* were martyred. Quéribus held out until 1255.

Cathar ideals and tolerance coexisting with a dash of humour has a strong appeal. A century later, an Inquisition was held to try to suppress vestiges of the beliefs. Then, as France became the strongest nation in Europe, national pride played its part and Catharism seemed to be gone, apart from customs and folk memory. From the 19th century onwards, as certainties and the worship of Progress in turn failed, many Occitans looked back to the civilisation of the 13th century. A neo-Cathar church was founded in the 1890s in Carcassonne to the west of Tarn. At the same time, determined efforts were made to revive the language. Today, the heritage industry has seized on the name almost as a slogan to attract tourists. Stories, such as a link between Montségur and the Holy Grail are played for all their worth, and the pageants and songs of the troubadours of old have been revived.

Note 8. A *bastide* is a pragmatic combination of stronghold and market town. Most were created in the 13th century under the patronage of the local landowner or even royalty. The site of the new town would be chosen carefully for its natural advantages and would be centred on the market place (often under cover). As new towns, many *bastides* were set out on a gridplan. Even today, a rectilinear town-plan at the centre of a village suggests its origins. The privileges used to attract inhabitants were all set out in the *bastide's Charte de Fondation* which was a legal document. The settlement can therefore date its origins with certainty.

Note 9. Excavations show that pottery was made near Lavaur. Busque, to the north of Graulhet was also the site of a number of Gallo-Roman potters.

Note 10. A *confrérie* was originally a religious brotherhood. It came to mean a craft union or guild. Nowadays, many associations of enthusiasts use the term, because in France *Association* and *Société* carry strict legal definitions. The Confrérie des Potiers produced everyday and specialist or luxury items such as dinner services and apothecary jars. Collectors still look out for Giroussens ware with pale orange and sea-green designs in light relief.

Note 11. In 1356, the English won the battle of Poitiers, but between 1369 and 1377, the French under Bertrand du Guesclin regained most lost territory. In 1415 the English under Henry V won the battle of Agincourt and briefly enjoyed control of the French court, but between 1429 and 1453, they once again lost their territory. Joan of Arc, burned at the stake in 1431, had a brief but dramatic influence on the campaign. The war can be described as having lasted 100 years, but there was a significant period of truce in the middle.

Note 12. Two local poets lived there in the 1650s. They called themselves troubadours, a description usually reserved for poet/musicians of earlier times. A connection which has not been proved is with Jean-Baptiste Poquelin 1622-1673, the famous playwright who took the name Molière, i.e. the feminist. In their time, his plays were controversial, and he was glad of the protection of liberal patrons such as François Jacques d'Aubijoux. He certainly stayed with him at Albi in 1647, and *Graulhétois* like to believe that he came also to his patron's home town.

Note 13. Henry IV (1589-1610) was succeded by Louis XIII, a comparatively weak king, who allowed too much power to provincial noblemen. He died in 1643 leaving the country in the hands of regents who governed the country (again, attending too much to the interests of powerful factions) in the name of the infant Louis XIV. It was not until Louis attained manhood that the period of strong centralised government associated with the 'Sun King' began.

Note 14. The area of French influence in North America was once vast. While the Spanish searched for gold further south, and the British clung to the eastern seaboard, the French went inland, colonising Quebec and almost the entire Mississippi basin belonged to them in theory.

Note 15. The *commune* literally means 'within the same walls' but in fact it applied not only to the village but also to the area around, rather like a British parish. The *commune* is administered by an elected *conseil d'administration* headed by the *maire*, literally the major citizen. The *mairie*, roughly the equivalent of a town hall in Britain, was the *maire's* office, one for every commune. In Graulhet, this used to be in a small square north of the high street. It is now in a larger building to the south. A town such as Graulhet would be the administrative centre of a *canton*, a group of communes. Larger towns and cities are divided into *arrondissements*.

In 1820 there were 44,000 *communes*. As the population has gradually shifted towards the cities, there has been a decline in the number of viable ones. For example, Le Bruc is now part of Montdragon.

Note 16. The *département*, derived from the French word to separate, was to be the new logical unit of government, replacing the old system of provinces, based as they were on local history and rivalry. French Basques, for example, were to be distributed among three *départements*, the Occitans among eight or so. Thus Graulhet found itself in the *département* of Tarn while Toulouse was in Haute Garonne. In each departmental capital was the *Conseil Général*, elected by the citizens of Tarn and also a *Préfet*, directly answerable to Napoleon in Paris. The boundaries of each *département* were drawn up in such a way that the Prefect on horseback could reach any part of it within a day. In this way, the head of state was in theory 'only one handshake' away from any other French citizen. As boundaries were drawn up based on geographical and political considerations, departments vary greatly in wealth and population, so often had to be subdivided. Tarn has a *sous-préféture* at Castres.

Note 17. The *Grandes Écoles* were to bring high quality training to the selection and education of the senior administrators of the new France. The École Polytechnique in Paris for engineers, the École Nationale d'Administration, and the École de Ponts et Chaussées for civil engineering were among these as was the École de St Cyr for the military. There were political motives. The new technocrats with direct allegiance to central government were totally independent of the old, provincial universities such as the University of Toulouse, a seat of excellence for centuries. These universities, then and now, help to keep alive regional affiliations.

Note 18. Before 1816, coalmines such as the ones around St Étienne to the east of the Massif Central used stationary steam engines. Any railway was short and worked by people and horses. The efforts of Trevithick and the Stephenson family were duly noted and steam transport was planned. The first public railway using mobile engines was proposed in 1821 to link the coal mines with the River Loire, then an important artery for goods traffic. The 17 kilometre line was open for freight in 1827 but the first passenger service did not begin until 1832. A number of changes were made to the cumbersome laws so that future proposals could proceed more quickly.

Note 19. La Loi Legrand was important in two respects. By 1837, a railway system for France was planned by the engineer Legrand as a strategic whole, much superior in his opinion to the piecemeal system growing up in Britain and the USA. Every part of France would be linked to the network, following the route which offered the straightest and most logical course, rather than being deviated in response to local interests. The railways would converge on Paris, giving the planned map the appearance of a star, with Paris at the centre.

The second part of the Railway Law had to do with implementation. The cost would be enormous, one thousand million francs, and the Government did not wish to raise it all through direct taxes. By 1842, it was arranged that Central Government would deal with the compulsory purchase of the necessary land and arrange for major engineering works to be put in hand. Local Government was obliged to pay two-thirds of these costs. The routes would be divided up into concessions which would then be awarded to private companies. These companies would pay for laying the track, purchase of locomotives and rolling stock and for any necessary buildings.

Private capital would be invited to build and stock the concession and recoup its investment once the line was running. The idea was not new, neither was it always successful. The technique of 'farming' out state projects had existed before the Revolution. The individual or company which was awarded the concession was known as the concessionnaire.

Note 20. Les Chemins de Fer Paris Lyon Méditerranée (PLM) linked Paris with the southeast of France. It included the St Étienne line in its network. The Compagnie du Midi (Midi) ran the southern sector and the Paris Orléans (PO) the south-west. These two had interests in the Languedoc area and were powerful local rivals.

The *Grands Réseaux* were the railway companies running the main lines stipulated by Legrand, and other standard gauge lines allowed for as the century wore on. They consisted of the three companies mentioned above and the Nord, Est, Ouest and État. These served the northern, eastern and western (Brittany) sectors of France with État strong in the mid-west sector. État and Ouest were merged fairly early on. After World War I, the Compagnie d'Alsace was formed when France was ceded Alsace-Lorraine. A few standard gauge lines ran independently of the *grands réseaux*, and the *grands réseaux* in turn could be involved directly or indirectly in the running of minor railways.

Note 21. The *réseaux sécondaires* or secondary lines were basically to complement the *grands réseaux* which could not bring all parts of the extensive land area of France within easy reach of a railway. Unlike the major lines which were supposed to obey strict guidelines laid down by Paris, much greater latitude was allowed to local administration. The *département* or commune could approve the plan, administer the railway for themselves or seek a *concessionnaire*. Subsidies were put on an official footing and the restrictive legislation applying to more profitable lines was streamlined. As narrow gauge was considered more economical, even from this date, most concessions were sought in narrow gauge.

Another boost to light railway construction was the law of 1880. As well as providing a *guaranteed* income to concessionaires, a provision which had to be modified, the class of 'tramway' was recognised. This, like an urban tramway, could be built at the roadside thereby much reducing the cost of construction. Feasibility studies had all suggested that an independent railway line linking Graulhet would be too costly. The tramway clause probably provided the vital impetus for the project.

Note 22. The Decauville Company went through various changes from the time that the Coville family moved from Normandy to the Paris region, adding 'de' to the name on the way. The first factory was built at Petit-Bourg 30 kilometres from Paris in 1853 by Amand Decauville. It was a sugar refinery for beet produced on the family farm. They built their first railway when they opened a quarry. In 1865 a short line taking the stone to to be loaded on river barges cut the price of building stone dramatically and increased profits. In late 1871, Amand died, and his eldest son, Paul took over the firm.

The link with portable railway began in 1875, when it was used with great success to load sugarbeet directly from the fields. In those days before caterpillar tracks were invented, Decauville Aîné as the firm was then known soon became major suppliers to agricultural and constructional concerns. Paul then took the major step of bidding to become a public carrier, by tendering to build the railway serving the Paris Exhibition of 1889. It was there that he met M. Bonnet and the story of the TVT began. *See also Note 71.*

Note 23. The *Cahier des Charges* was literally a book giving details of regulations, which, though less onerous than the ones which applied to main lines, ran all the same to a full volume. The *cahier* set out the rules governing all aspect of operation. The most famous of these were the 'Three Fifteens': a 15 tonne locomotive running on track weighing 15 kilogrammes per metre was subject to a speed limit of 15 kilometres per hour. If an application for a proposed secondary railway was successful, that is, it was agreed that the line was of public utility, a *cahier des charges* was drawn up for the line, with the national rules plus particulars. As the word *charges* suggests, fares and tariffs were also regulated. The *cahier* did allow for certain changes, for example in what the railway could charge. *See also Note 68.*

Note 24. La Societe Internationale des Travaux Publics, and later La Société de Construction des Batignolles, were invited to do the construction work. It was assumed that another organisation, such as the *Département* itself, would organise the finance and oversee running the line. As the names suggest, railway management was outside the remit of both companies. The Chemins de fer Économiques was a company specialising in managing railways, i.e. concessionaires, if the profit or subsidy were sufficiently attractive. This depended on how well operating conditions combined with subsidies. These operated according to formulae laid down by Paris and paid for by the *Département*, and were known as the guaranteed return.

Note 25. The Exposition Universelle of 1889, known as the Paris Exhibition, celebrated the centenary of the storming of the Bastille and the beginning of the French Revolution. The exhibition grounds were in a memorial park called the Champs de Mars beside the river Seine and the Eiffel Tower was constructed especially for the occasion.

Note 26. The Monsieur Bonnet who approached Paul Decauville at the Exhibition was Marius-Dominique Bonnet. He was born on 21st January, 1818 at Lavaur and was to die on 4th December, 1906 at Toulouse. His son was Joseph-Marie Bonnet. He was born in Toulouse on 27th December, 1854 and died in Laboutarié on 28th April, 1941.

A *correspondant*, literally 'one who communicates by letter' had come to be understood to be a representative.

Note 27. The Exhibition Railway demonstrated how even a lightly engineered line could keep to a timetable transporting passengers at reasonable speed. The impressive 3,000 m^2 Decauville pavilion offered company information on freight transport under the most exacting conditions, with an agricultural section. A second display area showed construction railways. A third explained how narrow gauge could transport passengers in unrivalled comfort with information on the Festiniog Railway, the Darjeeling, and lines in Tunisia and Ethiopia. The fourth showed military transport. Owing much to work done by Prosper Péchot of the French Artillery, the latter showed how apparently fragile track laid on the lightest of foundations could support incredible loads with the right equipment. To make the point, a 48 tonne field gun was on show, mounted on a four-bogie wagon, each bogie running on eight wheels. Modern roads, prepared at great expense with the most up-to-date equipment have difficulty coping with lorries of this weight.

Note 28. La Société des Mines de Dadou had to guarantee traffic of 10,000 tonnes of ore annually before they would be offered a connection. As the leather trade from Graulhet was of the order of 3,000-4,000 tonnes, this requirement may well have seemed unreasonable. *Note 29.* The D63 from Montredon to Réalmont, now a departmental road, was at one time a *route nationale.* The GC 86 through Graulhet and Briatexte in time was to become the N631, also a *route nationale.* It is now a departmental road the D631. The D87 to Gaillac was originally called the GC87. The PO asked their commercial agent in Gaillac for a reference. He recommended turning down the proposals, less on engineering or commercial grounds, than because M. Maire was associated with a number of bankruptcies.
Note 30. The Chambre Syndicale des Patrons Mégissiers de Graulhet was the association of the owners of the leatherworks. This still exists at La Rigaudié, 1 Rue Cardinal Roques. The Syndicat des Ouvriers was the equivalent organisation for employees.
Note 31. When the line was 13 kilometres long, four trains each way every day was not too taxing a schedule. When the Lavaur extension opened, the four-times-daily service continued although distances were longer. By the eve of World War I services were running down a little but there were still three daily services in each direction, and two on the Lavaur line. After the war, services were gradually restored but never to a pre-war level. Three daily trains each way were promised when the St Sulpice extension was opened, but this was soon reduced to two. After 1930, trains were gradually replaced by buses.
Note 32. Though more than one abbreviation was used, the railway is normally referred to as TVT in this book. The Head Office, *siège social,* of the firm moved three times. At first it was a small office in Laboutarié, close to M. Bonnet's house. With his successor came the move to Toulouse. At first it was in the Allées de Brienne, then the rue Sainte Marthe, finally the rue Raymond IV. The manager's office, once the same as the *siège social,* was transferred to Graulhet station when the latter moved to Toulouse.
Note 33. In 1892, a group of shareholders demanded that Paul Decauville and his brothers appear before the Tribunal du Commerce de la Seine. The Tribunal appointed a liquidator. The Bank of France suspended credit, and in consequence the Government Ministries cancelled their orders. By September 1893, receipts had plummeted. Shareholders, chief among them Woldemar Ramirez, succeeded in winding up the Éts Decauville Aîné and replacing them with the Société Nouvelle des Éts Decauville Aîné. Woldemar Ramirez engineered for himself the post of liquidator of the old company. All members of the family were expelled from the new Board. Paul Decauville stayed on as *maire* of Evry-Petit Bourg until 1900 and then left for Paris. He flirted with 'lighter than air dirigibles' before realising that the future belonged to the aeroplane. He founded a new company called Établissements Paul Decauville at Neuilly, a smart quarter of Paris, which made compressed air tools. He died in 1922. *See also Note 71.*
Note 34. In 1926, the franc was devalued dramatically. The exchange rate which had been 19.3 cents to the franc was reduced to 4 cents. Within France, the effect was high inflation. From 1926, price rises were regularly authorised on both the TVT and the Tramway de Réalmont, but though receipts rose, prices rose even faster. The devaluation was supposed to make French exports more competitive. For a time, it seemed to help firms such as Decauville. Between 1926 and 1930, profits picked up, though an element of the rise was just inflation. Profits collapsed in the four years to 1934, reflecting difficult conditions throughout the world, but climbed once more during the years leading up to World War II as Europe rearmed. There was no revival for the TVT and many other secondary railways.
Note 35. Between 1954 and 1961, there was enormous activity throughout France as the US Marshall Plan backed government-sponsored expenditure. Civic projects such as the new sports ground, *stade,* and *habitations à loyer moderé,* blocks of flats for low rent, which can also be seen in the photograph, blossomed in Graulhet and most other French towns.

Note 36. The bridge, built in the late 19th century, was called the Pont Neuf to distinguish it from the Vieux Pont which dated back to the 13th century. The Pont Neuf is also known as the Pont St Jean because it leads to the suburb of that name. Both cross the Dadou within a few yards of each other.

Note 37. Jean Jaurès, not to be confused with Admiral Jaurès, was a politician and man of letters. Born in Castres in 1859, he was firstly Professor of Philosophy at Albi Grammar School, then elected Député to the Assemblée Nationale, the French Parliament, at the age of 26. A confirmed socialist, he was assassinated a few hours after the outbreak of World War I.

Note 38. According to the amended Railways Act of July 1880, the guaranteed return on a project was worked out according to Central Government formulae. If a concessionaire provided the capital to build, equip and run a railway, the State and *Département* guaranteed a fixed rate of interest on the investment, an annual subsidy, and topped up this subsidy if the receipts were lower than an agreed figure. In return, Central and local government received a share of the receipts. There was scope for abuses, and modifications were made to the law but the basic provisions remained. The important step was to achieve classification as a *ligne d'intérêt local*, either as a railway or as a tramway. *See also Note 24.*

Note 39. Equal to the cynicism and weariness of the nation was a mood of optimism now that the war was over. The general feeling was that if the goods and services were provided, customers would then come forward to justify the investment. This third extension of the line was in its own way a leap of faith, providing the service first and then expecting feepaying traffic to be thereby generated.

Note 40. Fraisse Frères of Albi appears in another history as Fraise & Frères. They ran one of 12 industrial railways of Tarn which used mechanical traction. The Industrial Railway Society can supply more details.

Note 41. The Tramways of Ardèche were a metre gauge system which was centred on Aubenas, a town in the valley of a tributary of the Rhone. Constructed in 1910 by the Société des Tramways de l'Ardèche (TA) some sections closed four years later. The TA folded up in 1922. Part of the system struggled on until 1929, under new management.

Note 42. La Société Anonyme des Transports Économiques Départementaux operated from Toulouse, and so the *Département* referred to in its title was in fact Haute Garonne, adjoining Tarn. The name suggests that it was a semi-official bus company, operating with the express blessing of the Toulouse Town Hall. The next company with which the TVT allied itself would have been a small local concern.

Note 43. At that period, logging enterprises were expanding in the French African colonies of Gabon and Congo. A few of the locomotives and rolling stock were purchased and sent there where it is conceivable that something may survive.

Note 44. *Collège d'Enseignement Général* is a secondary school, roughly equivalent to the post-war British secondary modern. The equivalent of a grammar school would have been a *lycée*.

Note 45. The *Bâtiment des Voyageurs*, meaning literally 'passenger building' is what in English would normally be called the station building. The French would argue that the goods shed, *halle à marchandises*, and engine shed, *remise*, were equally buildings and equally part of the station.

Note 46. The *halle de transbordement* was the transhipment shed. One was built at every main line connection. Transhipment, the source of problems for every narrow gauge branch line, was a slow and labour intensive job. Goods risked being spoiled in bad weather if there was no shelter available.

Note 47. Notre Dame de Besplaux is dedicated to Mary. She could be either Our Lady of the Keys, or Our Lady of the Forests. The leather works is the Mégisserie Calmes, built here upstream of all pollution.

Note 48. The *Conseil d'Administration* would be the equivalent of a Company Board in English. In accordance with French Law, the Articles of the new company had been received by a *Notaire*, in March 1894 and the *Conseil Général* of Tarn had recognised the company as the successor to Messers Bonnet and Mandement. Marius-Dominique was the new Director, but his son Joseph-Marie was clearly on the Board because it was he who signed the invitations to the Grand Opening.

Note 49. The recipe varied according to company Policy and it is not quite clear what process if any, the TVT favoured. The PLM would add carbonate of soda in proportion to the hardness of the water. The Compagnie de l'Ouest would boil up a mixture of powdered quebracho (an Argentine hardwood,) and water. Caustic soda was added to the solution. The Compagnie de L'Est had a precise recipe : 16.7 kilogrammes of sodium carbonate: 5.2 kilogrammes of extract of logwood: 1.7 kilogrammes of extract of quebracho: 72 litres of water. The dry ingredients were added to the water in a wooden vat and stirred. An average of two litres of cleaning solution was used per boiler per day. The Compagnie du Nord followed British practice in relying upon purifying water before it was used.

There are seven different kinds of quebracho. Quebracho colorado, literally 'tinted axe-breaker', was a particularly rich source of tannin. The botanical name of this native of Argentina and Paraguay is *loxopterygium loretzii*. Once it could made soluble it was useful as a source of acid to break down limescale and for curing heavy duty leathers. The *mégissiers* would have known it well.

Note 50. The extension was already open to passengers though not to goods. The Ministre de la Marine would be the senior politician to whom the French Navy answered, a Government Minister. As well as paying his respects to Admiral Jaurès and the railway, he opened the newly built École Gambetta. Gambetta was a prominent politician who came from nearby Cahors. He led French resistance to the invading Prussians after the Emperor abdicated in 1870. If Admiral Jaurès was to be honoured, it was logical that so should Gambetta.

Note 51. After World War I, every commune in France erected a *Monument aux Morts*, naming residents who had been killed fighting. This Memorial was always in a prominent central place, though in the years since, some have been moved. In the case of the Graulhet Memorial, it has been moved to the Cimetière St Roch, still close to the river but downstream of the Town Centre. St Roch became associated with graveyards because he dedicated his life to nursing victims of the plague. The story goes that he cured some who were dying by virtue of his cross-shaped birthmark.

Note 52. Behind the *Monument aux Morts* there used to stand the Hôtel Terminus which derived its name from the railway; Graulhet was after all for eight years the terminus. The name hôtel can also mean lodging house or even office accommodation. In this case, the Hôtel Terminus fulfilled a number of functions. An hotel in the English sense was on the ground floor with a popular café, flats were above and in the attics were drying rooms for leather. The building was destroyed by fire in 1970 and has been replaced by the Post Office, known as the Hôtel des Postes.

Note 53. The original church was first dedicated to Notre Dame de la Capelle (Our Lady of the Chapel). It received its name Notre Dame du Val d'Amour, literally Valley of Love, from a gentlewoman who was brought to Graulhet as a bride and requested that it be renamed after her home church in what is now Ariège. In the vaults of the church are a number of noble tombs. The *halle*, local indoor market, was built onto its back and earned its nickname as Graulhet Cathedral when the Bishop of Castres made it his headquarters, all a long time ago. The building was demolished in 1848 and replaced in 1850 with the present church. It is decorated with *trompe l'oeil* murals executed by Joseph Bastié.

Note 54. The lower reaches of the Verdaussou brook provided for centuries fresh water for the town, and a sort of natural moat. Even until the late 19th century washerwomen were to be seen on its banks. Soon after, the little gorge become a noisome ditch, with the 'smallest room' of local *appartments* jutting out above it and drinking water was piped to the Théron. In 1927 the brook became once more the town's water supply. The stream was dammed about a kilometre above the town, the superintending engineer being a local man, Maurice Degove. A reservoir called the lac de Miquelou was formed, with a purification plant and pumping station. The water problems of the town and of the railway were solved.

Note 55. St Projet was a local saint, once Bishop of Montpellier. A small chapel dedicated to the saint was built in the space between two lanes, the Impasse Mère Ango and the rue Mattéotti, just outside the medieval town. The church dominated the important junction of the D631 going east-west and the north-south D84. This soon became the commercial quarter of the town and St Projet its protector. The saint or at least his statue was persuaded to take his place on a niche above a café on the crossroads.

By the 1890s, the chapel was disused and demolished to make way for the École Gambetta. This remarkable product of the bricklayer's craft with fancy brickwork and neo-romanesque arches still houses a primary school and nursery. As before mentioned, Camille Pelletan opened the school in 1903 when he inaugurated the Lavaur line.

Note 56. The original village in the area was Touelles, but this was destroyed by Simon de Montfort in the Cathar Wars. Briatexte, founded by Simon the Headcruncher, Seneschal of Carcassonne, was the second of two local *bastides* designed to replace it. The first was St Gauzens a little to the west, founded in 1270 by Amalric, viscount of Lautrec. St Gauzens failed to thrive, perhaps because Simon the Headcruncher was such a persuasive champion of his own *bastide*, perhaps because the Seneschal of Carcassonne was more prestigious than a Viscount, perhaps because Briatexte was more strategically placed.

Assured good defenses to the west by the Dadou river, there were originally fortifications to the east. An arcaded market square, the Place du Foirail, dates back to the period. The town was embroiled in the *guerre de Rohan* which took place during a period of weakness of central government. The walls were demolished in 1629, but the castle, a gatehouse and many original buildings survived. After the 1789 Revolution, the town would have acquired its *mairie* as did all other communes.

Note 57. Giroussens-Parisot was later to be called La Ramière when Giroussens was awarded its own halt on the St Sulpice line. Parisot is on the road up to the important commercial centre of Gaillac. It was to be a halt on the tramway proposed by M. Maire in 1890 which was rejected in favour of the successful Bonnet proposal. If the line had been built, it would have followed the same course as the TVT until this point. At the crossroads, it would have left the D631 and headed north along the D87. Within half a kilometre, it would have had to negotiate a slope of 14 per cent before the hamlet of Imberts, some crazy curves and then the hamlet of Les Galiniers. The next 3.5 kilometres were relatively straightforward. The watershed was crossed and then gradients were generally down. There was a river to be crossed, on a bend in the road, and then the village of Parisot.

2.5 kilometres beyond Parisot was the crossroads with the D14 which led north-west to Lisle-sur-Tarn, a 13th century *bastide*, and south-east back towards Briatexte over very rough country. Almost immediately there was a bridge, and another one a kilometre further on. The second bridge especially was on a sharp bend in the road. Before Montans, 6.5 kilometres on from the D14, there were two more streams to be crossed. Montans is situated on a meander of the Tarn. The road had to cross two streams, each requiring a sharp bend and then had to cross the Tarn itself before entering Gaillac. The town of Gaillac has existed since Roman times and is a centre of wine production. The main line skirts the western side of the town on the far side of the N88. Any proposed minor railway would have had to cross the river, the town and the *route nationale* before it could reach its terminus. It would, however, have been a most interesting and scenic ride.

Note 58. The SNCF, which stands for La Société Nationale des Chemins de Fer Français is the French national railway system which replaced the *grands réseaux*. Outright nationalisation was first proposed by the Socialists such as Léon Blum in 1919-20. For political reasons, these proposals were not carried through but, by 1931, the Depression had made the idea of a State buyout attractive to the companies concerned. Needless to say, it was hard to agree on a price but, in 1937, a compromise was reached. The network was valued at just under 1.5 billion francs and the State and the old companies became fellow shareholders in the new SNCF. The company was legally ratified on 31st December, 1937.

The buildings on Midi land at Lavaur station would thus briefly have passed back into the possession of the Midi before it was absorbed by the SNCF.

Note 59. The church, also spelled Syriaque or Siriaque, celebrates a sixth century Bishop.

Note 60. The existence of Giroussens as a *bastide*, that pragmatic French combination of fortress and market town dates back to the end of the 13th century. The local church, dedicated to Saint Salvy and dating back to the 14th century, has noted sculpture. The decoration behind the altar is the boast of the village. Giroussens became a noted producer of pottery by the 17th century. At around that time the residence of the Royal Gamekeeper was built.

Note 61. Port de Salles, literally a port or some place where a river crossing can be undertaken, was the place where a ferry crossed the Agout. The local hamlet which it served is called Salles. St Lieux is the *occitan* for St Léonce. His feast day is 4th May.

Note 62. The *député* represented the people of Western Tarn in the Assemblée Nationale, the lower House of the French Parliament. There were, in 1990s, 491 *députés* altogether.

Note 63. Also spelt Vaast, Wast and Waast, but generally Vast, the saint is Gaston, Bishop of Toul. He was an adviser of Clovis, king of the Franks, another influence on the development of France.

Note 64. The Ateliers de Construction A. Popineau were absorbed into Établissements Viset. Ats de Constr. A. Popineau were in the Plaine St Denis near Paris. Like Decauville, the company was established in the second half of the 19th century as a supplier of industrial and portable railway equipment. Ranging from locomotives to sections of track, the company manufactured a range of turntables. The working diameter of a turntable was less than the quoted measurement 'from lip to lip' of the connecting rails. For example, a turntable of diameter 1.2 metres spanned an actual distance of 1.52 metres. This might explain why the Directors of the TVT confused their order.

Note 65. VFIL stands for *Voie Ferrée d'Intérêt Local*. If a proposed line was given this status, the *Département* was obliged to ensure that it was built, underwriting any potential loss. Central Government would make a contribution, almost invariably less than half the building costs and little, if any of the operating losses.

Note 66. This stretch of the Tarn is sometimes known as the Vallée d'Amitié, in contrast to the wild territory of the Gorges du Tarn. The valley bottom has traditionally been good for cereals. The soil is alluvial, the fields reasonably flat, and the crops protected from stress caused by high winds. The valley slopes have always suited cultivation of vines and the most celebrated vineyards of the area are to be found around Gaillac. The uplands are less suited to cereals or vines but provide pasture and forest.

Trade in the varying natural resources was originally made possible by rivers such as the Tarn. Railways at first complemented and then themselves became arteries of trade. It is possible that the planned railway might have established new patterns of trade in the area, but on the whole not enough thought was put into this vital aspect of the project.

Note 67. Salvagnac dates back to the 15th century as its castle attests. It has eclipsed nearby St Urcisse, a 13th century *bastide*. The local church is decorated with frescoes, bearing witness to the ambitions of a town that would not be outdone whether in the sacred or the secular. More recently, a museum has been established, full of exhibits on 'loan' from neighbouring towns. The *Mairie* has the local Syndicat d'Initiative and so the little town has the ear of all visitors, business and government officials.

Note 68. The proposed line was declared of *utilité publique* on 15th February, 1913. This made the company eligible for a number of grants towards rolling stock, as required by the *cahier des charges* stipulated by Central Government, how many locomotives were required per kilometre of new line and how much wagon capacity. The grants in fact amounted to a leasing arrangement whereby the *département* purchased the rolling stock and in return retained nominal ownership of the goods and received a share of the profits over a certain level. *See also Note 23.*

Note 69. The *Statuts de la Société* correspond to Company Articles. In France, these must be deposited with a suitable *notaire*, i.e. lawyer. The contemporary term for the initials on the shield was *sigle*, derived from the Latin *singulae litterae*, i.e. initials.

Note 70. As the reader can see, the first / second class carriage supplied when the Lavaur branch was opened bears the inscription Tramways à Vapeur Laboutarié à Lavaur. On the railcar is inscribed Chemins de Fer à Voie Étroite du Tarn.

Note 71. What is known as 'the Decauville Company' went through numerous name changes. In 1875, when Amand Decauville was the head of the firm, the title was Ateliers de Construction de Petit-Bourg Decauville Aîné (Decauville Workshops of Petit-Bourg, a town in Seine et Oise near Paris). Decauville Aîné, i.e. the older, was inserted in case any of his other brothers wanted to start a business and use the family name. On 22nd September, 1887, the less ungainly name of Société Decauville Aîné was assumed when the company, now led by Paul Decauville, bid for the Great Exhibition railway franchise. As he was Amand's eldest son, the title Decauville Aîné was retained. When they were successful and were awarded the responsibility to build the Exhibition Line, the company prudently reformed itself (1889) as one of limited liability and was renamed the Société Anonyme des Établissements Decauville Aîné. Paul was now the Director.

After two heady years, the company was reduced to near bankruptcy. On 16th June, 1894, Paul Decauville was expelled from the Board, the company restructured its debt, retreated into its area of core business and renamed itself La Société Nouvelle des Établissements Decauville Aîné. After World War I, the company was once again in financial difficulty and in 1921 was taken over by the Société des Petits Fils de François de Wendel et Cie. After World War II, the company was accused of collaborating with the Nazis; a tactful bomb seems to have destroyed most company records! In July 1956, the company was renamed Decauville S.A. (Société Anonyme). As narrow gauge and industrial railways followed their inexorable decline, a shift in company policy was required and on 28th August, 1986, the company was reformed as La Société Industrielle Decauville S.A. As of the early 1990s it makes cranes and earthmoving equipment. *See also Notes 22 and 33.*

Note 72. The Établissements Weidknecht, Boulevard Macdonald, Paris had a history of subcontracting for the Decauville Company, especially in their days of expansion. After 1894, the two companies pursued a more independent course, with Weidknecht tendering on its own behalf to supply narrow gauge locomotives, which it continued to do for the TVT until 1913.

The Tramways of Royan, Charente Maritime in Western France, were a network centred on the resort of Royan. They extended from the Gironde estuary to the Isle d'Oléron, linking a number of holiday places. In 1890, concessions were awarded to the S.A. des Éts Decauville Aîné to build and run short railways radiating from Royan. As briefly mentioned in *Note 71* the Decauville Company overreached itself with this and other enterprises of the period and in 1894, the network became the responsibilty of the newly formed Société Générale des Tramways de Royan. Extending 42 kilometres during the period between World War II, the network was closed in 1945 after extensive war damage.

Note 73. The Musée des Transports de Pithiviers is the heart of a preserved railway which exists on part of the once extensive 60 centimetre Tramways de Pithiviers à Toury on the plains of Loiret, north of Orléans. In September 1891, the S.A. des Éts Decauville Aîné signed a contract to build and run the line. In July 1894, in parallel with events at Royan, the line became the responsibilty of the Tramways de Pithiviers à Toury. The TPT officially closed in 1965, but the Museum and a short stretch of line were saved, a pioneer in railway preservation.

Note 74.   The Chemins de Fer de Calvados, CFC, was a 60 centimetre network in Normandy. In 1881, the Decauville Company was awarded the contract to build and run a network around the resort of Luc-sur-Mer. Later on, even after the company became enmired in financial difficulties, it was involved in building a line from the nearby resort of Grandcamp-les-Bains. The Société des Chemins de Fer de Calvados was formed in 1895, was renamed the Société des Courriers Normands in 1937, and the network was closed in 1944.

Note 75.   In the 1920s, the Société des Automobiles Berliet had become a major supplier to minor railways who wished to avail themselves of the new technology of internal combustion. In common with the Decauville Company, it had a chequered history but Marius Berliet is now commemorated with an Institute and Museum in the precincts of the original company.

Note 76.   In 1911, the price of a return ticket from Graulhet to Lavaur was 2.1 francs. Prices were stable until after World War I and until 1926, there were no significant fare increases. Therefore, 106,000 francs was roughly equivalent to the cost of 50,000 full-price tickets. In the heyday of the line, more than 100,000 journeys were made each year, but many of them were even shorter than the trip to the main line, to a local market or a fête.

Note 77.   Col d'Ambres, between Graulhet and Lavaur, was considered the most testing part of the line, consisting of a kilometre of gradients approaching 2.5 per cent and never less than 2 per cent.

Note 78.   On a French railway, the *fourgon* served the function of guard's van, brake van and also often mail van.

Note 79.   Various factors led the authorities to seek in 1903 a supplier other than Decauville. Decauville were in financial trouble, and had pulled out of a number of civilian projects therefore at the time, they would not have been considered reliable suppliers. Carde, on the other hand, had the advantage of being nearer; Bordeaux is of the the order of 200 kilometres away whereas Decauville's offices were nearly 700 kilometres. There may also have been regional jealousies. As mentioned elsewhere, reviving antiquarian interests had helped to engender a stronger sense of regional identity.

Inspection of photographs suggests that Carde were primarily coach builders and bought in parts such as the bogies. The bogies almost certainly came from Decauville.

Note 80.   The Chief Engineer would have been known simply as *l'Ingénieur*. The Board of Control was created by Central Government to regulate railways in France

Note 81.   Bergerac is on the Dordogne river, in that *département*. An explosives factory, *poudrerie*, existed at the western side of the town, served by freight sidings off the main line going south. In 1916 a temporary 60 centimetre line was built linking the factory with the town centre making access easier for workers; the principal need was therefore carriages rather than wagons. The TVT supplied four carriages but a larger contribution came from the Société du Tramway de la Trinité à Étel in Morbihan, Britanny, which lent three Orenstein and Koppel 0-6-0 tanks and seven carriages. The Munition Works had some of its own stock, including a Decauville 0-6-0 tank. At the end of the war, the line was dismantled and the rolling stock returned.

Note 82.   The Decauville Company was once again seeking business. In 1921 the Société Nouvelle des Établissements Decauville Aîné had been taken over by a respectable banking company which was seeking a vehicle for investment. Thanks in part to the cash injection, sales (and profits) which had fallen sharply at the end of World War I rose steadily until the Recession which took hold of France in the 1930s. *See also Note 71.*

Note 83.   The box cars were probably made by the Magor Car Company of New Jersey, closed 1973, or the American Car and Foundry Co of Milton, Pennsylvania which (in 1990)

was in existence as ACF. The most authoritative description and drawings are in Richard Dunn's book *Narrow Gauge To No-Man's-Land*.

Note 84. Truck is the word used in the record of the sale. Best translated as 'wagon' such were probably used for track repair or train breakdowns. The dump trucks, skips and bolster wagons were probably employed on the reconstruction which was started at Graulhet just before the final phase of the railway. It is also conceivable that these wagons may have been used for work on the aborted Salvagnac line.

Note 85. The *département* is roughly the equivalent of a British County. The local *département* is Tarn, with the chief city at Albi. *Note 16* gives a fuller description of the *département* system. Chapter Two describes the major contribution made by the ratepayers of Tarn to the building of the St Sulpice branch.

Note 86. The concession awarded to the TVT in 1921 was to run until 31st December, 1963. In point of fact, most companies running secondary railways did not see out the entire period of their concessions. The privilege of being able to run a railway at a loss was hardly valuable! *Note 19* gives more information about concessions and the way that French railways were run.

Note 87. The line ran through the communes of Laboutarié, Montdragon, the Canton of Graulhet, Briatexte, Ambres and Lavaur. The section which is of particular interest ran through the communes of Giroussens and St Lieux, then on to St Sulpice. The *département* sold some of the land to individuals, some to the communes in which the property lay, but kept what it could not sell. Granting of wayleave could therefore be complicated. *For more details see Note 15.*

Note 88. The last surviving network of the area was the metre gauge network around Castres which was run by the Société Auxiliaire pour les Chemins de fer Secondaires (SACFS) from 1953 until its closure in 1962.

Note 89. The *département* in which Toulouse is situated is Haute Garonne. To its west is Gers on the Gascony plain, to the north, Tarn et Garonne, Tarn and Aude on the eastern boundaries with Ariège and the border with Spain to the south.

Note 90. The VFDM, the Voies Ferrées Départementales du Midi de la France was over 100 kilometres in extent, reaching into the neighbouring *département* of Tarn. It was unusual but not unique in that it was electrified, running on 1,500 volts.

Note 91. As can be seen from the names adopted by organisations such as railways, the French never lost their regional affiliations. *Note 3* describes how some old names officially returned in the 1980s though Toulouse has become the chief city of the region which has been given the politically neutral name of Midi-Pyrénées.

Note 92. By declaring a railway to be of *intérêt publique* it would be eligible for massive subsidies and in return would surrender almost all freedom of action. *See also Notes 23 and 68.*

Note 93. Weidknecht no longer trades under that name, nor do the Établissements Popineau. Companies such as Renault, Berliet and of course Decauville have long since ceased to supply narrow gauge railways.

Note 94. Salins du Midi are literally the salt-pans in the South. This was an established company which extracted salt from the Mediterranean in the neighbouring *Département* of Aude. The narrow gauge system had been installed at its Lapalme works south of Port La Nouvelle to move salt from the salt pans to the refinery. Geographical conditions have helped the industry. Behind the long straight beaches which front the sea are a series of salt inlets, the *étangs* which provide calm conditions and rapid evaporation.

Note 95. The Lac d'Artouste line, in the *Département* of Pyrénées Atlantiques, is 10 kilometres long. It extends to Pic de la Sagette, almost on the Spanish border. Built in 1924 as a quarry line, it was retained for tourists. When the SNCF came into existence, it ran the line until the RDSAPA took over and, as of 1985, were still running it.

Note 96. Before the advent of industrial vehicles on caterpillar tracks, a quarry or a construction site would have used portable track to create new configurations of railway as the task required. Portability meant flexibility.

Note 97. These *tape-culs* were based on a design used by the Chemin de Fer Forestier d'Abreschviller, another preserved railway up in Alsace. Originally opened in 1885, a section was saved by the Association (ACFA) and became a preserved railway in 1969, six year before the CFTT. ACFA solved problems such as how to turn rolling stock designed for freight into passenger carriages. Many of their solutions were copied by the young ACOVA.

Note 98. Traditionally, every French village celebrates the feast day of the local saint, usually the one to whom the church was dedicated. Nowadays, the fête is celebrated with a party and a disco, bringing the most remote of rural communities to ear-splitting life.

Note 99. The name is derived from a design of pitchfork used for turning over hay. Not entirely complimentary, the Association applies the term as a joke to particularly enthusiastic and nosy members.

Note 100. This company mined coal at Sainte Marie and Cagnac les Mines between Albi and Carmaux in Tarn.

Note 101. The line from Labouheyre to Sabres was a standard gauge light railway 19 kilometres in length. Opened in 1889, it was closed by its parent company in 1969 to be reborn the next year as a preserved railway.

Note 102. The Mines de Carmaux, operating round the town of that name on the railway north of Albi, were within a few kilometres of the Houillères du Midi (Coal mines of the Midi) in the most important mining and industrial area of the *Département*. There is a report on present day coal mining there in Issue 148 of *Voie Étroite*. Virtually all the industrial railway network has gone but of the surviving 3.5 kilometres there was a short 6 centimetre spur (in 1995). There is still an open-cast mine at Sainte Marie about two kilometres south of Carmaux station.

Note 103. The Sucrerie de Maizy, Aisne is in northern France in an area noted for the production of sugarbeet, hence the existence of the sugar refinery. The Decauville Company had a long association with sugarbeet since the occasion upon which Amand Decauville devised portable track to carry his own harvest out of the muddy fields.

Note 104. Facultatif means optional. Usually it is the organisation, not the individual which exercises the option.

Note 105. The Plaine de Salles is the flat area around Salles, the village on the valley bottom. It has a riding school. Giroussens is approached up a lane which crosses the line of the railway at right angles then turns west to climb the escarpment.

Note 106. The Société Anonyme Couillet, was a Belgian manufacturer of narrow gauge steam locomotives based in Hainaut. Between 1870 and 1887, virtually all the small 0-2-0 tanks supplied to Decauville customers seem to have been Couillets. The most celebrated were: *The Prince of Wales* which, if sales literature is to be believed, was carried overland by elephant to take up its duties on the North West Frontier of British India; the 3 tonne *Ma Camarade* which appeared at the 1889 Paris Exhibition; and *L'Avenir* which appeared on stage in a theatrical production. The association with Couillet continued until 1891. At that time, the Decauville company was trying to move into running complete railways, therefore small industrial locomotives seemed of little interest. Decauville was also looking more steadily to Weidknecht as a subcontractor. Soon after, there was the crash in Decauville company fortunes. Couillet continued to make industrial and agricultural locomotives up World War I.

Monuments Historiques, as with their British equivalents, are listed and protected by law from destruction.

Note 107. The motto roughly translates as: In praise of wine and of coal, referring to the owner's interest in drink as a member of the Guinness family and to his interest in steam engines.

Note 108. The electric transmission system was used in four railcars supplied to the 60 cm Tramways de la Savoie. The chassis of railcars Nos. A3 and A4, constructed by Decauville survive, one at St Eutrope and St Trojan.

Note 109. Crochat also developed petroleo-electric locomotives for the army in standard gauge mainly for shunting. There was an 0-4-0 22 tonne locomotive series LT1 to 130 and a 44 tonne bogie-mounted 'double' version series LT201 to 290. A few survived World

War II when most of them were rebuilt and converted to diesel. Two members of the 22L series are known to have remained in original condition. One in was sold by the Ateliers Industriels de l'Aeronautique de Clermont Ferrand in 1993, the other by the Ateliers de Chargement, St Florentin, Yonne in 1964.

Note 110. Établissements Patry, as well as dealing in secondhand equipment, produced locomotives for specialist mining purposes and also some for military use. Some years before the CFTT opened, the Forges d'Audincourt had sold Progrès No. 1111 to Patry which had restored it and then sold it on to Mr Guinness.

Note 111. European co-operation in the matter of aircraft meant that there a number of links between engineering works near Oxford, and ones in Toulouse.

Note 112. The Plâtrerie de Marssac, west of Albi, was a plasterworks, the Four à Chaux de Ronel, industrial limekilns, also in Tarn.

Note 113. Berga is in Catalonia in north-east Spain, *carbones* being coal mines.

Note 114. The *matériel remorque*, literally material that could be towed, were the wagons and carriages of the enterprise. The TVT had a *parc de matériel* because it had locomotives.

Note 115. The Code Napoléon, as explained earlier, was a legal system drawn up on the orders of Napoleon Buonaparte. It dealt with rights of inheritance. France obtained a reputation as a patriarchal society; universal male suffrage was introduced in 1875, but women had to wait until 1945 for full voting rights. In this respect, it was the then colony of Australia which led the world.

Note 116. 60 centimes, 0.6 francs would have been a reasonable price for a five kilometre journey. In comparison, the 13 kilometre trip from Laboutarié to Graulhet cost 1.3 francs. Inflation was pronounced in the following years because of the devaluation of the franc and difficult economic conditions.

Note 117. The STED, the Société des Transports Économiques Départementales of Toulouse, also took over services on the Graulhet to Lavaur line. There too they proved costly.

Note 118. A *sauterelle* is literally a little leaper and *araignée* a spider (see later in text). One wonders if M. Benoît had invented other devices in his previous 65 years.

Note 119. The *remise* would normally be the carriage shed. The one at Réalmont was a small, all-purpose building combining with the functions of goods shed as well. As there was no waiting room let alone a proper *BV*, no wonder that passengers liked the Hôtel Combelles.

Note 120. The summer coach is shown in a photograph. It has three compartments, with benches facing each other, each bench taking four people. We know that the end platforms had space for 12 standing passengers, implying that they were approximately 73 centimetres long (like the smaller of the all-weather coaches). Again assuming that dimensions were standard because of Government regulations (the *Cahier),* the compartments must have been similar to those of the open Decauville carriage on the Chemins de fer de Calvados which were of the order of 1.4 metres long. The dimension given for the CFC coach is an interior one, and there was seating at the ends, making accurate comparison impossible.

Note 121. Records of some carriage dimensions exist. At 2.4 metres, the overall height was comparable to that of the TVT one, allowing 20 centimetres for the additional height of the bogies. The overall length (excluding couplings) of the TVT carriage was 9.04 metres, the distance between outer axles 6.87 metres, giving interior dimensions of the platforms at each end of 90 centimetres. There were nine windows on each side of the TVT carriage, fitted into a length of slightly over seven metres, implying that the width of each window including frame was of the order of 75 centimetres. The larger of the Réalmont coaches had five windows in a distance of 3.65 metres, giving them approximately equal dimensions. The smaller coach, with a compartment 2.1 metres long, would have had three windows. The drawing and one photograph show one interesting difference. The TVT was supplied at least one carriage with planked sides, but other photographs show carriages with plain bodywork and similar to Réalmont ones.

Bibliography

Chemins de Fer Régionaux et Urbains, Journal of FACS Numbers 113 (4/1972), 127 and 190 (4/1985). Articles by Jacques Chapuis, Martial Respaut, and Jacques Daffis, in No. 190 give a full history of the railway, of the Réalmont Tramway and of the first 10 years of the Tarn Tourist Railway. Enquire from FACS, 134, Rue de Rennes, 75006 Paris for back copies.

Chemin De Fer Touristique Du Tarn. This is an illustrated guidebook of the Tourist railway, in French. It is available at St Lieux, or by post from ACOVA/CFTT, BP 2040, 31018 Toulouse, CEDEX.

Decauville Catalogues, keep your eyes open for second-hand copies or reprints!

Decauville: Ce nom Qui Fit Le Tour Du Monde, Roger Bailly. In French, this is a copiously illustrated history of the Decauville Company. If not available in this country, enquire at Éditions Amatteis, 77350 La Mée sur Seine.

French Minor Railways, W.J.K. Davies. Once more in print, this book has a useful introduction and then concentrates on the minor railways that were still operating in the late 1950s. English language.

Graulhet Réflet Du Passé, Ville de Graulhet, 1991. In French, this book is available from Librairie FITA, 81300 Graulhet.

Guide Michelin

La Grande Époque Des Petits Trains, Louis Briand and the Carto-Club Tarnais. With postcards and text, it gives a history of secondary railways in Tarn. It is available from CCT, 88 rue Courteline, 81100, Castres.

La Voie De 60 Sur Les Fronts Français De La Guerre De 1914-18, Dr Christian Cénac (available from author at 23, rue des Martyrs de la Libération 31400 Toulouse)

Le Siècle des Petits Trains - Calvados Pour Les Petits Trains Dieuleveult, Blin, French language.

Les Chemins De Fer PLM, Chaintreau, Cuynet, Mathieu (in French).

Les Petits Trains de Jadis, Henri Domengie Volumes 6, 7, 8 particularly Volume 7, Le Sud-Ouest. The text is in French. The series aims to cover all the secondary railways of France.

Les Petits Trains du Loiret, Bouchard, Duclos and Giraud (in French).

Narrow Gauge To No-Man's-Land, Richard Dunn. The text is in English, giving a full account of US Army narrow gauge transport during World War I.

Tarn, Adolphe Joanne. This French language description of the department originally appeared in 1902, but was reissued in 1997 by Lacour-Redeviva.

Voie Étroite magazine, back copies are available from APPEVA BP 106 80001 Amiens CEDEX.

Index

Note: References to drawings, maps and photographs are in **BOLD**.